MW00795657

Sanctified Revolution is an incalculab cleric and student. Dr. Ovell Hamilton has compiled, analyzed, and curated volumes of information and given to the Church of God in Christ a fact--based comprehensive history of our beloved church. This book places in context our glorious struggle to become a relevant religious organization and provides many answers to legitimate questions ask of our congregants. I enjoy the fact-based reality and quantitative presentation packaged within our colorful sanctified personality. This book will bless a new class of generational leaders around the world. Dr. Hamilton's work should be placed alongside the books of other notable COGIC historians and authors.

Reverend Dr. Matthew L. Brown
Senior Pastor of Greater Community COGIC
Bishop Designate to the Democratic Republic of the Congo

Building on the tradition of Dr. Ithiel Clemons' embryonic work, Ovell Hamilton's *Sanctified Revolution*, is a welcome testament to the great history of the Church Of God In Christ, America's first religious organization established and operated by Blacks. Included in this thoroughly researched and comprehensive work, his chapter on female adherents further enlightens readers on their massive contributions, a sometimes unheralded yet underlying cause of the Church's rapid growth.

Glenda Williams Goodson, Historian
Church Of God In Christ International Department of Women

I applaud Dr. Ovell Hamilton for bringing to fruition this magnificent research on the history of The Church of God in Christ. His many years labouring on this book will certainly enlighten, educate and bring clarity for lay members, ministers and scholars as well on COGIC's legacy. As a fellow minister in this great denomination serving in the country of Brazil, I am humbled by the opportunity to contribute as the publisher of this great work.

Elder Eneas Francisco
COGIC Brazil Jurisdiction, Public Relations
& Publisher at UPBooks

DR. OVELL HAMILTON

SANCTIFIED REVOLUTION

THE CHURCH OF GOD IN CHRIST:
A History of African-American Holiness

books

Itapira, SP - Brazil
2021

Copyright © 2021 by Ovell Hamilton
ISBN 978-65-88545-11-9
UPBooks [Casa Publicadora Bereana Ltda. ME]

Rua Francisco Otaviano Queluz, 103
Braz Cavenaghi - Itapira SP
CEP 13033-280 - Brazil

Cover design: **César Franca**
Layout: **Carla Montebeler**
Editor: **Eneas Francisco**

Cataloging-In-Publication (CIP)
(eDOC BRASIL)

Hamilton, Ovell.

H219s   Sanctified revolution: The Church of God in Christ: A History of African-American Holiness / Dr. Ovell Hamilton. – Itapira, Brazil: UPBooks, 2021.
    280 p. : 16 x 23 cm

    Includes bibliography
    ISBN 978-65-88545-11-9

    1. Church of God in Christ – History. 2. Church of God in Christ – Doctrines. I. Title.

DDC 289.3

Prepared by Maurício Amormino Júnior – CRB6/2422

CONTACT US:

www.upbooks.com.br / e-mail: contato@upbooks.net.br
Phone: +55 19 98430-7994

TABLE OF CONTENTS

DEDICATION

A fter a long journey of over twenty-five years of research on the Church of God in Christ, I have finally reached the terminal point of my research. I would like to thank my advisor, the late Dr. Jacqueline Rouse for her keen insight, superb professionalism, and expertise in supporting my efforts to finish this process. She had been guiding me in writing about COGIC history since 1997, when I completed the history of the COGIC Church in Georgia. This project could not have been successful without her valuable insight. Also, I would like to extend thanks to Dr. Glen Eskew, who has also served faithfully on my master's thesis and dissertation committees. I appreciate the constructive input that he provided to my research on COGIC history. Additional thanks to Dr. H. Robert Baker and Dean Harold Bennett for also guiding me through the completion of this great journey, also for Dr. Bennett's valuable contribution to the publication of this work.

On a personal note, I want to give a great love and thank-you to my parents, the late Hughdell and Durene Hamilton. In that small town of Poplar Grove, Arkansas, my father served as the griot/historian for our community and church, Star of Bethlehem Missionary Baptist Church, and encouraged me to cherish the legacies of family and community. My mother provided strong guidance on being successful, no matter what obstacle was in my path, and she always gave me a helpful proverb. Much gratitude goes to my siblings, who helped to pour wisdom into my life: my sisters Bobbie Jean Williams, Shirley Ruth (deceased), Audrey Lynn (deceased), Bettnie Faye (deceased), and my brothers Eric and William Bruce. Additionally, I want to give a great special thanks to my wife, Ericka Davis-Hamilton and my son, Ashton

Hamilton for encouraging me to do my best and persevere through the hard times of reading, studying, and writing. With the love and encouragement from my wife and son, the stressors of this process were conquered; and by the help of the Almighty, the comprehensive history of the Church of God in Christ is now complete. I would also like to recognize my late mother-in-law, COGIC Missionary Dora Jean Thompson Davis, who contributed valuable primary sources to this project.

Continuing the gratitude toward the pioneers in the Church of God in Christ, I must give a major appreciation to the late Bishop J. Howard Dell and his late wife, Mother Evelyn Jean LaFlora Lewis-Dell. Without their primary COGIC resources that included original minutes from the COGIC Elders' Council, letters from COGIC leaders, diaries, and COGIC authors, this comprehensive work would have been impossible to complete. Bishop and Mother Dell were key leaders in the Church of God in Christ and their work gave me the greatest perspective in writing history. Moreover, I want to recognize my pastor, Bishop Matthew Brown, who encouraged me to teach and research every aspect of this religious movement. Other COGIC appreciation goes to Pastor Leroy James, Bishop Adrian Williams, the late Mother Cleo Willis who served as my foundation in researching COGIC state history. I would like to give thanks to the members of Power House COGIC in West Helena, Arkansas along with Pastor and Bishop Alex Smith, Greater Community COGIC of Marietta, Georgia, the Christ Temple COGIC members of Atlanta, Georgia, Paradise COGIC of Jonesboro, Georgia with Pastor and Bishop Paul Fortson, Missionary Glenda Goodson who leads the Texas forum on COGIC History, COGIC Scholars, COGIC History Facebook Page Groups, and all of the benefactors who support this COGIC History Phenomenon.

A very special "sanctified" thanks to my two brothers of the Church of God in Christ, Publisher Eneas Francisco and Elder Elbert Hicks. Elder Hicks was very instrumental in coordinating the meeting between myself and Elder Francisco of UPBooks Publishing. He also was a great motivator on researching the history of COGIC in Pennsylvania, as we became friends on the Facebook Pages, COGIC History & Truth and COGIC History Page. Elder Francisco oversaw the superb organization of producing a book that could reach people locally and on a global scale. He has made this historic project a complete success with his outstanding professional leadership. Both men have been a pillar of support and encouragement providing me with keen insight on completing this journey. I am eternally grateful for the visions of both men in helping me to publish my work and make this dream a reality.

LIST OF ABBREVIATIONS

AIM   Auxiliaries in Ministry
COGIC   Church of God in Christ, Incorporated
             Triumph the Church and Kingdom of God in Christ
             Church of God in Christ, Congregational
             Glorious Church of God in Christ
             Congregational Church of God in Christ
             True Glorious Church of God in Christ
             Church of God in Christ, Jesus Apostolic
             Evangelist Temple House of Refuge for all Nations
                     Church of God in Christ
             Church of God in Christ, United
             Church of God in Christ of America, Incorporated
             Church of God in Christ, International
             Church of God in Christ International
             United Church of God in Christ
             Lighthouse Church of God in Christ of Canada
             Church of God in Christ America, Incorporated

UNAC   United National Auxiliaries Convention

YPWW   Young People Willing Workers

YWCC   Young Women's Christian Council

LIST OF KEY TERMS DEFINITIONS

BAPTISM OF THE HOLY SPIRIT
The acceptance of the Holy Spirit is considered the third and final phase of salvation in the Pentecostal faith. Pentecostals believed that a person must speak in tongues as evidence of receiving the Holy Spirit. The second chapter of Acts is used as the model for the belief in tongues. The Holy Spirit, believed by Pentecostals, accompanied the believer in everyday endeavors.

CONFESSION
According to the Holiness-Pentecostal tradition and other Christian faiths, this is the first phase of salvation. The sinner confesses his or her sins to Christ and is saved from the sins according to Romans 10:9-10. Jesus's death is the focal point of this phase because Jesus died so the world could be saved.

COME-OUTISM
The idea of Pentecostal members leaving the traditional organized Churches such as the Baptists and Methodists. Many members testified that God had brought them out of darkness (Baptist and Methodist Churches) to the marvelous light of the Holy Ghost.

DANCING
Pentecostal Christians, especially COGIC members, have a long time tradition of dancing in the Spirit. Sometimes the word "shouting" is used to mean the same thing as dancing.

District

A number of COGIC Churches and their pastors in a particular area of a state who are under the authority of a superintendent. The local churches make up districts and the districts make up a jurisdiction.

Elder

A title given to male preachers in the COGIC faith which indicates reception into the ordained ministry. The position of the elder is one level above a minister. The position makes one ready to become a pastor of a church. Ordinarily, elders serve alongside a pastor before leading their own church. In the Church of God in Christ, women are not eligible to hold the office and titles of minister, elder, pastor, superintendent, and bishop.

Glossolalia

To speak or utter in an unknown language or stutter speaking as a result of being overshadowed by the Holy Spirit.

Holy or Holiness

A lifestyle that was espoused by Christians in the mid-1800s. Holiness living among Christians was a lifestyle that advocated the non-participation in or avoidance of immoral actions of the private sphere: fornication, lying, adultery, drinking alcohol, smoking, going to secular clubs, and other activities that were deemed unbecoming of Holiness.

Jurisdiction

A designated COGIC entity composed of districts and local churches. The jurisdiction is led and managed by a state bishop who has been installed by the COGIC General Assembly. COGIC bylaws state that in order to be a bishop over a jurisdiction, the bishop must have 30 local churches under his authority.

Megachurch

A church that is composed of more than 2,000 congregants (members or non-members) on a given day of weekend worship. [1]

MIRACULOUS HEALING
Healings usually occurring during Pentecostal revivals where people testify of being healed of lameness, diseases, and other ailments. Some testimonies proclaimed that people had grown new limbs and were raised from the dead. Also known as divine healing.

PENTECOSTALISM
A religious movement that occurred at the beginning of the twentieth century that combined Holiness living standards and the concept of speaking in tongues upon receiving the Baptism of the Holy Ghost. Allan Anderson referred to this version of Pentecostalism as Classic North American Pentecostalism that emerged during the Azusa Street Revival in 1906 in Los Angeles, California.

PROSPERITY GOSPEL PREACHING
A preaching ideal that is based upon 1 John 1:9, which states that a Christian should prosper and be in health as their soul prospers. Thus, Christians are taught that they should be millionaires and never be sick. The Prosperity Ministries are dominated by mandatory tithing and offering practices that order the Christian to give their money to God.

SANCTIFICATION
A concept embraced during the Holiness Movement and then expanded by the Pentecostal Movement as the second phase of salvation. In sanctification, the believer is expected to live a holy and moral life before God. The sanctification process was taken to extreme measures, first during the Holiness Movement and then later in the Pentecostal era.

Women could not wear pants, makeup, and dresses had to come below the ankle. Men and women could not drink alcohol, gamble, listen to Jazz or Blues music, or go to parties. Some denominations preached against drinking tea and coffee, using toothpaste, and took water instead of grape juice for Communion.

SHOUTING

Occurs when a Christian screams out, usually, in agreement with the preached Word of God. Many times, Pentecostal Christians use this word to mean that they are praising God in a dance.

SPIRIT-LED/SPIRITUAL

A Christian belief that one's life should be led by the power of God's Holy Spirit. To note, Holy Ghost and Holy Spirit are used interchangeably.

SUPERINTENDENT

A COGIC clerical position that ranks above a pastor. The superintendent position is under the position of state bishop. The superintendent oversees, supports, and advises the pastors of his district who are under his authority.

THREE BLESSING THEORY

According to Pentecostal historian, Vinson Synan, the Third Blessing came after "sanctification" and was called the Baptism of the Holy Spirit.

TITHING

A practice governing financial stewardship base on Malachi 3. Each Christian is required to give 10% of their income to the Church as if they were giving it as a tithe to God. Tithing is the foundation of the COGIC Church's financial strength.

TWO BLESSING THEORY

According to Synan, the Second Blessing was "sanctification." Sanctification occurred when the person denounced the willingness in succumbing to immoral behavior.

WORD/SEED FAITH

In the Pentecostal tradition, this practice was started by Reverend Oral Roberts. The concept is enacted when the preacher asks for Christians to "sow a seed" of certain amounts of money to be blessed by the Lord.

In the COGIC faith, some preachers have lines of giving. One line may give 100 dollars, another line, 50 dollars, etc. When the Christian "sows the seed", they are to look for a blessing from God by believing in the Word of God that was preached by the minister. A common phrase with the Word/Seed Faith Ministries is "name it and claim it." The Christian only had to ask God for what they wanted, and then claim that the want would happen by faith.

XENOLALIA

To speak in a recognizable foreign language under the power of the Holy Spirit. For example, a Christian may speak Chinese, Spanish, or Arabic when possessed by the Holy Spirit.

INTRODUCTION

When viewing the historiography of Africans coming to the Americas, one feature in the merging of African culture into a transformative African-American culture has been the prevalence of religion, especially Christianity. Spiritual forces dominated the lands of Africa ranging from the worship of indigenous gods to Islam to Coptic Christianity, and a common religious heritage developed from the assimilation of the spiritual legacies of Africans in the Americas.[1] Beliefs about a "High God", spirits, and other forces dominated the countries of Guinea, Ghana, Sierra Leone, and Nigeria. Many Africans were taken from West Central Africa and the Gold Coast to be enslaved in America. A common religious heritage developed from the assimilation of the spiritual legacies of Africans in the America.

Organized African-American churches began to grow after the First Great Awakening period. African-Americans formed Black Christian denominations in the United States with the advent of the first Black Baptist Church in 1773 in Silver Bluff, South Carolina outside Savannah, Georgia.[2] The Church was formed under the supervision of the slave master from the Bryan Plantation who allowed David George and George Liele to preach the gospel to the slaves on the plantation, ensuring that slaves had a chance to become Christians. Another prominent African-American Christian denomination was the African Methodist Episcopal (AME) Church. The AME Church was berthed from controversy in 1816 as its founder, Richard Allen refused to pray in the "Black" section of the church, choosing to defy the standard by coming down to the altar in the front of the local church.[3] After Allen was forced to leave the area, he chose to create the AME Church as a separate organization from the segregation policies of the White dominated Methodist Episcopal Church in Philadelphia. Scholars and historians have recorded how the doctrines of Black Baptists and Black Methodists were driving forces for Black freedom, social equality, and economic empowerment.

With an early start in the 1700s, the Black Baptist Church, later forming the National Baptist Convention, USA, has been recorded as the largest Black organization in terms of membership, boasting around 7.5 million members.[4] In a surprising fashion, the second largest Black Church is not the AME Church, but a latecomer on the scene known as the Black Pentecostals whose founder was Bishop Charles H. Mason. One of the earliest formations of the Black Pentecostal Movements occurred in 1897 as an offspring from a Black Holiness sect called the Church of God in Christ (COGIC). One of its founders, Bishop Charles Harrison Mason, believed in the charismatic preaching about the inward dwelling of the Holy Ghost, righteous living, and total dedication to God. Additionally,

unlike the Black Baptist Church and the AME Church, the COGIC Church is the only Black Christian denomination in America that was solely berthed from the African-American religious experience, without being a byproduct of major White Christian denomination. It boasts of a religious fervor derived from the American slavery experience. Black Baptists and Black Methodists originated under White religious leadership and ecclesiastical orders. The Church of God in Christ incorporated

African influences with call-and-response preaching styles, musical renditions in song and instruments, and Spirit-possession.

The author's purpose for this research is to create a comprehensive historical work on the Church of God in Christ while highlighting the formation, development, and transition of the only Black Christian mainstream church body in America that was, solely, founded, organized, and fully controlled by African-Americans. Existing since 1897 in name, the COGIC denomination has had few analytical works dedicated to its contributions to Christianity and to the secular world. The legacies of the COGIC experience are mostly in the abstract categories of spirituality and faith, which challenged the complacency of modern Christianity. This research will showcase the COGIC legacies of charismatic preaching, often performed by a leader who claimed a God-appointed mandate to preach to the world, like the founder, Bishop Charles Harrison Mason. Also, demonstrative worship characterized by holy dancing, shouting and the desire to evangelize the world were integral practices of this Holiness-Pentecostal group that had a major impact on the religious forces in the United States and around the globe.

Chapter Two opens with the positioning of the Church of God in Christ and its foundations in the Black Baptist, Holiness, and Pentecostal traditions and how the Church became a powerful, spiritual and politically polarizing force during the Third Great American Religious Awakening period, characterized by the birth of the Pentecostal Movement in 1906 at Azusa Street in Los Angeles, California. The major features of the Third Great Awakening period were the ideals of racial and gender equality. At Azusa Street, women such as Florence Crawford and Clara Lum held key administrative positions under William Seymour's leadership. Florence Crawford later pastored several churches along with the prominent female Pentecostal leader, Aimee Semple McPherson, pastor of the Church of the Foursquare Gospel. Additionally, at the death of Seymour, his wife Jennie Brown-Seymour took charge and became the pastor of the Apostolic Faith Mission. In contrast, the first two periods of national religious revivalism occurred during times of slavery and when White women had specified second-class citizenship. The Third Great Awakening Pentecostal explosion crossed racial barriers of segregation and gave many women a chance to assume leadership roles in church administration and preaching.

The COGIC Holiness-Pentecostal Movement started as an egalitarian religious trend that was characterized by Black and White people worshipping together in the segregated South of the early 1900s, namely in Mississippi, Arkansas, and Tennessee.[5] The religious worship services that housed both Black and White worshippers existed several decades before the Civil Rights Movement. This Pentecostal experience followed the socio-political egalitarian movement of Populism and came before the socio-economic egalitarian movement of Communism. Pentecostal preachers and followers transformed the American religious and social landscapes by conducting mixed raced services, overlooking both gender and racial barriers. Years before Pentecostalism, Populism in 1896 transcended racial barriers evidenced by Georgia's son, Tom Watson who called for the protection of one of his Black Populist members who had been threatened with violence by irate Georgians.[6] On the same note, the Bolshevik Revolution of 1917 spurred a transcendence of race and gender pronounced by the written ideals of Nickolai Bukharin and Evegeni Preobrazhensky. These two Communist followers authored a Communist agenda called The Program. In the Communist agenda, racial and gender equality were priorities that were to sustain the Communist Movement, and make the revolution a worldwide phenomenon. Much like the Pentecostal Movement, the Communist Revolution embraced equality for all people regardless of race or gender. Moreover, The Program advocated a doctrine of hard work and perseverance, and the authors gave an indirect scriptural reference from 1 Thessalonians, which states "if a man did not work, he should not eat."[7] The Pentecostals also believed in the same biblical scripture as ardent fundamentalists. All three movements transformed generations of people and all three movements were not popular because of their anti-capitalist views. Pentecostalism, Populism, and Communism espoused a level playing field for all people regardless of race or gender. Pentecostal preachers like Bishop Charles Mason were often accused of being a Communist and a Socialist because of his theological stance on everyone being equal in God's Kingdom and his sermons that advocated caring for the poor people worldwide.[8] Furthermore, Pentecostal church services in the early 1900s, conducted by Seymour and Mason, displayed an equality that ignored a person's skin color and status in society.

Chapter Three commences with the biographies of Elder Charles Price Jones and Elder Charles H. Mason prior to Mason's journey to Los Angeles to attend the Azusa Street Revival led by Apostle William J. Seymour. Jones and Mason's biographies give a view of their theological backgrounds and their propensity to preach Holiness, even as they were ejected from the Black Baptist Church. Like other Holiness preachers, Jones and Mason believed in a second dispensation of grace called sanctification.[9] Sanctification meant that the Christian was set apart to do the works of God, not partaking in the immoral behaviors of society. Christians were encouraged to live a holy lifestyle that denounced drinking, smoking, dancing in clubs, cursing, lying, and other behaviors that were deemed immoral by Jones, Mason, and other people who embraced a holiness ethic. In the Black Baptist churches, the first phase of salvation was only preached, and the first and final phase was called confession. With confession of Jesus Christ as God's Son, Baptists believed that salvation was complete. In the mid to late 1800s, Methodists, especially White Methodists began to acknowledge the second work of grace called sanctification.[10]

In the beginnings of the fledgling COGIC Church, Mason and Jones were shunned by the Black Baptists and Methodist churches for being followers of a religious doctrine that espoused a more radical life in Christ, spiritually. Jones and Mason preached Holiness and sanctification as a prescribed lifestyle for all Christians and focused on conquering unethical behaviors that were not conducive to a holy lifestyle. The Black Baptists and Methodists became, in the eyes of Jones and Mason, rigid organizational structures that sought to serve humans and not God. Mason and Jones as Baptist preachers wanted the spirituality of Holiness, a Christian's life led by God, not by the doctrines proposed by boards of the Baptist and Methodist churches. Mason and Charles Jones rejected the idea that salvation ended when one confessed Christ, but maintained that a Christian had to be sanctified and live holy according to God's Word with the objective of achieving spiritual perfection.[11]

After disagreeing with the Baptist doctrines on the finality of salvation upon confession, Mason and Jones were excommunicated from the Black Baptist Church and began to preach a message of Holiness and sanctification throughout Arkansas, Mississippi, and Tennessee. As a general rule, their preaching appealed to the masses of rural farming communities throughout the South as they became a nemesis to middle-class African-Americans and Whites, who viewed Holiness groups as cults.[12] Being shunned by the Baptists and Methodists gave Mason and Jones preaching ammunition; both men used the prideful actions of the middle class Baptists and Methodists for the purpose of showing new lower class converts that God wanted the poor and downtrodden even though men may look down upon them. By the Holy Spirit, Mason led many campground meetings in fields and on farms, bringing the Gospel to the poor with shouting and praising God for giving them a holy and righteous life. Mason and Jones were free to preach without any worries of supervision or doctrinal oversight that could deter their message of being saved and converted to live sanctified in the Holy Spirit. Many people were converted to Christ under Mason and Jones's preaching, creating a renewed focus on living a life free from the bondage of sin. Mason and Jones preached against smoking, drinking, dipping snuff, secular music, dancing and drinking Coca-Cola. On the issue of drinking Coke, during the late 1800s and the early 1900s, Coke contained real cocaine. According to Mason and Charles Jones, the new spiritual life in God would not a holy person to succumb to the immoral standards of the world. The holy life in the Spirit of God, as a belief, kept the saints from smoking, drinking, and cursing, and other vices. Overall, Jones and Mason wanted to be led by the Spirit in all facets of their lives, professionally and personally. In the initial development of the COGIC Church, Mason and Jones's preaching was free from the responsibility of organization. Both men served as roving evangelists who preached in several areas and then moved on to preach to other crowds.

However, these loose bands of believers eventually needed organization and administration. Mason had received a name for the organization in 1897, calling the new spirit-led church, the Church of God in Christ. According to COGIC ideology, Mason received the name for the Church of God in Christ from God as he walked down Gaines Street in Little Rock, Arkansas; the name was based on the biblical scripture, 1 Thess. 2:14.[13] The passage of scripture stated: For ye, brethren, become followers of the Churches of God which in Judea are in Christ Jesus.... In an ironic twist, the Church of God in Christ became organized with administrative heads in Mississippi, Arkansas, and Tennessee. No matter how the leaders maintained that a church should be led by the Holy Spirit, secularization, in an organizational manner, had to take place in order for Mason and Jones to successfully manage the affairs and concerns of their newly found converts. Much like the early Church in the Roman Empire, the original Christians did not have much organization; however, when they perceived that Jesus was not coming back within several years, the Christians settled down and organized churches. Many of the followers of Jones and Mason believed that Jesus was coming soon.[14]Nevertheless, much like the early Christian Church, reality set into the new sanctified believers so they began to establish churches and have services until the Second Coming of Jesus Christ. Mason and Jones had to take on the secular attributes of church structure and produce doctrines for the sanctified believers.

Thus, Charles Jones and Mason proclaimed a Christian should live a life that was separated from the immorality of the world and was contrary to the Baptist theological concept that salvation was complete and final at the phase of confession. Many of the teachings denounced drinking, smoking, adultery, going to clubs, and proclaimed a "modest" dress code for men and women.[15] Also, the union between Jones and Mason spurred the African-American movement of Holiness in the South. This early "movement" went through a naming phase. First, Jones and Mason's group was called the "Movement;" then the two preachers were calling their movement, the "Church of God."[16] However, not wanting to be confused with the White Pentecostal Church of God in Anderson, Indiana and Cleveland, Tennessee, Jones and Mason desired another name. In 1897, Mason received a divine inspiration from God to name the Church, "Church of God in Christ." This marked the beginning of the only African-American religious Christian denomination founded, organized, and administered exclusively by African-Americans without being a by-product of any White Christian denomination.[17] From the beginning of Mason's conversion to Holiness and sanctification and before traveling to Azusa, this point in COGIC history was called the Pre-Mason Era because Mason was not the main leader in the Church of God in Christ, Unincorporated. Charles Price Jones was the General Overseer of the newly formed denomination.

Mason's Pentecostal religious experience began at the services conducted by Apostle William Seymour at 312 Azusa Street in Los Angeles, California, another Black preacher who defied racial prejudices and stereotypes. African-Americans, White Americans, Latinos, Africans, Germans, Englishmen, and a plethora of other races and ethnic groups worshipped God collectively without regard to the social climate of racism and prejudice. The worshippers claimed that the power and authority of the Holy Spirit impacted their lives. The key to the cooperation was that all members acknowledged the presence of the Holy Spirit which destroyed prejudice against gender and color. Everyone was a child of God, and everyone could be saved and speak in tongues as the "Spirit gave utterance."[18]

In a similar historical trend dating back to the early Christian Church of the Roman Empire, the Church of God in Christ (COGIC) proclaimed its existence as a Bible-following, Spirit-led group of believers who did not conform to the standards of the world. Testimonies of COGIC members often boasted that they were in the world but not of the world, meaning that they were living for God hoping to be in heaven when their natural lives expired. As the only major Christian denomination in the United States that was originally founded by African-Americans, the Church of God in Christ produced legacies that impacted Pentecostalism and all other areas of Christendom with a renewed fervor of righteous living and spiritual revivalism. The spirituality of the Church of God in Christ was embodied in the personal life of Bishop Charles Mason. His life was dominated by the spirituality of Holy Ghost possession, dancing and shouting, speaking in tongues, and living a holy life.[19] Mason believed that the Holy Spirit had eminent power in church affairs and should take priority in the lives of the COGIC followers and believers. Around the late 1890s, Mason was preaching to thousands of people in the areas of Arkansas, Mississippi, and Tennessee with much charismatic conviction and spirituality that had been prevalent in the secret slave church meetings that were forbidden by the masters.[20] Mason led services that were dominated by prayer, preaching, shouting, dancing, and singing. The major focus of Mason was that all Christians or saints should be led by the Holy Spirit.

Chapter Four records the events that prompted the beginning of the Mason Era and the end of the partnership between Mason and Charles Price Jones, triggered by Mason's new belief around the issue of glossolalia. Before Mason became the sole leader of the COGIC Church movement, he was an Assistant Overseer of Tennessee under the leadership of General Overseer Charles Price Jones. Jones was the original leader of the COGIC movement.[21] He and his group, according to records of Calvin McBride, did not decide to use the Church of God in Christ moniker until 1906.[22]

To explain the difference of Mason's Church of God in Christ,

Incorporated, which formed after the split between Jones and Mason, and the first Church of God in Christ led by Jones, Church records display the disagreement between a spirit-led, tongue-speaking Mason and a practical student of theology, Charles Jones. Mason's spiritual tendencies were pitched against Jones's academic reasoning over the issue of speaking in tongues after receiving the Baptism of the Holy Spirit. Mason's renewed spirituality was a by-product of his visit to the Azusa Revival under William J. Seymour in 1907.[23] Mason's spirituality clashed with Jones's practical view of speaking in tongues as being one of the signs of the Holy Spirit. In the aftermath, a court case ensued, Frank Avant vs CH Mason, which determined who could keep the Church of God in Christ name along with the churches.

The theological dispute occurred in the Shelby County Chancery

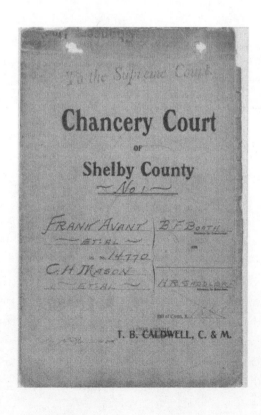

Court in Memphis, Tennessee. In March 1907, Mason left the South with John A. Jeter and David J. Young to attend the Azusa Street Revival in Los Angeles, California. The three men were seeking to confirm the news of a great outpouring of the Holy Ghost upon Christians, causing the people to speak in tongues.[24] When Mason, Jeter, and Young returned to Tennessee and Mississippi, the proclamation of tongues by Mason was met with resistance by General Overseer and leader of the early COGIC Church, Charles Price Jones. Mason's theology, which was an extension of Seymour's interpretation, made tongues a requirement in receiving the Baptism of the Holy Ghost. At that moment in time, Mason advocated and agreed with a third dispensation of salvation: The Baptism of the Holy Ghost with fire and evidence of speaking in tongues. His friend and leader, General Overseer Jones, disagreed with the tongues proclamation accompanying the Baptism of the Holy Ghost. Jones believed that glossolalia was not a mandatory sign of the Holy Spirit.[25] The disagreement over tongues led to the dissolution of Jones and Mason's relationship as leaders of Holiness. Beginning in 1907, the politics of tongues played out in the Chancery Court in Memphis, Tennessee and the state supreme court in Jackson, Tennessee. [26] At the end of the court case, Mason led the Church God in Christ into Holiness-Pentecostalism.

Ironically, a court case decided who would lead the Church of God in Christ into the twentieth century. For this study, historical evidence will show the transition of a charismatic church leader and a loosely configured association of individual congregations to an organized and bureaucratic institution of religious and political power. Previous evidence recorded Mason's early secular practices that overshadowed his spiritual tendencies, that evidence was the court case involving Mason's faction and the Frank Avant faction, displayed by the legal fighting over the mandatory action of speaking in tongues upon the Baptism of the Holy Ghost.[27] So, the age-old question arose, can any church maintain the quintessence of spirituality in a world filled with overwhelming egos and pride, and can egos and pride be eliminated from the church organization? As a trend, a church seems to be more spirited and less secular when it is persecuted and secluded from mainstream society.

After settling down in to an organized Church of God in Christ, Mason decided to pursue his fervent passion in being Spirit-led and Spirit-filled. Mason's Holy Ghost experience prepped him for moving the Church of God in Christ from a Holiness group to a Pentecostal-Holiness group. When Mason attended the Azusa Revival, he stated he had a renewed spiritual life after experiencing the phenomenon of speaking in tongues. Glossolalia was a mandatory sign, according to Pentecostal belief structure, that a person had received the Baptism of the Holy Spirit.[28]

When Mason returned to the areas of Memphis, Tennessee, and Jackson, Mississippi, his newly found spirituality with the evidence of speaking in tongues was not received by Overseer Charles Jones.[29] An argument ensued between Mason and Jones over whether believers needed to speak in tongues as evidence that they possessed the Holy Spirit. Mason's stance caused Jones to react with a theological explanation that tongues was one of the signs of the Holy Spirit[30], and the argument eventually led the two men of high spirituality into the secular realm of a court case. Considering the situation, two men led by the Holy Spirit were driven to the secular sphere of local courts to settle a theological debate. The court case proved to contradict the perception of Pentecostal Christians praying over their differences in the Holy Spirit. However, these specific disagreements were being decided by a secular judge who did not necessarily believe in the authority and power of the Holy Spirit. In 1910, at the end of the court cases, Mason was awarded the authority to use the name, Church of God in Christ, and Jones had to change his church name to Church of Christ (Holiness).[31] Nevertheless, after the trial, Mason sought to maintain the characteristic of his life and church in being guided by the Holy Ghost. From 1910 to 1961, Charles Mason was the face and example of spiritual living and power which dominated COGIC's existence as a national and international religious force.

Chapter Five casts light on the internal growth of the Church of God in Christ under the leadership of Mason. Furthermore, Mason's Azusa Street Revival experience and leadership of the COGIC Church marked the continuous impact of the Mason Era on the COGIC history timeline. Mason and his followers mimicked the Azusa tradition in wanting to preach, pray, sing, and testify under the power of the Holy Spirit. Evangelism helped Mason and the preachers under his supervision to spread the message of Holy Ghost possession with the evidence of speaking in tongues. Mason sent preachers like E.R. Driver, who was a minister under Mason's leadership at Saints Home COGIC, to Los Angeles, California, and he sent other preachers to evangelize in Chicago, Detroit, New York, and other major cities.[32] Under Mason's supervision, preachers were advised to preach sanctification and Holiness with the final phase of salvation being the Baptism of the Holy Ghost.

Also in Chapter Five, Mason dealt with the issue of gender politics as he recognized the roles that women could play in the growth of COGIC. Mason acknowledged the power of the women in the COGIC Church as they were known as the prayer warriors, song leaders, supporters of preaching, and Bible Band leaders.[33] Mason, with Mother Elizabeth Roberson,established the Women's Department as a powerful organization within the COGIC Church. Women like Mother Roberson were stern advocates of holy living and being used by the Spirit. COGIC women wanted to maintain a standard of the holy, sanctified woman not only through love, peace, and joy, but also in dress and appearance. COGIC women could not wear pants, but had to wear long dresses below the knee. Also, COGIC women were to abstain from make-up, open-toed shoes, gaudy colors such as red, flashy hats,[34] and other dress and attributes that were deemed worldly like the modern woman of the early 1920s. COGIC women kept Mason's idea of a Spirit-led Church as part of their mission. Women started preaching in the northern and western parts of the United States, establishing missions and churches under the spirit of COGIC. Even though women had established many COGIC Churches, women could not be ordained as elders and pastors and had to yield the church to a male preacher.[35] COGIC women had played major roles in establishing local congregations in some of the most distressed areas of America. Despite the chauvinistic obstacles faced by COGIC women, the Women's Department thrived and supported Bishop Mason throughout his leadership tenure as Senior Bishop of the Church of God in Christ, Incorporated. COGIC Women possessed a passion that enabled their group to rely heavily on the Holy Spirit for guidance while following the examples of Mason. Mothers and missionaries of the COGIC Church displayed, evidenced by COGIC historical writers, Calvin White and Anthea Butler, a "closeness" to God, a prominent dedication to prayer, and a fervent passion to evangelize the world under the banner of the COGIC Home and Foreign Mission Department.

Chapter Five follows the Church of God in Christ, Inc's tremendous growth in membership under the dominant leadership of Mason. With the growth in membership, the Mason Era saw the rise of other COGIC factions that separated from COGIC, Inc. The first faction occurred in 1912 under the leadership of Elias Dempsey Smith. Other separations from COGIC, Inc., occurred in 1914 and 1932. In 1914, the Assemblies of God (AOG) was formed in response to White Pentecostal leaders leaving COGIC leadership, which was predominantly African-American. In 1932, Overseer Justus Bowe of Arkansas disagreed with Mason over the COGIC, Inc.'s, episcopal authority. Justus Bowe believed in a congregational authority.[36] So Justus Bowe and other ministers left in 1932 to form Church of God in Christ, Congregational.

Other factions formed after Mason's death over the validity of the office of Senior Bishop. Up to 1961, the top officer in COGIC, Inc., was the office of senior bishop. However, in 1968, COGIC, Inc.'s top religious leader became a Presiding Bishop, marking a transitional point from the process of senior spiritual succession to an election held every four years. The tradition of senior spiritual succession occurred when Senior Bishop Ozro T. Jones, Sr. assumed the role of national leader after the death of Mason. Jones was the most senior spiritual leader in the COGIC faith and he was the only living bishop of the first five bishops who had been appointed by Mason.

Even though Senior Bishop Mason was involved in one of the most defining court cases in COGIC history, his participation in the first court case of 1907 in reference to 1 Cor. 6:1-7[37] was captured by COGIC writer, Calvin McBride, as being an attack on the Holy Spirit with Mason being the representative of that Spirit. That first court case in 1907 set a precedence for other court cases involving the COGIC Church. This landmark court case encompassed the idea of who would lead the church after the split between Holiness members and Holiness-Pentecostal members. Another landmark court case on this scale occurred after the death of the Founding Father.

Mason continued to spread his newfound belief of the Holy Ghost Baptism evidenced by speaking in tongues. However, for most of his life, as witnessed by his family and colleagues, Mason exhibited a life full of faith, prayer, and fasting to preach with the Holy Ghost and fiery conviction. Upon his death, the Church leadership suffered a tremendous blow for there was no clear, selected candidate to assume the role as the spiritual leader of the Church of God in Christ. The year 1961 marked a critical point in COGIC history as a major shift from spirituality to secularization occurred with heated political battles over who should lead the Church.

Chapter Six chronicled the events during the second phase of the Mason Era as COGIC became an international institution. COGIC women leaders were instrumental in carrying the Pentecostal message to overseas territories and were involved in civic organizations on the home front. Under Mason's leadership, the Official COGIC Manual was revised by Bishop O.T. Jones, Sr. and Bishop J.E. Bryant. The COGIC Manual detailed the church's doctrine and displayed an extensive list of male and female leaders in several states and foreign territories. Additionally, this chapter outlined COGIC's participation in the Civil Rights Movement and the events that contributed to the volatile confrontations over future leadership after the death of Mason.

Chapter Seven examines events in COGIC in the years immediately following the death of Mason. COGIC leadership after 1961 was left in a state of confusion and plagued by opportunistic leaders, bishops and elders as the church entered the Post-Mason Era. After Mason's death, the spiritual ascension of Senior Bishop Ozro T. Jones was seen as the clear choice. O. T. Jones, Sr. was the assistant to Bishop Mason and was one the last surviving members of the first five bishops appointed in the Church of God in Christ. On the other hand, other members supported Robert Mason, Bishop Mason's son, and Mother Lillian Brooks-Coffey, Bishop Mason's close confidant as successors.[38]Even though Mother Coffey was a female leader, the COGIC constitution, at that point in time, did not strictly forbid women in holding the office of elder, pastor, or bishop because women had previously held the title of overseer, along with the male leadership. Lastly, there was the son-in-law of Bishop Mason, Bishop James O. Patterson, married to Bishop Mason's daughter, Deborah Mason. With many possibilities to consider for leadership, matters became more complicated when it was learned that Mason did not leave clear instructions on who should be his successor. This situation left a huge void, giving an opportunity for a significant group of bishops to defy the spiritual and executive authority of Senior Bishop Jones.

Scholars, Bobby Bean, Robert Owens, and Calvin White have labeled the years 1961-1968 as the "Dark Ages of the Church of God in Christ" or the "Years of Wilderness Wanderings."[39] However, the names for those years have been tainted by biased leaders and scholars who did not support the leadership of O.T. Jones. Interestingly, Senior Bishop O. T. Jones disappeared from the COGIC history timeline. Moreover, the concept of senior spiritual leadership was replaced by the acceptance of a quadrennial election of a leader called a presiding bishop. After all the infighting against O.T. Jones and all the usurping of power over the leader who had served under Bishop Mason, the COGIC Church found its way back into court in Memphis, Tennessee. The court case, A.B. McEwen, J.O. Patterson, Complainants vs. O.T.

Jones, R. E. Ranger, O.T. Jones, Jr, Defendants, determined the future process of how COGIC leadership would be chosen in officiating the affairs of the Church.[40]

In 1968, after the Chancery Court of Memphis instructed the COGIC Church to create a General Assembly to elect its leaders, Bishop James O. Patterson, Mason's son-in-law, began the age of a secularized/political Church of God in Christ when he became the first Presiding Bishop along with eleven members, who composed the first COGIC General Board.[41] The spiritual leadership example set by Bishop Mason disintegrated and O. T. Jones, the last contact of Mason's spiritual legacy was left out of the process by a court generated assembly. The most glaring example of the secularization of the Church of God in Christ was the election of the Presiding Bishop and the General Board. The Presiding Bishop and General Board were elected for a term of four years and the elections took place in November. The essence of Bishop Mason's model for spiritual leadership was overtaken by a secularized imitation of the national political-presidential leadership process.

Since the death of Bishop Mason, who has been immortalized in the annals of Pentecostal history, the COGIC Church has been constantly trying to recapture the Holy Ghost movement that propelled sanctification and spirituality to the forefront of Christian lifestyles. Each Presiding Bishop of COGIC has tried to re-create the Azusa Street Revival experience for his tenure by conducting Holy Ghost Conferences and meetings that focused solely on prayer, Holy Ghost Spirit-focused gatherings, fasting, and preaching.[42] The attempts have been admirable; though the same leaders had been responsible for the secularization of the COGIC Church. Before Bishop J.O. Patterson died in 1989, he issued a profound statement, that "we" need to take the politics out of the Church. On the contrary, J.O. Patterson was mainly responsible for bringing politics into the COGIC Church; politics characterized his ascension to the office of Presiding Bishop. Politics, power, and ambition dominated every sphere of COGIC spaces during and beyond the 1970s. Furthermore, several mainstream denominations have advanced through the phenomenon of being institutionalized, where politics trumped spirituality.

As the research focused on national politics in the COGIC faith, Chapter Eight outlined the rise in power of the first COGIC Presiding Bishop, James O. Patterson, Sr. and some political endeavors on the state level. Using the state of Georgia as an example, COGIC state leaders felt the impact of 1968 and other policies enacted by the church's national leadership. Georgia had leadership problems that were handled by one of Mason's leading overseers, Bishop Riley Williams. Most recently, the current Presiding Bishop, Charles Edward Blake had to handle some succession of leadership problems in Georgia that dealt with replacing, not only a state bishop, but the former COGIC Presiding Bishop, Chandler D. Owens. Georgia often required the attention of the national leadership to solve issues of leadership immorality, abuse of authority, and the unwillingness to obey and respect the office of the state bishop. Many of the events in Georgia mimicked the events on the national scene, especially the politics surrounding leadership. Nevertheless, the politics of leadership and details were, for the most part, kept from the public view of the congregations. The circle of leadership had details of the political events, but the lay members were not privy to many of the facts and specific actions of leadership. Generally, COGIC members were instilled with the motto: "Always obey leadership", since the early years of Bishop Mason.

Chapter Nine highlights the succession of presiding bishops, after the death of Bishop J.O. Patterson, Sr., and their administrations will be highlighted up to the tenure of the current Presiding Bishop, Charles E. Blake. Key events occurred during each administration with connections to the state of Georgia. Moreover, each succeeding COGIC presiding bishop faced the many challenges of maintaining the standard of Holiness that was espoused by the founder, Bishop Mason. Some internal groups in opposition to the elected leadership developed during the quadrennial election process that caused friendships to end and political factions to develop around candidates running for the office of presiding bishop.

The Epilogue explores the legacy of Pentecostalism, in general, and the Church of God in Christ, specifically. Other movements that copied the characteristics of the Pentecostal Movement will be reviewed. Some criteria for showing Pentecostal connectivity is targeted, and the following criteria may not be all-inclusive for a movement to qualify as being connected to Pentecostalism: 1) The divine nature or reverence status of the leader perceived as God's anointed servant; 2) Mass gatherings of people who adhere to paying tithes and offerings in obedience to God's commandment; and, 3) Dynamic, charismatic preaching in services dominated by Spirit possession and demonstrative praise to God in the form of shouting and dancing, divine healing, prophecy, and the utterance of different kinds of languages or tongues.

COGIC Pentecostal legacies can be seen across the national and international spheres of religion. Many of the charismatic leaders in this modern era were connected to the Pentecostal Movement, and many were affiliated with the Church of God in Christ like preaching sons, Carlton Pearson and Paul Morton. Even though both preachers are no longer in the COGIC denomination, their COGIC backgrounds have been evident in their ministries. Carlton Pearson started the Azusa Conference, meetings that hearkened back to the times of the Azusa Street Revival. Paul Morton established the Full Gospel International Baptist Church Fellowship, merging Black Baptist and COGIC religious cultures, while adopting the leadership title of presiding bishop. Other Pentecostal legacies can be seen in the works of Jim Bakker and Jimmy Swaggart, prominent Assembly of God ministers who impacted the phenomenon of televangelism. In a negative light, these two preachers have been the source of scandals that have been connected to the Pentecostal Movement. Jim Bakker's affair with Jessica Hahn and his alleged homosexual activities embarrassed the spiritual followers of Pentecostalism. As devastating, Jimmy Swaggart's rendezvous with two prostitutes did not help the Pentecostal message of Holiness and righteous living.[43] The actions of Pentecostal preachers who had been placed on moral pedestals by their followers have caused many believers and non-believers to doubt the sincerity of a rigid Holy-Pentecostal lifestyle as the leaders fell into scandalous situations. Moreover, in recent polls, there has been a section of the population who have left the Church scene altogether, citing a morally bankrupt leadership core.

In the days of the COGIC Church's humble beginnings, the institution and its leaders faced the politics of race by preaching sanctification and Holy Ghost possession to all unbelievers. Moreover, early Pentecostal services not only broke down racial barriers but also destroyed chauvinistic ideals of women not being allowed to preach. Early Pentecostal churches and missions were launched by several influential women preachers such as Aimee Semple McPherson who founded the Foursquare Gospel Movement, Florence Crawford, a veteran of the Azusa Street Revival, and Elizabeth Woods Roberson, who established a powerful Women's Department in the Church of God in Christ, Inc. COGIC's standards of holy living obliterated racial and gender barriers in the early twentieth century. During a time of overt racial and gender discrimination, the COGIC Church produced an environment that espoused equality.

CHAPTER 1

BAPTIST AND HOLINESS
FOUNDATIONS OF COGIC

The Church of God in Christ, Inc. developed on a historical timeline via influences from charismatic leaders and Christian theological movements that occurred during the eighteenth, nineteenth, and twentieth centuries. Early COGIC leaders were influenced by the Black Baptist Church traditions, the Holiness Movement that occurred during the Post-Bellum era, and the Azusa Street Revival that initiated a Pentecostal explosion upon Christian worship around the world. Charles Harrison Mason, the founder of COGIC, Inc., took part in all three arenas of Christianity, and he carried his Black Baptist roots, his Holiness conversion, and his Pentecostal tongue-speaking experience into the formation of the Church of God in Christ, Inc. Observing this impact of religious triangulation, the COGIC Church adhered to a belief system that embraced the following features; (1) salvation by grace; (2) a set of values regarding private morality; and (3) an openness to an ongoing religious experience. These experiences were personal in nature and could not be specifically analyzed due to a plethora of inward experiences felt differently by various members in many parts around the world.

The purpose of this chapter is to capture the general essence of the COGIC experience in light of interpreting and annotating its complicated history, which is filled with testimonies of charismatic events, signs and wonders, miracles, faith healing, and emotionalism. COGIC church services resounded with spirited expression with powerful hypnotic music with the members chanting repetitive phrases in songs of worship.[1] While the idea of a deeper spiritual pursuit in religion was surfacing in the South, political struggles existed over the issues of what doctrines would prevail in the churches, what leaders would have control over the churches, and would the churches remain interracial or would the churchgoers separate according to race? Throughout this paper, the politics of religious doctrine, the politics of establishing leadership, and the politics of race dominated the religious landscape of Holiness and Pentecostalism. While the masses of people followed the ideals of a holy lifestyle, political battles were waged behind the scenes as people jumped and shouted without any care for the heated arguments about interpretation of scripture, court cases, and financial impropriety.

In some sense, the Black Baptist Church where Mason started preaching, was akin to the Black Pentecostal Church of God in Christ; the Black Baptist Church became the first political battleground over the doctrine of sanctification. Formed in 1773, from the ideals of slave preachers like Andrew Bryan and George Liele, Black Baptists were direct descendants of the slave religion practices that were characterized by singing, shouting, dancing, and praising God. The Black preacher was called to his office by God, as perceived by the Black followers and the preacher himself, and he exercised dominance because of his knowledge of the sacred book, the Bible.[2] The Black Baptist slave preacher not only served as the liaison between the slaves and God, but also between the slaves and White authoritative figures. Looking at the phenomenon of African-American duality, the Black Baptist slave preacher had to preach one sermon during the day in front of the master and the plantation overseer with a theme of pleasing the master; however, at night, a different sermon was preached.[3] The sermons at night had themes of freedom and proclaimed that the master was pharaoh, and pharaoh needed to let the enslaved people go. Sunday day sermons had the general theme of slaves being obedient to the master for obedience to the master was right in the eyes of the Lord. However, the sermons of freedom from slavery would translate into freedom in society and being free from the bondage of sin. The duality of the African-American religious experience was pronounced in the fight against slavery and the battle to live a righteous life in the eyes of God. Moreover, the charismatic preaching about freedom took place in Mason's theological stance against worldly sin, for he believed that a person could not live a holy and sanctified life without the help of God. Preaching to the secular world structure to change the people living in the unholy landscape of mainstream society was a mainstay with early COGIC preachers Charles H. Mason and Charles Price Jones. Early Black Baptists were preaching against slavery and the mistreatment of African-Americans as second-class citizens, giving rise to preachers such as Nat Turner who led a slave insurrection in 1831[4] and Hiram Revels, who became one of America's first Black U.S. senators, replacing Jefferson Davis during Reconstruction.[5] Without a doubt, the Black Baptist element was entrenched into the foundation and development of the COGIC denomination. The elements of the Black Baptist slave religion can be seen in Mason's straightforward preaching style which was accompanied by singing and dancing. Mason and Jones received their early training under the guidance of leading Baptist preachers. Both attended Arkansas Baptist College under the supervision of Elias C. Morris, the first president of the National Baptist Convention, USA in 1895.[6] The Black Baptists and the Black Holiness group, in the form of the COGIC denomination became swapping grounds for many members who oscillated back and forth between the two denominations.

The main theological concept that separated the COGIC denomination from the Black Baptists was the finality of confession. In the Black Baptist tradition, salvation started and ended at the stage of confession. After a person confessed to wrongdoing with an outlook on life to adhere to righteous behavior, then that person could be in salvation and stay in salvation without having to complete any further steps. On the other hand, Mason and Jones began to preach against that doctrine, plainly called "once saved, always saved", because the two preachers had been influenced by the Holiness Movement by the end of the 1800s.

Another characteristic of the Black Baptist Church that gave Mason an edge in developing the COGIC Church was loose organizational structure. The local churches and preachers in the Black Baptist body did not have a mandatory order to affiliate with any national organization.[7] The loose structure of the Black Baptist Church allowed Mason to explore other religious doctrines, movements, and theologies. As a local pastor, Mason had autonomous control of his church and had the moral authority to determine a righteous, godly path for himself and the members due to his status as a respected, spiritual leader. Additionally, Mason's path to Holiness was not, initially, hampered by the Black Baptist Church. However, Mason's leadership adhered to episcopal authority, in which Mason, the general overseer of COGIC appointed pastors. Unlike the congregational authority in some Black Baptist Churches where the congregation voted on the selection of a pastor.

1.1. The Holiness Contribution in the COGIC Church

Looking at the start of the Holiness Movement in America, during the 1860s, anew religious theology on living"holy" dominated several regions of America. Synan argued that Methodist spirituality prompted by its main leader, John Wesley, was passed down to his followers during the Holiness Movement.[8] The Holiness Movement gave the COGIC Church another pillar to add to its foundation of salvation. The Holiness doctrine went beyond the first stage of salvation by proclaiming sanctification and how a person should live holy. The Holiness Movement advocated, minimally, two stages of salvation: justification and sanctification. Synan explained how both stages were considered the two-blessing theory.[9]Furthermore, the ideal of sanctification along with living holy was the second phase of salvation, following the confession of a person. There were many do's and don'ts in the sanctified/holy lifestyle. In Holiness, Christians were forbidden to partake in behaviors like fornication, adultery, lying, stealing, and cursing. Holiness standards also took improper behaviors to another level by forbidding members to drink alcohol, smoke, or chew tobacco. One of the main practices of Holiness was the situation surrounding divorcees. Members of Holiness could get a divorce; however, the member could not marry another person until their former spouse died. If a divorced Holiness person married again while their former spouse was yet alive, then that person was deemed as a sinner and could be chastised by church leadership. The concept of not marrying another person until your divorced spouse was deceased was problematic for Mason during his early years of conversion to Holiness. The belief of Holiness stated that Christians had to act like Christians and not like the non-Christians who espoused to immoral behavior and did not confess salvation. The divorce situation would be a stumbling block for Mason in these early years of being a Holiness preacher. Ithiel Clemmons recorded that from 1891 to 1893, Mason had a failed marriage to Alice Saxton, a childhood friend. Saxton did not believe in Holiness and refused to abide by the doctrinal restrictions, so she and Mason divorced in 1893.[10] Clemmons also documented that Mason had a bout with depression during this troublesome time because he was a single, divorced preacher who could not preach by example.

As Baptist and later Holiness preachers, Mason and Jones preached the second state of salvation with conviction that prompted the Black Baptist Church to shut their doors to their preaching opportunities. Obviously, telling people that confession was not good enough and that one had to do more to live a Christian life, was not a very popular message to established Baptists and Methodists. The rise of Holiness after 1894 was a religious revolt that paralleled the political and economic revolt of Populism, and Holiness kept the "ole" time religion which denounced capitalistic Christianity which created poverty, irresponsible uses of wealth, and unhealthy living conditions.[11] The Holiness Movement hearkened back to a time when Christians prayed and worshipped together with a primary focus on saving souls for God. The doctrines of Holiness gave a general feel of a spiritual movement among White

Christians. However, Black Christians and followers of Holiness had a different feel, one inclusive of erasing barriers due to race and gender. Black Holiness preachers, male and female, proclaimed a gospel that erased the color lines in a segregated America.

As Holiness became popular and entrenched in the rural South, ironically, Holiness doctrines of Wesleyan perfectionism had its beginning in the North after the upheaval of the Second Great Awakening. Recorded by the Knoxville Daily Chronicle, in 1872, Northern Methodist ministers came to Tennessee to preach Christian holiness and perfectionism, the ability to live above immoral standards here on earth.[12] During the 1890s, Mason and Jones heard the message of Holiness and began to preach the message of spiritual perfectionism in the Black Baptist Church. The Black Baptist Church responded by excommunicating the two preachers because the Black Baptist Church did not believe that certain behaviors were not immoral, like alcohol consumption, sexual relationship between two unmarried consenting adults, smoking, secular dancing, and listening to jazz music.[13] Holiness preaching expressed the need for the Christian to abstain from behaviors that were considered evil and unethical. The purpose of Holiness preaching and living served as a benchmark on the limits of Christians becoming carnal and worldly.[14]

In the South, the Holiness movement identified with the poor and tried to imitate the Bible's proclamation in helping the poor.[15] The Holiness message of equality in the eyes of God and interracial revival meetings crossed a limited number of racial barriers that existed in the South. Mason, as a Holiness preacher, had preached to White converts and had several White ministers acquiesced to his leadership as a powerful, charismatic speaker of the Gospel. Mason believed in helping the poor which was one of his main themes of preaching to all people, regardless of their race, gender, or economic background. The Holiness message proclaimed all people were equal. Furthermore, this notion of equality was later transplanted into the Pentecostal Movement at 312 Azusa Street, Los Angeles, California.

From the Holiness Movement of the 1860s, the Pentecostal Movement emerged at the end of the nineteenth century. The Pentecostal Movement was the last leg in developing the foundation for Mason's theology on salvation and the transition of the COGIC Church. For the believers in Pentecostalism, there were three works of grace. The first work was confession, established by Mason's example of being a Black Baptist convert, in which, he began his early preaching career. The second blessing theory proclaimed the ideals of holiness/sanctification. During this phase, the Christian was concerned about living a life "free from the bondage of sin" and perfecting a life that exemplified righteousness. The third blessing theory was the final phase of salvation, the Baptism of the Holy Ghost with evidence of speaking in tongues. As Allan Anderson defined Pentecostalism, he stated that early North American Pentecostals, named Classical Pentecostals, discriminated against anyone who refused to believe that one had to speak in a tongue (glossolalia) to possess the Holy Spirit.[16] Mason's experience at Azusa Street, led by the preaching of William J. Seymour, converted Mason to the life of Pentecostalism. According to Mason's testimony, being Holy Ghost-filled enhanced his preaching, and caused him to extend beyond the second work of grace and plunge forward into Pentecostalism.[17]

1.2. From Holiness to Holiness-Pentecostalism

How did Mason transition, theologically, from a Baptist preacher to a Holiness preacher and finally to a Holiness-Pentecostal preacher? The answer to the question rest on the Pentecostal preaching of Apostle William J. Seymour during the Azusa Street Revival. Seymour was born in Centerville, Louisiana on May 2, 1870, and as a young lad, some records stated that he was a prophetic dreamer.[18]Leaving Louisiana at the age of sixteen, Seymour served in various religious denominations; a member of the Methodist denomination, the Holiness denomination, and, finally, the Apostolic Faith Movement.[19] Seymour eventually became a traveling Holiness preacher and evangelist after receiving the call from God to a life of ministry. Like many preachers of this era, both Black and White, Holiness preachers were not required to have a formal education. Once the preacher professed that God had called him or her, then they stood on their perception of God-given leadership and authority to proclaim the Gospel of Jesus Christ.

Before coming to Azusa Street, Seymour was a student in the class of Charles Fox Parham, a Pentecostal theorist who believed that tongues were a mandatory sign in possessing the Holy Spirit.[20] Parham was also labelled a racist and segregationist because Seymour was not allowed to sit in the classroom with White students. Seymour had to stand outside the classroom to receive his instructions. Later, Seymour received an invitation to pastor a small Holiness congregation in Los Angeles, but was dismissed from the pastoral position due to his preaching on "tongues" as mandatory evidence of receiving the Holy Ghost. After leaving the congregation, Seymour was allowed to have a pulpit on the front porch of Richard and Ruth Asberry's home located on 214 Bonnie Brae Avenue.[21] Seymour preached hard against evil behaviors, advocated divine-faith healing, and offered salvation in the light of the third work of grace, the Baptism of the Holy Ghost with evidence of speaking in tongues. According to COGIC Presiding Bishop Charles Blake, the modern Pentecostal Movement began in 1906 when Seymour started preaching at 214 Bonnie Brae Street and received the Baptism of the Holy Ghost and spoke in tongues.[22] The house at Bonnie Brae Street eventually became too small to accommodate the large crowds seeking the Spiritual Baptism with tongues as the onlookers gazed at the folks shouting, screaming, dancing, singing, and other types of non-rational, ecstatic religious experiences. Outgrowing the Asbury's' home, Seymour moved the group to an old livery building at 312 Azusa Street, and the charismatic movement was named the Azusa Street Revival. This religious phenomenon was characterized by people claiming salvation or being saved, divine faith healing, miracles, and most of all, the Baptism of the Holy Ghost evidenced by speaking in tongues.[23]

A year later in 1907, Mason ventured to Los Angeles, California to investigate the rumors of people being baptized in the Spirit and uttering in tongues. Mason spent five weeks at the Azusa Street Revival and was convinced that he had acquired a new anointing evidenced by speaking in tongues, divine healing, Godly wisdom, and the exorcism of demons.[24] Mason's Pentecostal experience enhanced his Holiness commitment by placing emphasis on a physical manifestation of the Holy Spirit in the form of tongues. Different kinds of tongues existed among the Pentecostals. One tongue, a "babbling," was when a member experienced possession by the Holy Spirit, and the other form of tongues was actually a spoken foreign language. Under Seymour's teachings, Mason believed that everyone had to speak in tongues if he claimed a Holy Ghost experience. The act of "speaking in tongues" was the discriminating factor that distinguished the dedicated Christians from the marginal Christians.

However, Mason's newfound doctrine of a mandatory tongue-speaking experience under the power of the Holy Ghost was not received by the leading preacher of Black Holiness Movement in the southern tri-state areas of Arkansas, Mississippi, and Tennessee. In 1907, Mason returned to Mississippi from California. Charles Jones disagreed with the new doctrine of mandatory tongues proposed by Mason. Jones maintained the strict doctrines of Holiness and resisted anything that resembled spiritism, mysticism, and hypnosis.[25]Tongue-speaking was often observed when people were in a hypnotic, spiritual condition. From that point, Mason and Jones split into different religious organizations. Charles Jones stayed with the Holiness doctrine while Mason combined sanctification and the doctrines of Holiness with the new Spirit Baptism and tongues. Also, Mason continued, well into the twentieth century, being the key leader and face of the COGIC denomination.

After analyzing the three-religious phenomenon (Black Baptists, Holiness, and Pentecostalism) that are pillars in the COGIC faith, Mason, even in the postmodern era, has remained the dominant face of Black Pentecost. Therefore, the history of the COGIC Church has three main eras: Pre-Mason Era, Mason Era, and the Post-Mason Era. Chapter Two will display the events and key persons in the Pre-Mason Era and the following chapters will highlight the Mason Era and Post-Mason Era. Mason's life was dominant in all the research materials on the COGIC faith. His Holy Ghost experience and proclamation of miracles, as perceived by his followers, created the legend of Mason as a holy man who could heal the sick and cast out devils.[26]

As Mason continued in the path of Pentecostalism, Charles Jones maintained the doctrine of Holiness. For the most part, the concept of "speaking in tongues" has never been officially adopted by COGIC leadership. In many parts of the United States, some COGIC members dogmatically believe that a person should "speak in tongues", while other members do not believe that "tongues" are a mandatory sign for the Holy Spirit. Nevertheless, the COGIC denomination owe great debts to the Black Baptist organization, the Holiness Movement, and the Pentecostal Explosion at Azusa Street. Mason led many followers of the COGIC movement and with great influence, many preachers of the Black Baptist and Black Methodist denominations converted to COGIC. Mason, as a premier Holiness-Pentecostal preacher, was so influential, that White members and preachers began to follow him. Elder James Logan Delk, a white COGIC preacher, was so inspired by Mason's preaching in Conway, Arkansas; he wrote a book about Mason called, He Made Millions Happy.

Even though Mason's preaching converted many people and crossed racial boundaries, Charles Jones saw the glaring contradiction of the Pentecostal belief on "speaking in tongues." According to Charles Jones, the "tongues" doctrine was not mandated by the Bible and was not practical because a person could not understand a preacher who preached in "tongues." Many times, Charles Jones' common sense approach was trumped by the emotionalism of the Pentecostal Movement despite having no biblical proof. The showdown between Jones and Mason over "speaking in tongues" caused a rift between Holiness and Holiness-Pentecostal Christians that has not been addressed or answered, even in this present age.

Evidently, the rift between Mason and Charles Jones over "tongues" had the same implications and problems as in the case of sanctification. In 1899, Reverend Elias C. Morris had a rebuttal to Charles Jones and Mason's interpretation on sanctification. Morris expounded on how sanctification was being misinterpreted by Jones and Mason as they preached sinless perfection and bodily holiness.[27] Jones and Mason were expelled from the Baptist Convention because Morris believed that the word "sanctify" meant to be set apart or appointed to service. Morris refuted the perfection claims of sanctification by citing erroneous teachings that were not supported by sound biblical doctrines.[28] Since Mason and Charles Jones refused to stop preaching the perfection doctrines of sanctification, Morris had both men expelled from the Baptist Convention. The doctrine of sanctification preached by Jones and Mason upset many Baptist and Methodist preachers because a different standard of Christian living was being publicized. In the Holiness-Pentecostal faith, parishioners and clergy were supposed to set an example of righteous lifestyle that did not promote immoral practices.

The mediocrity of Christian living, according to the views of Mason and Jones, was unacceptable and a higher standard of holiness should be preached around the world. Holiness standards denounced lying, pre-marital sex, adultery, stealing, cursing, and any action that was not condoned by the Bible, as interpreted by the followers of sanctification. Furthermore, the Holiness living standards were taken to many extremities because many people wanted to live according to the Bible. Some extreme Holiness living standards included the following infractions: smoking; drinking alcohol, and in some churches, drinking tea or coffee; women could not wear pants according to a verse in the Book of Deuteronomy that stated a woman should not wear anything pertaining to a man; men, initially, could only wear bow ties because the neck tie, according to some members of the older COGIC generation, gave a man a proud look, and God hated a proud look; at some churches, women could not wear the color red because red was the color worn by prostitutes; children could not participate in varsity sports at school; and, members could not participate in secret societies, fraternities, and sororities. COGIC had set very high standards for a person to live holy and sanctified, which caused a great confrontation with other religious denominations not living by the standards of Holiness and Pentecostalism.

One of the most heated debates in the Black Pentecostal Movement under Mason was the ordination of women to clerical leadership positions of elder, pastor, superintendent, and bishop. As a Black Baptist preacher, as a Holiness preacher, and finally as a Pentecostal preacher, Mason led a COGIC faith that historically refused to ordain women to serve in positions of the church hierarchy.[29] According to the COGIC Manual, women cannot be considered for the offices of elder, pastor, superintendent, and bishop.[30] Women, in COGIC, have, for a long time, supported the doctrine that they should be teachers and not preachers. The trend of not ordaining women to preach in the Black Baptist and Holiness Churches continued in the Pentecostal faith, even though many women had established churches and preached to thousands of converts. The problem still exists today even though many other denominations have lifted the ban on ordaining women. However, women under the leadership of Mason developed an interdependent Department of Women that has supported the COGIC Church financially, physically, and spiritually. Women have "unofficially" held the titles of pastor, but have not been able to be nationally recognized as an elder/pastor. This issue will continue to be a problem for COGIC leadership well into the twenty-first century.

CHAPTER 2

THE PRE-MASON ERA: JONES AND MASON PROCLAIMED HOLINESS

In analyzing the backgrounds of Charles Jones and Mason, the Black Baptist theological foundation was prominent in both of their lives. Jones was born in Floyd County outside of Rome, Georgia on December 9, 1865.[1] Jones was reared by his mother, Mary Jones, in the Black Baptist faith in Georgia. After his mother's death in 1882, Jones wandered from Kingston to Rome, Georgia, with a final destination of picking cotton on Cat Island, a land strip that separated the states of Arkansas and Mississippi. Jones was converted under the Baptist religious doctrine of being saved from his sins in 1884, and the following year, after being healed miraculously from a state of poor health, he felt he had been called by God to preach the Gospel of Jesus Christ.[2] Under the Baptist doctrine of being saved, Jones had only experienced justification. He had not yet experienced the two-blessing theory of justification and sanctification under the Holiness doctrine. Under the Black Baptist denomination, in 1887, he was licensed by Pastor George Dickey and proceeded to preach in the Arkansas towns of Forrest City and Helena.

His Baptist preaching counterpart, Charles Harrison Mason, was born on September 8, 1864 (according to the latest COGIC research) in Union Depot[3], which later became the town of Bartlett, Tennessee. Mason's birth year has been inconsistent throughout COGIC history.[4] He and Jones' mothers were affiliated with the Black Baptist faith and they were strong influences on their sons. Mason's mother, Eliza

Mason, was described as highly spiritual and dedicated to prayer. Like Jones, Mason also experienced a battle with sickness during the yellow fever epidemic that struck the area around Memphis, Tennessee around 1879. Mason recovered from the sickness, and this healing was viewed as a sign of God's calling the young man to ministry and to be dedicated to the spiritual matters of God.[5] As a note, both Charles Jones and Mason had a spiritual awakening in the form of a miraculous healing which was one of the foundations in the religious sects called Holiness. Both men followed a path to being exposed to religious and spiritual matters in the Southern Black Baptist tradition. This Baptist tradition infused the concepts and rudiments of the slave religion which exemplified charismatic preaching, shouting and praising God, and dancing under the influence of God's Spirit. The Black Baptist religion served as the foundation for Charles Jones and Mason's early theological views of the world in relation to the salvation of Jesus Christ. However, as both men claimed to have received a "calling"[6] from God on their lives, Mason became more of a travelling, evangelical prophet while Jones became more of a pragmatic theologian who viewed shouting and dancing as physical expressions that did not guarantee the presence of God's Spirit.

Mason was licensed to preach in 1891 and married a young lady named Alice Saxton.[7] After only two years of marriage, the new Ms. Mason refused to acclimate to the life of a preacher's wife, so they were divorced in 1893. Not having a wife at that time was detrimental to Mason as he fell into a state of depression over his failed marriage and then his inability to live fully in the life of Holiness. Mason lived in an era when divorce was shameful, especially if your occupation was an African-American preacher who was expected to uphold the sanctity of marriage in front of the people in the church and community. Nevertheless, after the bouts with depression, Mason decided to continue his ministry and to pursue an education. Mason preached his first sermon on sanctification at the Mount Gale Missionary Baptist Church in Preston, Arkansas around 1893.[8]

Charles Jones and Mason met in 1895, representing two different preaching backgrounds and styles in the Baptist religion. Jones was the pastor of Mount Helm Baptist Church, that would later split over the issue of Holiness and Sanctification. Both men were mentored by Elias C. Morris, one of the key supporters of the historically black college, Arkansas Baptist, and the first leader of the National Baptist Convention. Both Jones and Mason attended Arkansas Baptist College; Jones completed his courses, however, Mason attended for about three months and dropped out of the educational process. According to Mason's testimony, he did not need the schools and that there was no salvation in schools.[9] However, after a careful study of Mason's tenure at Arkansas Baptist, evidence of Mason's educational background was at a minimal level. Entering a college without any record of graduating from high school would prove to be a difficult task for anyone. During this time, only one in ten persons graduated from high school, and the numbers were probably lower among the non-White population.

Even though they possessed different views on education and theology, both men agreed on the doctrine of Holiness. Jones and Mason latched on to the doctrine of a Holiness lifestyle, seeking more than the first phase of salvation and the finality of salvation which was taught to them in the Black Baptist Church. The finality of salvation of the Black Baptist religion was summed up in the popular phrase: "Once saved, always saved." This doctrine did not set well with Jones and Mason and they searched for more answers to their spiritual walk in the ministry.

The opportunity for Mason and Charles Jones to develop enhancements to the finality of salvation came through the doctrines of the Holiness Movement that was moving across the South, North, and West. Holiness preachers proclaimed a revelation that proposed a second stage or phase of salvation called Sanctification. The larger working-class Holiness minority in the South drew away from the worldliness and middle-class majority, while the middle class disliked the Holiness followers' puritanical and fanatical attitudes.[10] Furthermore, according to Anita Bingham Jefferson's research, the Holiness Movement in the African-American community started with Charles Price Jones.He realized that he did not need to feed the intellectual appetite of his congregation, but he sought to preach to their spiritual needs.[11] Jones became the first Black Holiness reformer to engage in the ministry of Sanctification and passionate teaching about the Holy Ghost. On June 6, 1897, Charles Jones advertised a meeting for all congregants who believed in Holiness and Sanctification to meet him in Jackson, Mississippi. Considered the first Holiness Convention for African-Americans, the roster included preachers such as Charles H. Mason, A.J. Scarborough, John A. Jeter, William S. Pleasant, and R. H. Morris.[12] This convention was significant in the transition from Black Baptist preaching to Black Holiness preaching which advocated the two-blessing theory with the addition of the second phase of salvation: Sanctification, a way of living a life wherein drinking alcohol, lying, stealing, illicit sex, gambling, cursing, and listening to popular music were considered immoral behaviors. Holiness reformers like Charles Jones and Mason preached against the denominational pride of churches, tobacco users, snuff dippers, whiskey drinkers, and lodge members. Holiness reformers gave a message of compliance on living holy, and if one did not live holy, that person was going to Hell.

The Holiness Movement started by Charles Jones had many obstacles. Charles Jones and Mason conducted several revivals, and it became apparent that Charles Jones's group needed a name to distinguish itself from the other denominations. At first, the Holiness outbreak in this early period around the Mid-South was referred to as the "Movement", and then the "Movement" changed to the Church of God. The name Church of God became problematic because the White Holiness group had the name with headquarters in Anderson, Indiana and Cleveland, Tennessee. 1897 became a key transitional year for the Baptist preachers in converting to Holiness. In that year, Mason preached in Lexington, Mississippi, but not at any of the Baptist churches. The Black Baptist churches had closed their doors to Mason and others who preached the doctrine of Sanctification and Holiness.[13] So Mason, a charismatic grassroots Christian evangelist, preached from the south entrance of the Holmes County courthouse in Lexington, and later Mr. John Lee provided Mason with the living room of his home to preach the new ministry based in Holiness and Sanctification.[14] Eventually, Mason's following outgrew the living room, so Mr. John Watson gave Mason and his followers permission to use his old abandoned gin house to hold services.[15] The old abandoned gin house technically became the first Church of God in Christ. The church was named Saint Paul Church of God in Christ. Jones and William Pleasant assisted Mason in establishing the first African-American independent Holiness Church which was not a by-product of any White established religious denomination. Another church was mentioned by COGIC researcher Calvin McBride. McBride stated that Mason had a church in Memphis, Tennessee, that was having services in a home, then the members moved to a tent, and then eventually built Saints Home COGIC in 1901 on the same property as the tent.[16]

How did the name Church of God in Christ come into being for the new Black Holiness Movement? In retrospect, before 1897, there existed a Church of God in Christ, Mennonite during the early 1800s in America. This group was evangelical in nature and had a strict, Puritan lifestyle. This group existed before Mason's revelation on the COGIC name. The Church of God in Christ, Mennonite were descendants of the Anabaptists and later they were greatly influenced, in 1536, by the former Catholic priest, Menno Simons, who was baptized and converted to the faith of the Anabaptists.[17] Thus, this new group became the Mennonites and did not believe in infant baptism, being involved in politics, or serving in the military. Their lives were supposed to be separate from the world in every way possible. Personal Christian doctrines of appearance were placed on men and women. Men had to wear beards and women had to wear a head covering. Due to persecution by Catholics and Protestant groups, Mennonites immigrated to the United States between the years of 1683 and the late 1800s[18], rivaling the development of Holiness and Pentecostal groups. Some similarities are noted in the development of the Church of God in Christ, Mennonite and the Church of God in Christ, Inc. Like the Mennonites, COGIC, Incorporated had a dominant founder who was converted from the Baptist faith to the Holiness faith, and then to the

Pentecostal faith. The Mennonites and COGIC, Inc. did not believe in infant baptism and both had grooming and dress code standards that were befitting to a "saintly" life. Mennonite women and some COGIC women wore covered headdress, and COGIC women could not wear pants or trousers. Nevertheless, no records have been discovered in determining whether Bishop Mason's revelation was influenced by the Church of God in Christ, Mennonite movement that had existed over 100 years before Mason's COGIC, Inc.

According to COGIC, Inc. history, the COGIC moniker was berthed in a rural African-American community on a fateful fall day in 1897. Mason was walking down 8th and Gaines Street in Little Rock, Arkansas and he proclaimed that God had spoken to him about the church name for the Holiness movement among African-Americans. Finally, Mason received the name "Church of God in Christ" which was based on the scripture, 1 Thess. 2:14 which stated, "For ye, brethren, became followers of the churches of God which in Judaea are in Christ Jesus......." So, the name Church of God in Christ became officially adopted, later in 1906, for the churches in Mississippi, Arkansas, and Tennessee under the Holiness leadership of Charles Price Jones.[19] The hierarchy of the new Holiness sect did not use leadership terms such as reverend, father, and bishop, because those were titles used by the denominations of Baptists, Catholic, and Methodists who refused to recognize the "power" to live free from sin in the Holy Spirit. Charles Jones and his followers adopted the title of overseer, denoting their authority to watch over the work of God and the people of God on earth. Charles Jones became the General Overseer and resided in Mississippi at Mount Helm Baptist Church. The overseer of Mississippi was William S. Pleasant. The overseer of Arkansas was John A. Jeter, and the overseer of Tennessee was Charles H. Mason. Under the leadership of Charles Price Jones, this COGIC timeframe is the Pre-Mason Era, since Jones was in charge of the newly formed African-American Holiness group known as the Church of God in Christ in 1906. This Church of God in Christ was unincorporated and was the foundation for Mason's rise to the helm of leadership for the group during and after the year of 1907.

Mason, the charismatic, signs, and wonders prophet, preached around the rural southern regions of Arkansas, Mississippi and Tennessee with passion and conviction. Beginning in 1893 at a revival meeting in Preston, Arkansas, Mason prayed earnestly to the Lord so that leading sinners in the community could be converted to Jesus Christ.[20] Mason always consulted God before preaching and laboring in prayer, sometimes all night, so that the souls of people could be saved from their sins. His preaching was based on living a "sanctified" life in Holiness, a freedom from bondage by a worldly sinful nature. In November 1893, Mason entered Arkansas Baptist College for the purpose of obtaining an education that would enhance his preaching. However, after only three months, Mason would depart from the school citing: "The Lord showed me that there was no salvation in schools and colleges; for the way, they were conducted grieved my very soul. I packed my books, arose and bade them a final farewell, to follow Jesus, with the Bible as my sacred guide. Not long after this, when I began to lift up Christ by word, example, and precept in the ministry, the Word drew the people from the streets, roadsides, and from the utmost parts of the country. Very soon the Word of God began to sanctify the people everywhere He sent me. Bless His holy name."[21] This belief established for Mason the precedence for his theology and COGIC preaching standards. Academic learning was not important and not the main focus of the COGIC mission in the eyes of Mason. When Mason stated that there was no salvation in schools and colleges, he equated the pulpit and the homiletical skill set for all preachers. Basically, preachers did not need a formal education in religion and theology, all they needed was the calling of God; Mason would later, in the Pentecostal era,add that preachers would only need the Holy Ghost. Since the majority of Mason's converts were often poor and uneducated, they focused on salvation and receiving a "heavenly" reward after their death. Mason became a populist phenomenon among the rural farming communities of Arkansas, Mississippi, and Tennessee. Mason's theological views promoted racial equality as he preached to Whites and Blacks about being under the influence of the

Spirit of God, and he promoted equal access to the COGIC pulpit by denouncing any educational requirements. Furthermore, during the late nineteenth century and early twentieth century, the socio-religious COGIC Movement led by Mason rivalled the socio-economic Populist Movement led by Tom Watson of Georgia. Both movements crossed racial barriers and promoted a solidarity that denounced American Segregation, practices and policies. Also, later, Mason's preaching came to be dominated by prayer and speaking in "tongues" which focused on the signs and wonders of God, instead of racial politics.

On the other hand, Charles Price Jones preached in a manner that combined education with salvation, focusing on a common sensible theology with practical holy living. Charles Jones was a student of theology graduating from Arkansas Baptist College in 1891. Charles Jones, upon his conversion to Holiness, cited the decadent and unspiritual conditions of the churches in the South. Unlike Mason, Jones did not concentrate heavily on signs, wonders, and miracles, but he focused on practical holy living according to biblical scriptures. As he pastored Mount Helm Baptist Church, he was taken through much litigation and finally put out of that church for preaching about Holiness.[22] As Mason became the grassroots common-man preaching phenomenon, Jones became an astute and scholarly leader in the theology of Holiness. Mason proclaimed the "spirit" of Holiness, which would eventually lead to his conversion to the Holy Ghost-focused Pentecostal faith.

Charles Jones and Mason's new movement captured the attention of both African-American converts and White American churchgoers. Both leaders established and organized the people under the banner of Mason's God-inspired name, Church of God in Christ. The title overseer was taken among these men to distinguish themselves from the Baptist and Methodist faiths that were prominent in the South during and after the years of slavery and Reconstruction. In early COGIC circles, many preachers stated that it was blasphemy to call a man "reverend" because "holy and reverend is God's name" according to Ps 111:9. The Black Sanctified/Holiness Church decided to call its state leaders, overseers, and the subordinate preachers under them were called elders. The lowest level of the preaching hierarchy belonged to the minister, and below the ministers, the deacons operated in support of the preachers. The Holiness movement proved to be a revolutionary interpretation of a Christ-centered life that called for the Christians to set a high standard of righteousness. The Holiness doctrine went against all things considered and interpreted to be worldly. Charles Jones and Mason, like other Holiness preachers, spoke against drinking alcohol, smoking cigarettes, drinking Coca-Cola (Coca-Cola contained real cocaine in the early 1900s), dipping snuff or chewing tobacco, adultery, fornication, lying, stealing, lust, greed, and other behaviors that were addressed in the Bible or interpreted as immoral acts by the Holiness group. Holiness, preached by Charles Jones and Mason, was not accepted among other religious groups because many of the immoral actions called out by Holiness preachers were common place among the Baptists, Methodists, Catholics, and other denominations. Preaching against drinking and smoking was not popular when many Americans, part of secular and religious groups, consumed those products. Also, most of all, Holiness preachers were displaying a lifestyle that was supposedly free from sin which was a derivative of Wesleyan perfectionism. Holiness preaching firmly established the ideal of a second work of Grace. The second work of Grace took place after the first work of Grace in which the Christian, a former sinner, confessed his sins and accepted the Lord Jesus Christ in saving him from his sins. After confession, the Holiness Movement stated that the person had to be "sanctified" and live holy in a lifestyle dedicated to God. This lifestyle came with high moral standards and guidelines.

Mason's preaching became legendary as he preached to thousands of people in the rural communities throughout the Mid-South region. According to James Delk, Mason preached to about two or three thousand people standing in a cotton wagon.[23] Also Delk stated that Mason showed a sweet spirit to all people regardless of race, creed, or color; and several White leaders of many different Holiness organizations stated that if Mason had been a White man, they would have gladly stepped aside and let Mason lead the organization.[24] The racism of the early twentieth century was in total conflict in having a Black man, despite being a religious leader, to lead throngs of White people. The Holiness Movement's racial solidarity and equality presented a stern defiance, based on spiritual beliefs, to the ideals and laws of Southern segregation and racism. Mason preached to diverse crowds with numbers ranging from 1,000 to 7,000. Crowds followed Mason as they heard about the miracles, signs, and wonders that were indicative of God ordaining his ministry. Around 1897, at Mason's first church in Lexington that was set up in an old gin house, someone fired shots amid the people while they were shouting and praying. Miraculously, no one was hurt, and the news of this event spread like wildfire in the community of Lexington and many people came to be saved and many came to be curious about the world of the "sanctified" folks.[25] Mason developed a following based on the idea that signs, miracles, and wonders from God were an integral part of his ministry. On the other spectrum of the Black Holiness Movement, Charles Jones concentrated on the organization, administration, and overall development of the newfound group. Charles Jones focused on creating a cohesive Christian unit that could promote Holiness. Before the end of the Pre-Mason Era, Charles Jones and Mason heard about the Pentecostal explosion of the Holy Spirit in Los Angeles, California. Mason's spirituality was headed for a direct conflict with Charles Jones' pragmatic theology.

Charles Jones and Mason agreed to survey the incidents occurring in Los Angeles, California in 1907. The event known as the Azusa Street Revival was led by William James Seymour. News of services filled with diverse people of all races, speaking in tongues, divine healing, and miracles being performed had reached the camp of Mason and Charles Jones. Eventually, Mason, with Charles Jones's consent, journeyed to Los Angeles, California to investigate the news surrounding and the outpouring of God's Spirit upon this group of people. David J. Young and John A. Jeter accompanied Mason to the Azusa Street Revival. The impact on Mason would transition the

COGIC timeline from the Pre-Mason Era based upon the Holiness Movement to the Mason-Era that combined the ideals of Holiness and Pentecostalism, accompanied by the doctrine of speaking in tongues as a definite sign for the Baptism of the Holy Ghost.

With Mason and Jones leading a profound religious movement in the South, these two African-American preachers had an impact on the racial climate and the way Christians viewed their religion as a personal walk with God. Charles Jones and Mason proclaimed salvation for all people without regarding race or economic status. These two preachers were only concerned with living a holy life according to the Bible, mainly, like the early Christian Church in the Book of Acts. The Black Holiness response was due to the fact that the living standards of Christians, in the eyes of Mason and Jones, was lowered by the teachings of Baptists and Methodists groups. Holiness, according to Mason and Jones, convicted the Christian into shunning worldly vices of smoking, drinking, fornicating, cursing, lying, cheating, and stealing. These radical views called for the professed Christian to set an example for the world to follow Christ by asking forgiveness for all acts of immorality.

Many Baptists and Methodist followers, including preachers, answered the call to Holiness by the process of come-outism. Come-outism was experienced by new converts to Holiness, and later Pentecostalism, after the converts experienced a renewed sense to live holy according to the Word of God. The Holiness Movement caused a wave of radical followers of righteous living to denounce their former religious practices that were not conducive to the Spirit of God. Preachers like Mason preached about healing the sick, raising the dead, healing the deaf and blind, along with other miracles of the Bible. These revolutionary ideals were based upon a sincere, fundamental belief in the Bible, unlike the standard Christian belief that biblical events, like miracles and healings, only occurred during the era of Jesus and the Apostles. Mason believed that the same events in the Bible could and did happen during his religious services.

Mason took his dogmatic beliefs in Holiness to the Azusa

Street Revival in Los Angeles and merged his ideals with the classic Pentecostal experience of "speaking in tongues", the approved sign that a person had received the Baptism of the Holy Spirit. Already considered a formidable Holiness preacher, Mason, yet, sought a higher religious experience that could help his ministry and establish more churches. After going through the Baptist phase, and then the Holiness phase, Mason embarked upon a journey into the last leg of a religious experience that made him the face of Black Pentecostalism from 1907 to his death in 1961.

Moreover, the Holiness Movement, and later Holiness-Pentecostal Movement shook the foundation of American Christianity. The Holiness life was characterized by a serious and dogmatic focus on following God with an intense focus on going to heaven after death. Other denominations like the Baptists, Catholics, and Methodists held church services dominated by formality and rigid protocol. The services in COGIC were open to people shouting, singing, dancing under the power of the Holy Spirit, speaking in tongues, interpreting the tongues, prophecy (foretelling the future), divine healing, and other impromptu actions that claimed to be influenced by God and the Holy Spirit. The Holiness-Pentecostal Movement re-emphasized the supreme instruction and authority of the Bible and the ideal of a church being led by the infallible Holy Spirit, not by the direction of fallible men. A church led by the Holy Spirit was the platform embraced by the leadership of Charles Jones and Mason.

CHAPTER 3

THE TURMOIL AROUND TONGUES
AND THE FIRST COURT CASE

W hen Mason, Jeter, and Young arrived at the Azusa Street Revival in 1907, they witnessed the outpouring of the Holy Ghost on different races of people. Seymour, the Pentecostal preacher, expounded on the Word of God for about fifteen minutes and then allowed the Holy Ghost to take control of the service and speak through the designated person who felt the Spirit was talking to him. Mason seemed to have assimilated into the flow of the services with no problems because of his similar charismatic preaching style and background. Also like Mason, Seymour had little formal education and adhered to a call by the "Spirit", with no emphasis on education or classism while preaching that everyone was equal in the eyes of God.[1]

The Apostolic Faith Mission located at 312 Azusa Street, pastored by Seymour, housed the Azusa Street Revival after moving from 214 Bonnie Brae Street, home of Richard and Ruth Asberry. Opening on April 14, 1906, services at the mission were dominated by prayer, glossolalia, miracles/signs/wonders, and divine healing. Religious services at the Asberry home could not contain the hundreds of people and spectators that marveled at the preaching, shouting, dancing, and tongue-speaking by way of the Holy Spirit. On April 20, 1906, the first African-American saved during the Azusa Street Revival was Mack E. Jonas,[2] who later became one of the pioneers in the COGIC faith under Mason, serving as an overseer in Georgia, Michigan, and Ohio, and in later years, a bishop. The Apostolic Faith Mission services had three stations: one station was the altar, for the people who wanted to be justified or saved from a state of unrighteousness; the second place was the prayer room, for persons who wanted to be healed from a sickness or had special and specific requests to God; the third place was the Upper Room, modeled after the biblical event of Pentecost in the book of Acts when the Holy Spirit fell upon believers for the first time in an upper room. The Upper Room at Azusa was the place designated for people to receive the Baptism of the Holy Ghost with evidence of speaking in tongues.[3]

When Mason, Jeter, and Young arrived at the Apostolic Faith Mission in March 1907, they walked into an atmosphere full of prophecy and testimonies of people being saved from drugs and delivered from sicknesses. Mason listened to Seymour's sermon on Saint Luke 24:49, "And behold I send the promise of my father upon you; but tarry ye in the city of Jerusalem until ye be endued with power from on high."[4] Seymour had also invited Mason and his friends from the South to the upstairs room in the mission. Seymour admonished Mason, Jeter, and Young that God was going to do great things for them if they did not follow worldly pleasures, but instead, follow the pleasures of God.[5]When Mason sought the Baptism of the Holy Ghost with the evidence of tongues, he stated,

The sound of a rushing might wind was in him and his soul cried, Jesus, only one like you. My soul cried and soon I began to die. It seemed that I heard the groanings of Christ on the cross dying for me. All of the work was in me until I died out of the old man. My soul cried, Oh, God, finish your work in me. Then the sound broke out in me again. Then I felt something rising me out of my seat without any effort of my own. I said, it may be my imagination. Then I looked down to see if it was really so. I saw that I was rising. Then I gave up for the Lord to have His way within me, and all of my being was filled with the glory of the Lord. So, when

I had gotten myself straight on my feet there came a light which enveloped my entire being above the brightness of the sun. When I opened my mouth to say Glory, a flame touched my tongue then ran down to me. My language changed and no word could I speak in my own tongue. Oh, I was filled with the glory of my Lord. My soul was then satisfied.[6]

At that point, Mason transitioned from a Holiness preacher to a Holiness-Pentecostal preacher accepting the third work of Grace by receiving the Baptism of the Holy Ghost with evidence of speaking in tongues. This kind of experience along with the testimony was common among the followers of Pentecostalism. Many followers testified of visions dealing with an "out of body experience", bright lights, and profound voices.[7] The following testimony from Mason recorded and summarized another version of his Pentecostal tongue-speaking experience:

The first day in the meeting, I sat to myself, away from those that went with me. I began to thank God in my heart for all things, for when I heard some speak in tongues, I knew it was right though I did not understand it. Nevertheless, it was sweet to me. I also thanked God for Elder Seymour who came and preached a wonderful sermon. His words were sweet and powerful, and it seems that I hear them now while writing. When he closed his sermon, he said, 'All of those that want to be sanctified or baptized with the Holy Ghost, go to the upper room; and all those that want to be justified, come to the altar.' I said that is the place [altar] for me, for it may be that I am not converted [saved from sin completely] and if not, God knows it can convert me... Glory! The second night of prayer I saw a vision. I saw myself standing alone and had a dry roll of paper in my mouth trying to swallow it. Looking up towards the heavens, there appeared a man at my side. I turned my eyes at once, then I awoke, and the interpretation came. God had me swallowing the whole book and If I did not, turn my eyes to anyone but God and Him only, He would baptize me. I said yes to Him, and at once in the morning when I arose, I could hear a voice saying, I see... I got a place at the altar and began to thank God. After that, I said Lord if I could only baptize myself, I would do so; for I wanted the baptism so bad that I did not know what to do. I said, Lord, you will have to do the work for me; so, I turned it over into His hands..." Then, I began to seek for the baptism of the Holy Ghost according to Acts 2:44 which readeth thus: 'Then they that gladly received His word were baptized,' Then I saw that I had a right to be glad and not sad. The enemy [devil] said to me, there may be something wrong with you. Then a voice spoke to me saying, if there is anything wrong [with] you, Christ will find it and take it away and will marry you... Some said, 'Let us sing,' I arose and the first song that came to me was 'He brought me out of the miry clay.' The Spirit came upon the saints and upon me... Then I gave up for the Lord to have His way within me. So there came a wave of glory into me and all of my being was filled with the glory of the Lord. So, when He had gotten me straight on my feet, there came a light which enveloped my entire being above the brightness of the sun. When I opened my mouth to say glory, a flame [a sign of the Holy Spirit] touched my tongue which ran down to me. My language changed, and no world could I speak in my own tongue. Oh! I was filled with the glory of the Lord. My soul was then satisfied.[8]

Mason had transitioned from a Black Baptist preacher to a Holiness preacher, and at this juncture, merged Holiness and Pentecostal beliefs within himself. Like Seymour, Mason believed that speaking in tongues or glossolalia was a mandatory sign of receiving the Baptism of the Holy Spirit. Mason's new experience and direct interaction, in which he believed that he was personally touched by God, would dominate his life and ministry for the next fifty-four years. His dogmatic stance in preaching about tongues was substantiated by his supernatural and holy call by God. The problem presented by this experience caused a permanent rift in the relationship between the African-American Holiness founding preacher, Charles Price Jones and the newly converted African-American Holiness-Pentecostal preacher, Charles H. Mason. Concerning Holiness groups and Pentecostal groups, all Pentecostal groups accept the ideals of Holiness, but not all Holiness groups accept the Pentecostal idea of a mandatory sign of speaking in tongues being evidence of the Holy Spirit. Thus, Mason, a Holiness preacher, added the Pentecostalism to his preaching repertoire. Mason, even though there was proof that he had previously preached under the Holy Spirit as thousands of people confessed salvation during his sermons, now believed that the Baptism of the Holy Spirit at Azusa was God's highest calling on his life, and the concrete evidence was given in the form of tongues. Furthermore, glossolalia or speaking in tongues was not a new format of worship among Christians. During the early to mid-1800s, British missionaries had contemplated about allowing the Holy Spirit of God (using the Book of Acts of the Apostles for an example) to come upon them so that they could speak the language of the African people who they were Christianizing. The practice never developed during Britain's Christian missionary works.

As stated earlier, the practice of speaking in tongues in the modern era was developed by a White Pentecostal preacher named Charles Parham. He founded a school in Texas based on tongues being a mandatory sign for the Baptism of the Holy Ghost.[9] One of his students, William J. Seymour, attended that school and started a church that took the concept of glossolalia to mainstream society with witnesses from around the world converging on the Apostolic Faith Mission at 312 Azusa Street. Seymour's Azusa Street Revival impacted the life of Charles Mason in 1907, and Mason took the "tongues" message to the South and to his Churches of God in Christ. Conflict arose as Mason preached "tongues" being a mandatory sign of the Holy Spirit which signaled the third phase of salvation, the Baptism of the Holy Ghost with evidence of glossolalia.

Seymour and Mason became friends during the Azusa Street

Revival. Seymour, in later years, needed Mason's friendship when the Apostolic Faith Mission began a downward slide into non-existence. The first religious blow to the Azusa Revival came in October 1906 when Charles Parham came to the mission and denounced the inter-racial services as N-word worship and Holy Rollerism. After being kicked out of the mission by Seymour, Parham started a rival mission in the building of the Women's Temperance Christian Union and drew many White members of Azusa to his upstart ministry.[10] The second major blow to Seymour's mission came in 1908 from a vindictive Seymour acquaintance. Clara Lum, a white female member, became upset with Seymour when he married Jennie Evans Moore, a Black member of the mission. No evidence is recorded of a serious relationship between Lum and Seymour, but Bishop Clemmons had stated that he had asked Mason about events surrounding Lum and Seymour.[11] Mason stated that Seymour had told him that Lum had fallen in love and wanted a marriage proposal from him, but Mason advised Seymour not to marry a White woman during the racially charged atmosphere of the times, so Seymour proposed to and married Jennie Moore.[12] Clara Lum reacted harshly by moving The Apostolic Faith, the mission's official periodical, to Portland, Oregon,[13]carrying the mailing lists of many Azusa Revival donors with her as well. Also, this action by Lum financially crippled the Apostolic Faith Mission and its great Azusa Street Revival. As Lum crippled the Azusa Pentecostal Movement financially, in 1911, a White preacher named William H. Durham paralyzed the great revival with his doctrine of "the finished work of Christ"[14] where sanctification is complete when a person is converted or saved, and there was no need to preach the other two stages of sanctification and Holy Ghost Baptism. This preaching was contrary to Seymour's doctrine of the three stages of salvation: conversion or being saved, sanctification or living holy, and receiving the Baptism of the Holy Ghost with evidence of tongues. Durham attempted to take over the Apostolic Faith Mission. Seymour locked him out of the mission. During the fallout, many of the Azusa members, especially the White population, left and followed Durham.[15]

After the Azusa Street Revival ended, and not without controversy, Mason rose to being one of the top Pentecostal preachers in the country. Mason often invited Seymour to preach at the COGIC Holy Convocations (the annual gathering of all COGIC members, occurring initially in the months of November and December). Mason's new preaching doctrines brought controversy into the Holiness organization that was controlled by Charles Jones. The doctrinal dispute on "tongues" became so heated that litigation had to settle the matter.

3.1. THE CHURCH OF GOD IN COURT, 1907-1909

After the Azusa "tongues" experience, Mason did not immediately return to the Deep South. He travelled to the Tidewater area of Virginia and he preached the Baptism of the Holy Ghost in a revival at Friendship Cathedral in Chuckatuck, Virginia. Many people from the tobacco and peanut fields attended the services and joined, greatly increasing the church's membership. Mason, a travelling prophet, left Chuckatuck for Norfolk, he and his cohorts were asked to leave the Grant Street Church after preaching about sanctification and the Holy Ghost Baptism experience at Azusa. Nevertheless, Mason started a street ministry in Norfolk under the threat of being arrested. Mason's street ministry blossomed and allowed the purchase of the first building on Goff Street, that became the first COGIC Church in Virginia. The church, in later years, became C.H. Mason Memorial COGIC because it was the "Mother" church that produced many pastors, bishops, and other churches. After Mason organized the COGIC saints in Virginia, then he headed for Memphis in late July 1907.[16]

When Mason, Jeter, and Young returned to the South, doctrinal divisions and splits began to occur in the newfound African-American Holiness group known as the Church of God in Christ. Mason started preaching about tongues being a sign of the Holy Spirit and that the Baptism of the Holy Ghost with tongues was the third and final phase of salvation. To annotate this process of salvation considering the Pentecostal experience, the first phase of salvation was confession, dealing with a person asking for the forgiveness of sin. Mason and Charles Jones were trained under this theology when both were members of the Black Baptist Church clergy. The Black Baptist Church considered this the first and final phase of salvation and that there was no need to seek or bring out any other phases. Again, many Baptist believers accepted the idea that when a person confessed salvation and was saved, he would always be saved. Then Charles Jones and Mason converted to the Holiness Movement and accepted the idea of a second phase of salvation that dealt with living holy and sanctified (set apart from the world) in the eyes of God. Mason then travelled to the Apostolic Faith Mission under Seymour during the Azusa Street Revival and experienced the Baptism of the Holy Ghost with evidence of speaking in tongues, which became the third and final phase of salvation according to the classical Pentecostal tradition.

Charles Jones, General Overseer of the Churches of God in Christ, disagreed with Mason's new doctrine and theology. Charles Jones maintained that "speaking in tongues" was one of the signs of the Holy Spirit but not a mandatory one. The argument was debated at the General Assembly organizational meeting in Jackson, Mississippi; however, two opposing factions emerged. The assembly split into preachers who stayed with the Holiness Movement under General Overseer Charles Jones and those who believed in the new doctrine of tongues aligned themselves with Overseer Mason. In November 1907, Mason called an assembly of preachers and followers of the idea of the Baptism of the Holy Ghost with evidence of speaking in "tongues" to meet in Memphis. The following preachers responded to the call: Eddie R. Driver, Justus Bowe, R.R. Booker, Robert E. Hart, Emmett M. Page, David J. Young, Daniel Spearman, W. Welsh, A.A. Blackwell, R.H. I. Clark, James Brewer, and J. H. Boone.[17] White preachers also were affiliated with Mason's tongue-speaking Pentecostal Church.[18] Moreover, this first assembly of preachers and members called by Mason would, in later years, morphed into Mason's vision of a Holy

Convocation, an annual meeting for all COGIC saints to meet at a designated place for prayer, fasting, singing, and preaching.

Before Mason called an assembly that followed his COGIC doctrine of "tongues", in October 1907, Frank Avant, a member dissatisfied with Mason's preaching on "tongues", filed a lawsuit to remove Mason from the church he pastored and founded in Memphis, Tennessee called Saints Home Church of God in Christ. The court case was heard in the Chancery Court of Memphis, Tennessee beginning on April 18, 1908. Two general concepts were key in this court case: 1) Mason's continuation or termination as pastor of Saints Home COGIC; and 2) The Church of God in Christ moving forward as a Holiness organization or a Holiness-Pentecostal organization. General Overseer Jones and Overseer Jeter were key witnesses against Mason on the principle fact that Mason was preaching a different doctrine centered around speaking in tongues. Benjamin Booth, a prominent African-American attorney in Memphis, prosecuted the case for Frank Avant and the Charles Jones faction, while the Mason led group acquired the services of Henry Saddler, another African-American lawyer. Both Booth and Saddler were members of the Collins Chapel CME Church.[19]Attorney Booth brought many cases against Tennessee's laws of segregation and helped Ida B. Wells-Barnett in her case against a Memphis railroad company. His presence in Memphis court rooms, the state supreme court in Jackson, Tennessee and the US Supreme Court was remarkable, making him a nuisance to the racist laws in the South. [20]

Overseer Jeter was questioned initially by Attorney Booth. During Jeter's questioning, Booth established that "speaking in tongues" was not a part of the original doctrine of the Sanctified Churches of God in Christ. Jeter testified that Mason spoke in unknown tongues and interpreted the tongues himself because no one else in the services understood his preaching in tongues. For that reason, Mason's preaching was not a part of the original doctrine of the Holiness Church and that "speaking in tongues" was the main reason Mason was excommunicated from the Churches of God in Christ.[21]

General Overseer Charles Jones was the next witness questioned by Attorney Booth. Jones testified that he and others had two councils with Mason, and Mason refused to retract his doctrine of tongues being a mandatory sign of receiving the Holy Ghost. Charles Jones also stated that Elder Eddie R. Driver and Elder Robert E. Hart were excommunicated as they followed the doctrine of tongues taught by Mason. Another interesting point, during this case, Elders Driver and William Roberts said that they had experienced tongues but did not preach or prophesy in tongues like Mason, and could not interpret the tongues, yet both men chose to follow Mason instead of Charles Jones.[22] With the testimonies of Jeter and Charles Jones, Booth had provided enough evidence that Mason had been contrary to the original doctrine of the Church that he had named. The Church of God in Christ at this stage remained a Holiness denomination, excluding the doctrine of tongues which was prominent in classical American Pentecostalism. Also, Driver and other Mason sympathizers accused Jeter of experiencing the speaking in tongues phenomenon at Azusa Street, but he changed his stance on tongues when he came back to the South under Charles Jones' leadership. The tongues dilemma split the founding preachers of the Black Holiness Church of God in Christ. Charles Jones and Jeter stayed with the doctrine of Holiness, while Mason extended his religious experience to Pentecostalism.

Saddler, in the defense of Mason and the tongues sympathizers, provided a convincing argument that Mason's tongue doctrine was not contrary to the doctrine that Jones and others preached in Holiness. Saddler used the argument from the Bible that stated in the Book of Mark how those who believed in God would cast out devils and speak with new tongues. Charles Jones rebuttal using that Scripture was that speaking in tongues was a historical doctrine, like raising the dead.[23] In other words, tongue speaking, like raising the dead, was prominent in biblical history and events, but not so prominent in modern times. Charles Jones' analysis of tongues was that it was one of the several signs a person could experience upon receiving the Baptism of the Holy Spirit. Saddler also challenged Charles Jones's authority over Mason in the early Church of God in Christ on whether it was a legitimate organization with established doctrines and by-laws. Charles Jones upheld the facts that the Churches of God in Christ or Sanctified Churches had assemblies that met in Jackson, Mississippi, and excommunicated preachers who did not follow Holiness, and had a publication called The Truth, founded by Jones, himself.[24] General Overseer Jones plainly stated that speaking in tongues was not a part of the preaching platform in the Holiness lifestyle.

The defense attorney had Elder Eddie R. Driver to testify on behalf of the Mason faction. Driver was questioned about the legitimacy of the Churches of God in Christ's organization under General Overseer Charles Jones. His testified that matters were handled solely by the local church because the local churches did not have to answer to a higher administration. Booth, the prosecutor, presented evidence of a higher administration by displaying the pamphlet, Rules of Government of the Churches(sic) of God in Christ, adopted January of 1906, with General Overseer Charles Jones presiding over the state of Mississippi, Mason presiding over Tennessee, and Jeter presiding over Arkansas.[25] Booth questioned Driver on why Mason was advocating and preaching in tongues. Driver stated that Mason did not stray away from the original doctrine of Holiness, and that Mason and himself preached about tongues with a foundation confirmed by the chapters in the books of Saint Mark and First Corinthians.[26] Driver was a key supporter of Mason, and, after this court case, Driver became one of Mason's generals who travelled and evangelized the state of California, spreading the COGIC message on the Baptism of the Holy Ghost.

Another key witness in support of Mason's tongue theology was Elder William M. Roberts. Roberts, like Elder Driver, became another one of Mason's generals in the field of COGIC Pentecost, and both were members of Saints Home COGIC on Wellington Street in Memphis. Mason sent Roberts to the state of Illinois and Roberts pioneered the COGIC faith in Chicago. Both Driver and Roberts became the first overseers of their designated states. Roberts testimony was also in support of Mason's "tongues" theology.

Attorney Booth questioned Roberts on when Mason began to preach in "tongues" and "unknown tongues," and it was after he returned from the Azusa Street Revival.[27] Roberts affirmed that Mason spoke in "tongues" under the Spirit of God, and Booth asked Roberts did he ever speak in tongues, and could he speak in "tongues" at that moment. Roberts stated that he had spoken in "tongues" before, but could not speak at that point because he was not under the Holy Spirit of God. He testified that "tongues" and other styles of worship like falling on the floor, shouting, or dancing were common occurrences in the African-American [Holiness] Church experience.[28]

The other key testimony of this court case came from Charles Mason. Mason appeared to have been viewed as a modern-day prophet who brought signs, wonders, and miracles to those under the influence of his preaching and evangelical circuits. Mason's "tongues" was part of the signs, wonders, and miracles trio due to the many testimonies of Mason speaking in known and unknown languages under the Spirit of God. Other testimonies also claimed that Mason laid hands on sick persons and they were healed; thus, Roberts and Driver were drawn to Mason and his prophetic preaching. During the court proceedings, Mason used the Bible as his creed and the reason for his preaching in "tongues," stating that he did not stray away from the original doctrine of Holiness because the original doctrine of Holiness was based on the Bible.[29] Therefore, he should not have been excommunicated from the Holiness fellowship. Mason also quoted from the Book of Mark, proving that "tongues" were Biblical and his preaching on "tongues" was not out of line with the principles of Holiness.[30] Also, Attorney Saddler had Mason testify to the fact that Frank Avant, the person who filed a lawsuit against Mason and his "tongues" preaching, was not a trustee of Saints Home COGIC; therefore, he may or may not have the proper position of authority to bring a lawsuit against a pastor.[31]

After all testimonies were given from both sides and after both lawyers had wrestled with questions about the Bible, Holiness, and "tongues," the Court decided in favor of Frank Avant and General Overseer Charles Jones. On July 28, 1908, the Chancery Court, Shelby

County in Tennessee, presided over by the Honorable F. H. Heiskell ruled that Frank Avant and all adherents to the original faith and order were entitled to the use, occupation and enjoyment of the Saints Home Church of God in Christ, called the Sanctified Church which was situated on the east side of Wellington Street near Vance Street in the city of Memphis, Tennessee.[32] Also, Mason's agents, friends, and sympathizers were barred from preaching or attempting to preach at the church or anywhere on the church property, and the Mason faction was ordered to pay the costs for the lawsuit.[33] A copy of the Judge Heiskell's decision can be found in Appendix A.

The Mason faction decided to appeal the case to the state Supreme Court in Jackson, Tennessee. In a strange turn of events, the state Supreme Court, on May 24, 1909, overturned the decision of the Chancery Court. The state Supreme Court in Jackson claimed that there was an error in the degree of the Chancery Court, and the decision, was therefore, reversed.[34] The state courtconfirmed Mason's "tongues" doctrine was not contrary to the original Holiness faith and he was entitled to the church that he had been pastoring for about seven years. After the victory for Mason and his newfound Pentecostal fervor, the Mason Era began with a newly formed Holiness-Pentecostal Church of God in Christ. Mason's ideals and persona dominated the mission of COGIC until his death in 1961. The results of the Mason Faction's appeal are chronicled in Appendix B.

In basic terms, the Tennessee Supreme Court ruling was based on the fact that the Church of God in Christ was not legally incorporated in 1906; therefore, the superior council led by Overseer Jones had no authority over individual churches, and the council's actions could only be enacted in an advisory manner.[35] Moreover, two important events occurred after this decision. Mason was allowed to maintain his church and he was allowed to keep the name "Church of God in Christ." With the beginning of the Mason Era, the Church of God in Christ transitioned from being a Holiness Church to a Holiness-Pentecostal Church with people "speaking in tongues" as the Spirit came upon them. Charles Price Jones and his followers remained a strictly

Holiness organization. So, after the court decision in 1909, Jones and his followers established the Church of Christ (Holiness) organization, not following the "tongues" movement of the Pentecostals.[36]

General Overseer Charles Jones gave a critical assessment of the "tongues" phenomenon that divided his Holiness organization. He contested that no one gift is the specific sign or evidence of the Holy Spirit's presence, and he also stated that the Scriptures did not ascribe categorical evidence to any gift or gifts of the Spirit.[37] This was a direct objection to the theology of Charles Parham, William Seymour, and, now Charles Mason. Moreover, Jones criticized Mason's followers like David J. Young, who "would make holy jumpers out of all of us; unless we snorted, frothed, and jumped; we did not have the Holy Ghost."[38] In many Pentecostal circles, regardless of the racial makeup, people thrived on the ideal of spirit possession that made a person shout, dance, holler, or jump. Many Pentecostals believed like Elder Young that the Holy Spirit did not move in the service unless people were jumping and shouting. Jones disagreed with the application of emotionalism and mysticism that the "tongues" movement promoted in Pentecostalism. The "tongues" movement caused Mason and Jeter to denounce their initial experience of receiving the Holy Ghost while they were Holiness preachers, and both proclaimed that they had received the "authentic" Holy Ghost experience with "tongues" under Seymour's preaching. This idea did not set well with Jones. Even though Overseer Jeter eventually denounced the "tongues" experience after returning to the South, Overseer Mason was excommunicated for his dogmatic stance claiming that "tongues" was a definite sign for a person receiving the Holy Spirit.[39]

The "tongues" movement of the Pentecostal explosion severed a lot of Jones' Christian friendships. As he lost Mason to the Pentecostal "tongues" explosion, he lost another friend, D.G. Spearman. Jones considered Spearman an intelligent preacher, great orator, deep thinker, and good singer.[40] Nevertheless, Spearman went into a depressive state. Spearman never recovered from this spiritual fall; he became a follower of the Pentecostal "tongues" doctrine and prophesied to Overseer Jones that God would make an example of him for opposing the doctrine of "tongues." Spearman, on the other hand, was imprisoned for check forgery and claimed that a spirit caused him to, spontaneously, mutter gibberish (Spearman blamed his propensity to talk or babble incoherently on the church services that were dominated by people babbling in tongues) against his will.[41]Jones stayed the course of Holiness and held his position that the "tongues" doctrine was not a requirement to receive the Baptism of the Holy Spirit.

As the African-American Holiness team disintegrated, Mason emerged as the face of the "tongues" movement in the South as he took control of the Church of God in Christ.

What is the founding year of Mason's newly formed Church of God in Christ?[42] Different years exist under the leadership of Charles Jones and Mason. Under Mason, the COGIC body was initially registered in Mississippi as the Church of God in Christ of America, not Church of God in Christ, Incorporated.[43]

Mason's church would, eventually, come to be known as the Church of God in Christ, Incorporated with a founding year of 1907, following his excommunication from Jones' Holiness organization. The Mason Era were the years of growth and organization for the Church of God in Christ, Inc. Mason's doctrine of "tongues" spread like wildfire throughout the South and led to testimonies of signs, wonders, and miracles being performed. Mason's services had many followers who catapulted his ministry as a strong force in the South, and eventually impacted Christianity in America and around the world with a Pentecostal message.

Even though Mason had a significant number of preachers to follow him in developing the Church of God in Christ, Inc., was he or Charles Jones correct in their interpretations of the Bible on the concept of "speaking in tongues" as a mandatory requirement for the Holy Spirit? Jones observed the emotionalism of people experiencing the "tongues" and declared that a person did not have to "speak in tongues" in order to be filled with the Holy Spirit. As Mason preached in "tongues", Jones complaint was that people could not understand the language spoken by Mason; therefore, the people could not be converted if they could not comprehend the preaching. On the other hand, many people in the rural South were drawn to the antics surrounding a person "speaking in tongues" because many followers assumed that the Holy Spirit had possessed that person's body. Also, Jones charged that Mason and the followers of the "tongues" doctrine did not have ample, biblical evidence to support the requirement. Complementing Jones' analysis, no scripture in the Bible stated that a person had to "speak in tongues" in order to receive the Baptism of the Holy Spirit. Moreover, historical evidence has shown that the Church of God in Christ, Inc. and other splinter COGIC groups have not codified "tongues" as a mandatory requirement for the Holy Spirit. Several COGIC Manuals of splinter groups have left the "tongues" requirement to the interpretation of the individual.

For the most part, "tongues" have never been included in the official doctrine, constitution, or structure belief system in COGIC, Inc. Depending on a COGIC follower's location and his age group, "speaking in tongues" may be mandatory among some older members in the South, while the act is not mandatory among the younger generations or among followers in the Northern and Western regions of the United States. Nevertheless, Mason was able to draw a large following of members and clergy due to the signs of miraculous healings and the wonders of "speaking in tongues."

CHAPTER 4

FIRST PHASE OF THE MASON ERA (1907-1933): COGIC DEPARTMENTS

D uring the years of litigation, Mason began to departmentalize his Holiness-Pentecostal organization to further the Gospel message of being filled with the Holy Ghost. Several key departments were established during the early 1900s: Sunday School, Women, Young People Willing Worker's (YPWW), Evangelism, and the Home and Foreign Mission. These departments had specific purposes and COGIC was able to reach people and to increase its membership, rivaling Black Methodist and Black Baptist denominations. The Sunday School Department attracted the educators, as the first National Sunday School superintendent was a college professor. Sunday School also helped to educate the farming communities, since many only had Sundays off from the life of sharecropping.

Mason also saw a need for a Women's Department. This department allowed the input of women into the world-wide ministry of the COGIC Church. Many of the moral standards of Holiness and teachings on moral purity were conducted by COGIC women. Out of the Women's Department came the rules of women not wearing trousers or make-up; the length of dresses had to come down to the floor; and, women could never show any skin.[1] Also, the women of COGIC served as domestic and foreign evangelists taking the messages of Holy Ghost and "tongues" across the United States and to the overseas territories in the Caribbean and Africa. The Evangelism Department focused on spreading the Pentecostal message in the

United States, and promulgate the belief that all Christians needed the Baptism of the Holy Spirit with evidence of "tongues." During the 1940s, one of the eras of African-American migration from the South, COGIC evangelists, many who were women, established churches in California, New York, Michigan, and Illinois.[2] These female evangelists had the COGIC clerical title of missionary to distinguish them from the male preachers who were referred to as ministers and elders. Commonly, in other Christian denominations, the missionary title referred to male and female workers whose purpose was to convert nonbelievers, usually in foreign lands. Evangelism in foreign territories was handled by the Home and Foreign Mission Department, with many of these evangelists being women. Also, COGIC female missionaries and male preachers worked tirelessly to bring the message of being saved, sanctified, and filled with the Holy Ghost to different countries around the world. Canada was one of the targeted territories for the COGIC Pentecostal message. However, with much disappointment, COGIC Inc.'s presence could not flourish in Canada due to a lack of support from the organization's headquarters in Memphis. According to testimony from Bishop Wayne Channer of the Lighthouse Church of God in Christ of Canada (LCOGICC), the General Board of COGIC, Inc. did not provide minimal financial support to establish missions and churches in Canada. So COGIC preachers in Canada, like Bishop Channer's father, Vinnel T. Channer, refused to support COGIC, Inc. headquarters since the headquarters did not support him.

The last COGIC department created during the early 1900s was the Young People Willing Workers (YPWW). The YPWW's purpose was to evangelize, indoctrinate, and teach young people about the Baptism of the Holy Spirit. The YPWW department encouraged young girls and boys to live a sanctified life in Christ, serving as an example to other young people in the world. Many of the leaders of the YPWW Department were young preachers who advanced ultimately being ordained as bishops in COGIC, Inc. Recruiting young people ensured that the COGIC faith would have a viable number of converts in the future to proclaim the Pentecostal message.

These departments were developed under Mason's leadership, not necessarily under his supervision or guidance. Mason was known as an excellent prophetic preacher and a man given to much prayer and faith. On the other hand, he did not possess many of the organizational and administrative skills in managing a huge religious organization that was growing bountifully and rapidly. Therefore, he needed the departmental heads and assistants to support his vision globally and nationally.

So, in 1908, Mason approved the establishment of the Sunday School Department to educate the COGIC saints on lessons in the bible. As noted in an earlier chapter, while a student at Arkansas Baptist College Mason stated that there was no salvation in the schools.[3] At this point, around 1893, he was not referring to educational units like the Sunday School that expounded on the Word of God, so there is no contradiction yet. The first Sunday School in the COGIC Church was organized in Lexington, Mississippi, by Professor L.W. Lee, a founding member of Saint Paul COGIC, who was saved under the leadership of Charles P. Jones.[4] With this newly formed Church, problems existed in the Sunday School under Mason's leadership. In 1924, Elder Frank Christmas succeeded Professor Lee. Christmas, in 1916, tried to introduce quarterly booklets for the COGIC members to prepared for the Sunday School lessons. Many of the COGIC members disagreed with Elder Christmas' attempt to hand out booklets on the grounds that they believed that the COGIC Church was a Spirit-led church (a church that waits for the leadership of the Holy Spirit); therefore, how could one know what the Spirit wanted the saints to learn three or four months ahead of time?[5] Despite the confrontations, the Sunday School Department issued quarterly booklets so that people could learn doctrines and beliefs of the COGIC Church based on the teachings of the Bible. A motto was adopted for the Sunday School Department: "A child saved is a soul saved, plus a life." In some parts of the country, "Reaching the unreached and bringing them in" was an added phrase to the Sunday School motto. The main focus of the Sunday School Department was to educate the members of COGIC on holy and righteous living and to teach mandatory obedience to God and His written Word, the Bible.

After the formation of the Sunday School Department, Mason decided to create a COGIC Women's Department. Mason declared that women needed a separate work and leadership; however, the Women's Department would be subordinate to the authority of Mason. Women were great supporters and moral leaders in the COGIC faith. So, in 1911, the COGIC Women's Department was established under its leading mother, Mother Elizabeth Woods Robinson, a pioneer in evangelism and religious education.Mother Robinson was born Elizabeth Isabelle Smith to Mose Smith and Elizabeth Jackson in Phillips County, Arkansas on April 5, 1860 and started reading the Bible at eight years of age. She was converted to the work of God during the late 1800s.[6] Mother Robinson, like Mason, had a key religious experience while she was a child. She heard someone calling her name, "Liz, Liz, Liz", but she did not know who was calling her. Her mother told her not to answer because, among African-American communities, a legend persisted that when a person heard his name, and no one was there, it meant that the person was about to die,[7] or in some interpretations, death was calling his name. Also, like Mason, Mother Robinson moved from the Baptist Church to sanctification and Holiness and then finally to Pentecostalism after hearing a COGIC preacher in Dermott, Arkansas. Before her conversion to Pentecostalism, she married William Henry Holt in 1880 and had one daughter, Ida Florence. Holt died a short time after the marriage and then she married William H. Woods and they attended a Black Baptist Church in Pine Bluff, Arkansas. Later she married Edward Roberson, a COGIC preacher, and they established a church in Omaha, Nebraska.[8]

Mother Robinson was a student at the Baptist Academy in Pine Bluff, Arkansas, but left the academy after receiving the Baptism of the Holy Ghost. She worked with Dr. Robert Hart in evangelizing the areas of Trenton and Jackson, Tennessee. In 1911, at the General Convocation in Memphis, she was appointed General Overseer of Women's Work in COGIC.[9] On another note, Mason considered appointing Mother Lillian Brooks Coffey, his close administrator and revivalist singer, to the Overseer of Women's Work position. However, Mother Coffey declined the position and advised Mason to choose a more seasoned woman because Coffey felt that she was too young, since she was nineteen years old.[10] Eventually, the position would belong to Mother Coffey in 1945, after the death of Mother Robinson.

Controversy surrounded the role of women in the Pentecostal Movement, in general, and posed problems for the COGIC faith specifically. The problem in COGIC was whether women could preach or not. Mother Robinson, along with Overseer Robert E. Hart, theorized the idea that women could "teach" the Gospel, and reserve the "preaching" of the Gospel to the ranks of the male clergy."[11] Mother Robinson stated that Jesus never called a woman to preach using the last chapter of the Book of Mark to justify her reasoning, as Jesus gave orders to the male disciples to go into all of the world and preach to every creature.[12] Despite the limitations on women preaching, Mother Robinson's appointment as an Overseer of Women's Work was a powerful position because she supervised over half of the COGIC membership. The title overseer also was in every way the same title given to the top male preachers in each state who supervised elders, ministers, mothers, missionaries, and lay members. There was no distinction in the perspective of the title overseer, which was designated for male and female leaders. Under Roberson, COGIC women provided valuable support in establishing churches and missions. The women were greatly responsible for the phenomenal growth in COGIC membership.

Two key auxiliaries were founded under Robinson's leadership of the Women's Department. The first key auxiliary was the Prayer and Bible Band. Mother Robinson received advice and training about creating a Bible Band from Joanna Patterson Moore, a white missionary who was the catalyst for African-American women to create Bible Bands in the Baptist and COGIC denominations. In Moore's magazine called Hope, she promoted Bible readings, mothers' training, and home schooling.[13] The Bible Bands in COGIC increased the literacy rates of women, and with those high literacy rates, women became the key readers for many COGIC preachers. For example, a tradition that existed among early COGIC services was the designation of women to read the scriptures for the text of the sermon during service. On several occasions, COGIC preachers were illiterate and needed the skills of a reader so they could expound on the bible scripture. As the women read aloud in the service, the preacher often repeated the textual passage and related its meaning to the congregation, often with a homiletical exhortation of telling the congregation to abide in "Holiness" or risk going to "Hell." Early COGIC preaching with the support of women readers emphasized the benefits of living holy and the dire consequences of living an immoral lifestyle. As the Bible Band served as a training ground and formal educational experience for mothers, missionaries, and female teachers of Sunday Schools, the male members and male clergy did not have access to a formal theological education. Dating back to the Mason's statement on no salvation in schools, many of the early COGIC preachers interpreted, from Mason, that they only needed the Holy Ghost to preach and pastor a church, while women had an educational jewel in the Bible Band.

The other auxiliary under the COGIC Women's Department was called the Sewing Circle. This division of the Women's Department, in its infancy, had a specific purpose. What was the purpose of a woman's auxiliary that sewed clothes? Well, in the initial developing years of the Holiness and Pentecostal Movements, many denominations claimed that women could not wear pants or trousers. The justification was found in the Book of Deuteronomy, 22:5, stating that a man should not wear anything pertaining to a woman, and a woman should not wear anything pertaining to a man. Therefore, the Sewing Circle women met to sew and transform trousers into dresses. Mother Robinson adopted this moral principle, mandating that women had to wear skirts or dresses, usually with a hem at the ankle or floor length.[14] Mother Robinson established the dress code for sanctified, holy women so that there was a difference in dress and lifestyles that distinguished the appearances of worldly women from the saintly women. Women were not to tempt the man by dressing provocatively. COGIC's mothers and members of this era had an earnest desire to live holy in life and dress. Mother Robinson wanted to set a standard of Holiness that required the respect for African-American women, denouncing the stereotypes of White racism. Mother Robinson and her COGIC Women's Department presented a moral front that denounced sin and proclaimed Holiness by living holy, acting holy, and dressing holy. Early COGIC women laid an enduring foundation that lasted to the modern and postmodern eras. Today, pants-wearing wearing women are not denounced as sinners by preachers as it was during the years of Mother Robinson. From the observation of the author, the issue of COGIC pants-wearing women not being looked upon as sinners started around the mid-1980s. In many services, women wear pants due to the modern interpretation of scripture that women and men in the Bible wore robes, not dresses and trousers. However, the older COGIC women tended to adhere to the standard of not wearing pants with a perceived notion that such behavior was connected to original Holiness and original Pentecostalism.

4.1. THE FIRST SPLINTER GROUP: TRIUMPH THE CHURCH AND KINGDOM OF GOD IN CHRIST

After the establishment of the COGIC Women's Department, Mason had a Charles P. Jones experience with a rebellious preacher named Elias Dempsey Smith. Smith had served as Overseer of Louisiana, working with James Feltus and Henry Feltus, Sr. Smith originated the theory of "never dying." Literally, Overseer Smith preached that a person in his physical body could live forever. He taught that once people became sanctified that they received an immortal body that would never die and never have pain, and there would be no need to take any medicine.[15] In 1912, Smith separated from Mason and the COGIC Movement proclaiming eternal life on earth and the earth being taken over and ruled by the Negroid race.

Smith established Triumph the Church and Kingdom of God in Christ with a Black Nationalist-sanctified doctrine. In the new movement's name, triumph and kingdom dealt with the prediction that Smith was preaching about Black people taking over the world by the help of God. Some authors recorded that Smith was prophesying about a king rising out of Ethiopia, and other authors stated that Smith proclaimed himself to be that miracle leader coming out of Ethiopia. Along with teaching about earthly immortality, Smith claimed that he was going to be the king that God would anoint to rise out of Addis Ababa, Ethiopia, becoming the ruler of world as God's vessel.[16] Mason witnessed the ritual of the Triumph members attaining a body that would never die. Mason gave the following eyewitness account:

> *It is very interesting to see how they do to get that body. They got down, prayed a while, then stop saying anything or moving for awhile. Then they declared themselves dead. They start a song and the pretended dead arise and shout, declaring themselves now clothed in their never-dying bodies. They were required to stand and tell what they heard and saw while passing through sham death. Some would tell one thing and some another. Then they would declare themselves in that body that will be here until Jesus comes, as that body cannot die.[17]*

In short, Mason took the same position that Jones took against him about the "tongues" doctrine. Mason used scripture to argue the point of immortality here on earth. Regardless of Mason's opposition, several people followed Smith with hopes of an immortal new world and the ability to reign over earth with their new God-chosen king, Elias D. Smith. However, Mason would have his vindication; in 1920, Smith travelled to Ethiopia with supporting funds from his members. People gave a lot of money to Smith because he preached that Blacks in America would take over the railroads, banks, and fine houses of White people. Mason witnessed people placing money in Smith's hands and making a wish, and Smith told them that they would receive whatever they wished for.[18] While Smith was in Ethiopia, he died. There were several reports on the cause of his death. One report stated the he obtained a fever and died, and the other report stated that he ate some food that caused his death. Bishop C.H. Stokes of Triumph the Church and Kingdom of God in Christ reported that Smith died during an African King wine-drinking ritual. The true African King lived after drinking the wine. Smith drank the wine and within seconds, the wine ate holes in his body and he died immediately.[19]

Now the problem for this splinter COGIC group was that their leader who claimed bodily immortality was dead in Ethiopia. What a devastating blow to their faith! After the death of Elias Smith, the Triumph Church members regrouped after the loss of their dreams and hopes that they had placed in Smith's doctrine. Minister Cleveland Stokes, one of the ministers under Smith's leadership, left the Triumph Church in Mount Hope, West Virginia and started a mission in Eversville, West Virginia in a two-room house. Seeking a new name for the church under his authority, Minister Stokes went on a three day fast in January 1921, and he stated that God had revealed to him to name his mission, the Glorious Church of God in Christ.[20] A meeting among former members and current members of Triumph the Church and Kingdom of God in Christ occurred on April 8, 1921 in Charleston, West Virginia, to reorganize under the name of the Glorious Church of God in Christ. Not all members of the Triumph Church agreed to separate, but maintained some of the doctrines and continued to exist as an organization well into the present day. Now Mason's COGIC proliferation had two more organizations: Triumph the Church and Kingdom of God in Christ and the Glorious Church of God in Christ. Later, the Glorious COGIC split to form the Original Glorious Church of God in Christ in 1954.

Smith's movement had a different perspective of Holiness and Pentecostalism which carried the COGIC moniker and placed it upon a Black Nationalist agenda. Another prodigy of Smith's movement was the renown, Prophet James "Papa" Jones of Detroit, Michigan. At the age of six, Jones joined Triumph the Church and Kingdom of God in Christ as a young mystic-prophet, and preached his first sermon in Birmingham, Alabama, as a teenager.[21] In 1938, Prophet Jones was sent to Detroit, Michigan, as a Triumph Church missionary. Prophet Jones began to receive large monetary gifts for preaching about God; however, he refused to turn the monetary gifts over to the leaders of the Triumph Church. So, Prophet James Jones separated from Triumph the Church and Kingdom of God in Christ and formed Church of Universal Triumph, the Dominion of God[22]in the city of Detroit. Using Holiness-Pentecostal methods, Prophet Jones proclaimed that he was the only prophet of God because God only spoke to him. Just like Elias Smith and Charles Mason, Prophet Jones was the main spiritual leader of his movement. Also, Jones' parishioners held services in a former theater building on Linwood Boulevard with a reputation of being one of America's noisiest religious sects.[23] During Prophet Jones' services, accompanied with loud music while people shouted, danced,uttered in "tongues", and gave monetary offerings. Like the Azusa Street Revival under Seymour, services lasted for hours, but Church of Universal Triumph services were often dominated by God-proclaimed rantings of Prophet Jones with many insulting remarks to the members.

Prophet Jones and Elias Smith had used the legacy of the Holiness-Pentecostal Movement of mass gatherings to manipulate the people under their authority. Both men raised significant amounts of funds. Smith's monies were poured into a futile claim that a Black King was going to take over the world, while Prophet Jones' simply used the funds toward his own personal wealth: a large 54-room mansion, a $13,500 mink coat, and a chauffeur-driven limousine.[24] The three leaders, Mason, Smith, and Prophet Jones, drew throngs of people to their ministries. With promises of a heaven's reward, blessings from God, healings from God, miracles, world-takeover, no wonder the poor people, especially the African-American population, in the rural and urban areas of the United States were drawn to these three modern religious leaders of spiritual and economic prosperity. While

Smith and Prophet Jones focused mainly on their personal agendas, Mason developed a church movement that fostered the development of men, women, and children in the COGIC departments of ministry.

4.2. 1914: THE YEAR OF YPWW AND THE SECOND SPLINTER GROUP UNDER MASON

Following the turmoil caused by Elias Smith and his Triumph COGIC, Mason and his followers established the YPWW Department in the Church of God in Christ. The youth were taught these concepts: 1) unification of Holiness; 2) to increase spiritual strength; 3) to keep a pure mind; 4) to stimulate more life in service; 5) to educate in Scriptural knowledge; 6) to keep the unit of the Holy Spirit; and, 7) to live holy. The motto for the COGIC youth department was taken from 2 Tim. 2:15, "Study to show thyself approved unto God, a workman that needth not to be ashamed, rightly dividing the word of truth."[25] The mission to convert young people to the Holiness-Pentecostal faith showed the innovation side of the COGIC Church. Mason's COGIC Church had a variety of activities and programs. Young people could sing in the choir, attend designated Sunday School classes, play musical instruments like the guitar, drums, and organ, participate in oratory contests, and recite poetry[26] along with biblical scriptures. So, the youth were engaged in the mission and life of COGIC, Inc.

The first president chosen for the YPWW Department in 1914 was Elder M.C. Green. Green, who only served as president for three years, and was followed by the most prominent and impactful YPWW president in the COGIC history, Elder Ozro Thurston Jones, Sr. Elder O. T. Jones elevated the YPWW Department to an organization of national and prominent status, holding its first convention in 1927 in Kansas City, Missouri.[27] Elder O.T. Jones started a COGIC legacy of the YPWW Department president being elevated to the status of bishop (created in the year of 1933) in COGIC, Inc. Several bishops, past and present, have held the office of YPWW president. Also, O.T. Jones, Sr.

became one of the first five bishops ordained in COGIC, Inc. and he succeeded Mason for the office of Senior Bishop and Chief Apostle of the COGIC faith in 1962.

The YPWW Department leaders mentored, trained, and produced some of COGIC's greatest leaders and bishops. O.T. Jones, Sr. served as the second senior bishop and the last senior bishop in COGIC history. Senior Bishop Jones provided strong leadership and direction for COGIC after the death of Mason in 1961. Other former YPWW presidents who became bishops included Bishop O.T. Jones, Jr. who served on COGIC' General Board and continued the expansion of his father's ministry in that state of Pennsylvania; Bishop Chandler D. Owens served on the General Board and became the third COGIC Presiding Bishop, and his COGIC tenure was marked by a surplus of funds in the church's budget; Bishop William James served on the COGIC General Board and as a prominent and influential bishop in the state of Ohio. Additionally, former Youth Department leaders, Bishop Jerry W. Macklin and Bishop J. Drew Sheard, currently, serve on the COGIC General Board and are leading bishops in California and Michigan, respectively.[28]

As the YPWW Department began to flourish with hopes for attracting young people to a lifestyle of Holiness, another splinter group emerged amongthe White clergymen of COGIC, Inc. For several reasons, the members of the White COGIC under Mason sought to separate themselves into their own Pentecostal organization. Mason, an African-American Pentecostal, preacher was basically the only convenient clergyman who had the power and authority to ordain preachers of the Pentecostal faith. Many Southern White preachers resented being under the leadership and authority of an African-American clergyman. To make matters worse, many of the White COGIC members were persecuted by their own race in the South for worshipping with African-Americans. Thus, the meeting in Hot Springs, Arkansas on April 2-12, 1914, was the founding meeting for the Assemblies of God. The Assembly elected Eudorus N. Bell as chairman (later, the position would be changed to superintendent) and J. Roswell Flower as secretary and the first executive presbytery.[29] The Assembly of God historical documentation does not include any recognizable ties to Mason's COGIC, Inc. Mason attended the Assemblies of God meeting in 1914, and did not show any ill feelings toward the White clergymen he had ordained and led. He bid them a godly farewell and blessed their assembly. Unlike the first two splits dealing with the Church of God in Christ, this split concerned race. The fights with Charles Price Jones and Elias Dempsey Smith concerned doctrine and the interpretation of biblical scripture. During the early years of the 1900s, several White preachers served in the COGIC faith. Eudorus Bell was under the leadership of Charles Jones when he decided to follow Mason and the doctrine of "tongues" that led to the Avant/Mason trial in 1908.

4.3. COGIC Evangelism and Foreign Missions

After the up and down year of 1914, Mason approved the formation of the Department of Evangelism in 1917. This department had the purpose of gaining new converts in spurring church growth. The motto for the department was, "The Flame of Evangelism Must Never Go Out." Early COGIC evangelists under Mason included the "Singing Evangelist", Lillian Brooks Coffey. As stated above, Coffey became the General Overseer of Women's Work after the death of Mother Elizabeth Roberson in 1945.[30] Other early pioneers of COGIC evangelism included the twins, Mary and Martha Renfro, Elder Utah Smith, and Elder S.T. Samuel. Elder S.T. Samuel evangelized in North Carolina, being its first overseer. Samuel also worked in Virginia and several other states on the East Coast.[31] The evangelistic fire of the Church of God in Christ under Mason spread rather quickly across the United States. The territorial legacy of COGIC began in Arkansas, Mississippi, and Tennessee; and these states were the proving and training grounds for preachers and missionaries. The women and men in the South branched out to plant churches in the urban areas of the United

States. In 1917, Lillian Coffey lived in Chicago, Illinois. No COGIC missions or work existed in Chicago, so Sister Coffey started a church, later named William M. Roberts Temple COGIC.[32] Coffey sent word to Overseer Mason for Elder Roberts to come to pastor in Chicago. Roberts was serving as Mason's assistantbut was sent to pastor the work in Chicago, thus making him the first overseer of Illinois.[33]Like Chicago, women missionaries also planted churches in Detroit and Los Angeles.

After the court case, Frank Avant v. C.H. Mason, ended in 1909, many COGIC churches started to develop under Mason's leadership in the South, and branched outward to states in the North, Midwest, and West. Mason was the General Overseer of COGIC, Inc., so he appointed overseers of the states of Arkansas, Tennessee, and Mississippi. Robert E. Hart was selected as overseer of Tennessee; David J. Young was appointed overseer of Arkansas, but according to Charles Pleas, Young left Arkansas in 1912, so Justus Bowe returned as overseer of Arkansas[34], and J.A. Lewis was appointed overseer of Mississippi.[35] Mason had the first COGIC Church in Tennessee, he pastored Saints Home COGIC and he established St. Paul COGIC in Lexington, Mississippi. Robert E. Hart was a convert from the Colored Methodist Episcopal (CME) Church, and he worked and assisted Mason in winning the court case, Frank Avant v. C.H. Mason, being an integral part of the appeal process. Hart was succeeded by R.H.I Clark as overseer of Tennessee before the title overseer was changed to bishop. Around 1914, in Arkansas, Justus Bowe was pastor of the First COGIC in Fort Smith, Arkansas.[36] Many COGIC churches that were built "first" in the designated states were named First Church of God in Christ. Other pioneer pastors of First COGIC of Fort Smith included Ozro T. Jones, Sr., who would succeed Mason in 1962 to become the second Senior Bishop of COGIC, Inc., and Junious A. Blake, Sr. served as a Jurisdictional Bishop in San Diego, California and as a long-standing member of the COGIC General Board. Bishop J.A. Blake, Sr was the father of Bishop Charles Edward Blake, the current presiding bishop of COGIC. In Mississippi, in the year of 1909, Jeff A. Lewis became the first overseer. Lewis was instrumental in establishing a COGIC school in the basement of St. Paul COGIC in Lexington with its first principal being Professor James Courts.[37] Overseer Lewis was succeeded by Stephen Rice in 1916, and Rice oversaw the construction for the first building on the forty-acre campus of Saints Academy in Lexington.[38] Mason sent Mack E. Jonas to establish churches in Georgia. Mack Jonas was recorded as the first African-American saved at the Azusa Street Revival, and he chose to follow the leadership of Overseer Mason.[39] Overseer Jonas arrived in Georgia in 1909 and started the First COGIC in Atlanta on the corner of Maury Avenue and Lansing Street. Jonas served the state of Georgia until 1917,[40] being reassigned to the Mid-Western states of Michigan and Ohio. Jonas was succeeded by B.I. Reese who served from 1917 to 1920. In California, Mason sent Eddie R. Driver to establish churches in the year of 1914. He served the state of California from 1914 to 1924,[41] and named his church Saints Home COGIC, the same name as Mason's first church in Memphis, Tennessee. The early COGIC churches started missions that grew tremendously as the message of being baptized in the Holy Spirit resonated with people who wanted a higher level of Christian experience, not settling for the finality of salvation at the point of confession. COGIC also had many converts from the Baptist and Methodist denominations. Tension between Black Baptists and COGIC members lasted well into the postmodern era as Baptist members, in a derogatory manner, called COGIC people, "them sanctified folks." Spreading the message of Holy Ghost power appeared to be steamrolling across America as COGIC missions and churches were planted in urban areas. COGIC's foreign missions program was more difficult.

In 1926, the COGIC Home and Foreign Mission Board was developed. The motto for the department was taken from Matt. 28:18, "Go ye therefore and teach all nations." The Home and Foreign Mission Board, a division under the Women's Department, had the mission of establishing churches in foreign countries and territories.[42] Mother Roberson worked diligently with the Home and Foreign MissionBoard. At one point in time, the President/Elder Searcy of the

House of Prayer International of Portland, Oregon joined COGIC, Inc. and led the Home and Foreign Mission Board; however, Searcy served only one year and returned to his own work.[43] After Searcy vacated the position, in 1926, Elder C.G. Brown of Kansas was appointed president of the Home and Foreign Mission Board. The Board was reorganized under Brown's tenure and became known as the Department of Home and Foreign Mission in 1937.[44]

Overall, foreign missions, especially, in Canada have had some disappointing outcomes. Bishop Wayne A. Channer of the Lighthouse COGIC in Canada stated that many of the COGIC, Inc. churches felt neglected by the COGIC headquarters. Channer explained that COGIC leaders only wanted the Canadian churches to send their reports to Memphis, but did not provide the pastors with any financial support or training for upstart churches in Ontario, Canada. Many of the COGIC foreign overseers did not reside in their designated territory. For example, the overseer of Canada resided in California, and the overseer of Haiti resided in Tennessee. Effective organization and leadership could not be accomplished by clergy leaders who did not have strong connections to the missions and people outside of the United States. Nevertheless, COGIC missions have been documented in over fifty countries around the world with several programs focusing on evangelizing Africa.

4.4. DEVELOPMENT OF THE HOLY CONVOCATION

As the COGIC denomination was being departmentalized, Mason established annual meetings for the clergy and lay members to convene in a specific town for worship and tend to the administrative business of the organization. In 1916, Mason led a meeting for all COGIC saints in Los Angeles, California, with hosts, Overseer Eddie Driver and Overseer Samuel Crouch. However, the first National COGIC Holy Convocation took place in Memphis at the Tabernacle, the meeting place for the Holy Convocation. First, the overseers and elders met from 1908 to 1924 at 392 South Wellington Street, which was Saints Home COGIC, the church Mason pastored. The Tabernacle, located on 958 South Fifth Street, was built in 1925 for all of the saints coming to Memphis from around the country and the world.[45] The early COGIC Holy Convocations were held between the dates of November 25 to December 14. The dates for the convocation gave farmer-preachers and evangelists a convenient time to receive money from their harvest so that they would have some funds to take care of expenses at the convocation.[46] The Tabernacle burned in 1936, so the saints moved to Mason's church, called Temple COGIC, located on 672 South Lauderdale Street in Memphis until Mason Temple was completed in 1945.[47] The Holy Convocation served as the Azusa Street Revival of Memphis, Tennessee. During the Holy Convocation, Mason began the meeting with three days of fasting and prayer so that people could concentrate on the Spirit and worship. This was considered a sacred time that charged the life, vitality, and vision of the COGIC saint in understanding the purpose of service to Christ and the COGIC church.[48] Seymour, Mason's mentor at Azusa, attended the Holy Convocation in Memphis, for Mason had invited him to preach on several occasions. Furthermore, the Holy Convocation, like Jerusalem for the Jews and Mecca for the Muslims, transformed Memphis into a COGIC Holy Land. During the years of segregation in the South, Memphis, as many COGIC members testified, did not allow African-Americans to stay in the hotels. Nevertheless, COGIC saints in Memphis opened their homes and kitchens to visitors from around the country. There was constant fellowship among the members inside and outside of the Church Tabernacle. Older members always became sentimental when talking about the sisterly and brotherly love shown by everybody. Living and worshipping together created bonds like the New Testament Church in the Book of Acts of the Apostles, as COGIC members shared "all things in common" with each other.

Before the convocations occurred with the masses of COGIC saints travelling to Memphis, between the years of 1917-1924, the General Board of Elders met in Memphis. In 1919, the 12th General

Convocation of Elders was chaired by Eddie R. Driver. The meeting's agenda concentrated on finalizing the publication of the ministerial roll, ordaining elders, and Mason's authority to appoint pastors to churches (Mason had episcopal authority because he was the sole leader of the COGIC Church, contrary to the ideal of congregational authority when church members elected a pastor). Also during the meeting, Apostle Seymour made a visit and stated that the Church of God in Christ was the greatest movement on earth. On a negative note, Mason issued several directives, one concerning the marriage of Elder Frazier. Mason said that the marriage was unscriptural for he had married another man's wife and was no longer to be considered a minister until he put the wife away (annul the marriage).[49] To bring light to the statement by Mason, Elder Frazier's marriage could have been legal, but in the Pentecostal tradition of marriage, a divorcee could not marry again until the other spouse died. Mason abided by this rule when dealing with the failure of his first marriage to Alice Saxton, and Mason married Leila Washington in 1905 after the death of Alice Saxton.

Moreover, improper and unlawful marriages, according to Mason's belief about Holiness, dominated the agenda of the 13th General Convocation in 1920, starting with charges against elders for unlawful marriages. The preachers' licenses were revoked, and they were banned from the pulpit. In 1920, the meeting established church reports.[50] Reports were financial assessments levied upon each COGIC local church in support of administrative expense in spreading the Gospel of Jesus Christ. The local church was ordered to give the monies to the overseer, and then the overseer gave the funds to the General Financial Board. This hierarchal assessment structure exists today in the COGIC Church with each church being assessed and each credential holder with a license to minister, male and female, being assessed a designated annual monetary fee.

The mass gathering of Holiness-Pentecostal followers in Memphis was dominated by the leadership-style of Mason. As a testament to his spiritual leadership, Mason had gained the trust of many followers due to his humble dress and "common-man" approach to material possessions. Unlike Prophet James Jones, Mason did not dress in a flashy mink coat or ride in a limousine. Mason sought to model the humbleness of Jesus Christ, whom he preached about constantly. Also, Mason had many proclaimed eyewitness accounts that he had laid hands on people and the people were healed, with many rumors that he had raised the dead. Unlike Prophet James Jones, Mason did not assess a fee for the healing. Followers from around the United States heard of Mason performing signs, miracles, and wonders from the Bible, so many people began to investigate COGIC, and eventually joined the movement that taught that the Holy Spirit was yet working among Christians in the modern era.

4.5. TROUBLE WITH THE U.S. GOVERNMENT: WAR AND CONSCIENTIOUS OBJECTION

With the ability to mobilize a large group of African-Americans and influence some White Americans also, Mason's ministry was viewed as a threat to the system of southern segregationist policies for his members saw him as God's leader over them. Adding to the troubles of being sanctified, in 1917, Mason was under surveillance by the Bureau of Investigations for preaching conscientious objection, telling his male parishioners not to fight in the war.[51] According to the files of the Bureau of Investigations and the War Department, Mason was preaching to 2,000 to 3,000 people in Lexington, Mississippi, in August 1917 admonishing that his church did not believe in bloodshed and that the COGIC was opposed to war. He also stated that if any members joined the armed services, those members did not have to go to war and did not have to register. Mason also stated that WWI was for the rich man, but the poor man had to fight; that the GERMANS were a good people who had always treated the Negro well, better than any other members of the White race. Mason went on to say that the Negro did not have a grudge against his

German friends and should not fight against the Germans.[52] Many of the Pentecostal Movements were under surveillance by the federal government because of their tight-knit communities that refused to participate in the war effort. Unexpectedly, the Church of God in Christ and its male leadership were enthralled with the politics of war. During wartime, specifically World War I, Pentecostal churches were forced to show support to the United States government's war efforts or be considered traitors to the country.

The Bureau of Investigations began to build a case against Mason in 1917 by using people to infiltrate the Lexington church services. Witnesses against Mason included J.H. Fuqua, Chancery Clerk of Holmes County, Mississippi, and T. Pullen, a resident of Lexington. Reverend A. H. Miller, Plummer Broome, and Willie A. Thurmond were actual witnesses who had attended the religious services to hear Mason preach. In June 1918, an arrest warrant was issued for Mason under the Disloyalty Act because there was not enough evidence to charge him under the new Espionage Act. Mason was charged with obstructing the draft by telling young men not to register but claim conscientious objection according to the scriptures. Mason was charged with making statements to promote the cause of the German Empire.[53]

The Holmes County Judge issued the warrant for Mason's arrest; however, Sheriff Bell, after arresting Mason for his alleged anti-war preaching, had to protect Mason from an angry White lynch mob. So, Sheriff Bell relocated Mason to Durant, Mississippi, and then to the federal prison in Jackson, Mississippi, avoiding a potential lynching scene.[54] Mason awaited his federal court date, and then he was transferred to Paris, Texas, to stand trial for treasonous activities.

Mason and his congregations were persecuted for their stand against actively participating in the United States' Allied venture in World War I. With mounting pressure from the federal government, Mason tried to ensure the government that COGIC members were patriotic and were not treasonous. During the sermon in the next paragraph, Mason urged his members to purchase war bonds and stated that male members could serve in the military, but should be assigned to non-combative roles. Moreover, the United States Army was segregated, not allowing African-American troops and White troops to fight together on the battlefield.

To further prove his loyalty, Mason's preached a sermon on June 23, 1918, called "The Kaiser in the Light of the Scriptures." However, the sermon was recorded by Elder William B. Holt, the General Secretary of COGIC.[55] Mason preached from Hab. 2:2,

> *The Lord answered me and said, write the vision and make it plain. Mason went on preaching saying that they tell me the Kaiser went into prayer and came out and lifted up his hands and prayed, and afterwards declared war. Let us see, what did he pray and for what did he pray? Surely, he did not pray thy Kingdom Come, because the Kingdom of God is righteousness, peace and joy in the Holy Ghost, Rom. 14:17. If he had been praying for peace he would not have declared war. The Apostle Paul declared in 1 Tim. 2:12, I exhort therefore that, first of all, supplications, prayers, intercessions and giving thanks be made for all men for kings and for all who are in authority that we may lead a quiet and peaceful life in all Godliness and honesty. If he had the spirit of this prayer, he himself would have endeavored to live a peaceful life.*
>
> *In 1 Tim. 2:8, the apostle says, I will therefore that men pray everywhere, lifting up holy hands, without wrath and doubting. This is the attitude to be in while praying with uplifted hands. The Kaiser prayed in wrath, with the purpose to work wrath, which was a vain prayer, as he had not the spirit of Christ or the authority of the Scriptures. Thus, the prayer of the Kaiser was unscriptural. He complimented the President, and showed he was in harmony with the Scriptures, as recorded in 1 Kings 8:33-45. In this proclamation calling the American people to a day of fasting and prayer, that they might confess their sins and shortcomings and humble themselves before the Lord, in order that they might find favor with him who causes wars to cease and who makes bare his holy arm in defense*

of a righteous nation, and was in harmony with him who taught us to pray, Thy Kingdom come, Thy will be done, on earth as it is in heaven. The Lord declared by the mouth of Isaiah, the prophet, Open ye the gates, that the righteous nation that keeps the truth may enter in Isa. 26:24. He now called attention of his vast audience to the spirit of the Christ that prayed. He quoted from the prayer of the Savior found in the Gospel of John 17:15, I pray not that thou shouldest take them out of the world, but that thou shouldest keep them from evil. The Kaiser is praying to the end that evil might come into the world; the Savior prayed that men should not be killed, but that God would keep them from evil. He[Mason] declared the Kaiser appeared to be the war beast of Revelation 13, causing all the world to wonder after the beast, and that his power came not from God, but from the dragon. (Mason began to refer back to the prophet Habakkuk) The vision was for an appointed time, but at the end it should speak. The prophesies were being fast fulfilled, and the present events proved that we are living in the last days and the end was near. Behold, his soul which is lifted up is not upright in him. The events of the present war proved that the soul of the Kaiser was lifted up in him, and in my estimation, he was not of God. He is a proud man; neither keeps a home; (then Mason quoted the Hab. 2:5) he enlarged his desire as hell, and is as death, and cannot be satisfied, but gatheredunto him all nations and heaps unto him all peoples.With the Kaiser's ambition to rule the world and the spirit of militarism that possesses him, he is fittingly described in this way. He does not want to keep at home, but is reaching out hands dripping with blood of innocent children and defenseless women sent to an untimely death by the barbarous method of submarine warfare, which is out of harmony with all laws of humanity and fair play and is a violation of all the principles of civilized warfare. The German Kaiser is seemingly attempting to gather to himself all nations and to rule all peoples. Not satisfied with the rape of Belgium, he has overthrown the governments of Romania and Montenegro, and through hypocrisy and deceit he betrayed Russia into a disgraceful peace. (Mason quotes Hab. 2:6) Shall not all these take up a parable against him, and a taunting proverb against him, and say, 'Woe to him that increased that which is not his; shall they not rise up suddenly? that shall bite thee, and awake that shall vex thee? because thou hast spoiled many nations.' All the remnant of the people shall spoil thee because of men's blood, and for the violence of the land of the city and all that dwell therein. Woe to him that covets an evil covetousness to his house, that he may set his nest on high; that he may be delivered from the power of evil. Thou hast consulted shame to thy house by cutting off many people, and hast sinned against thy soul. If anyone in this building hopes on the victories of Kaiser in the present war, their hopes are invain. Although he may conquer nations and devastate cities, in the end he has to meet God, and that the remnant of the Germans and all peoples saved out of the slaughter will rise up against him and cry, 'Woe unto thee because thou hast spoiled many nations; the people shall spoil thee.' Jesus Christ came to bring immortality and eternal life to light, to bind up broken-hearted and bring the glad tidings of salvation from sin and death to a lost and ruined world. The devilish spirit of the Kaiser that causes women to be ravished, infants to be dashed to pieces, and prisoners of war to be tortured and put to death by methods only equal by the Spanish Inquisition and the persecutions of the Christians under Nero. The Kaiser could not be of God, for the scriptures declared, 'If any man have not the spirit of Christ he is none of his.' Rom. 8:9. (Quoting from Luke. 9:54), And when his disciples James and John saw this they said, Lord, will thou that we command fire down from heaven and consume them-even as Elias did? But he turned and rebuked them, and said, Ye know not what manner of spirit ye are of. The disciples spoke as they thought men would do, or should do. (Mason quoted Jesus' answer, Saint Luke 9:56), The Son of Man is not come to destroy men's lives, but to save then. Future events showed, before he would kill, he offered up himself, and by His death came peace, and if the Kaiser had been willing to die rather than shed blood of his fellow man, we would now have peace. I cannot understand, after preaching the Gospel for twenty years and exhorting men to peace and righteousness, how I could be accused of fellowshipping with the anti-Christ of the Kaiser. (Mason goes on to answer the question that had been asked him many times), Is it right to buy Liberty Bonds? (Mason's reply), Yes! Yes! What does it mean to buy Liberty Bonds? It means to lend your country a certain amount of money. What says the scriptures? Matt. 5:42, Give to him that asks Thee, and from them that borrow of thee turn not away. Brethren, we are living by every Word of God-Matt. 4:4. Our government is asking us for a loan, and we are in no violation of God's Word in granting it, and not only to loan, but loan, hoping for nothing to gain. Luke 6:35. I have loaned the government, and have succeeded in raising for, for the help of the government, more than three thousand dollars, in taking out bonds, and as far as I am concerned, the Spiritual injunction stands. I have loaned, hoping for nothing in return.(Mason prayed for the time to come when the German hordes should be driven back across the Rhine, the independence of Belgium restored and victory of allied armies restoring peace to war torn world-especially for the coming of the Prince of Peace and the day when men would beat their swords into plowshares and men would learn to war no more.)[56]

With this proposed sermon[57] and a collection of papers in the Bureau of Investigations' files, Mason accomplished the task of alleviating two burdens that were hindering his ministry. Supposedly, the public denouncing of the Kaiser using Biblical Scriptures and a moral platform, Mason could distance himself from the accusations of treason, despite his conscientious objector's stance that he preached to his members. The alleged sermon also showed support for the United States government and its war efforts as Mason wholly supported the idea of COGIC buying liberty bonds. Again, Mason, allegedly, used the Bible to solidify his claims and to justify his actions. The reasoning by Mason was sound in supporting the country in order to deter allegations of treason and the fearmongering by Whites in the South who demonized the Sanctified Church for being pro-German and pro-Socialist. Another point that has not been raised by other authors or researchers is the validity of the sermon being fully or partially preached by Mason or not preached at all by Mason. Reason being, Elder Holt recorded the sermon that was supposedly preached by Mason, but, while analyzing the words and structure, Holt seemed to have injected some of his ideas in the sermon for the purpose of exemplifying patriotism, and to denounce German affiliation. In Mason's sermon, the idea of a German conspiracy was vehemently denounced. The anti-US evidence in the Bureau of Investigation's files contradict the pro-US stance by Mason in the "Kaiser Sermon." In another light, Holt, a White man affiliated with an African-American organization appeared suspicious, and he was perceived by persons outside of the COGIC Church as a German spy.[58] The question in many African-American communities was why were Blacks fighting Germans when the persecution was coming from White America. The Bureau of Investigations' files seem to support Mason's idea of sympathizing with the Germans, being contrary to the sermon preached on the Kaiser dated June 23, 1918. The investigators perceived that Mason's words for the Kaiser and against the US mistreatment of Black Americans were enough to arrest him for violating the old Disloyalty Act.[59] During this time, African-Americans were still being lynched in cities across the nation. The early 1900s was characterized by race riots in Atlanta, Georgia, Tulsa, Oklahoma, and Elaine, Arkansas. American Whites had plenty reasons to fear an alliance composed of African-Americans and their White allies who supported Socialism and Communism.

In returning to the scrutiny of Mason's Kaiser sermon as recorded by Holt, the sermon appeared more formal and more analytical than the other sermons or testimonies preached by Mason. Also, the Kaiser sermon was not compatible with Mason's apolitical lifestyle, because in the sermon a political position was taken to strongly support the United States' war efforts. The sentence structure and grammar had a professional tone, and very few slang words were used by Mason, unlike the format of Mason's earlier court testimony and sermons. Another glaring feature of this sermon is the antithesis of Pentecostal spirituality and its defiance against worldly matters. Obviously, Mason has made a theological turn from his early Pentecostal stance on not being involved in worldly affairs for he preached "ye are in the world, but ye are not of the world." The Kaiser sermon was placing Mason directly in the heart of a worldly matter that involved a war between several worldly nations. The sermon specifically talked about beating the Germans back across the Rhine, making the sermon a geopolitical argument to defeat Germany. Holiness and Pentecostal believers, in general, denounced any participation in war, politics, and social organizations like Free Masonry, Shriners, and the Red Cross. At this juncture, along with the first court case of 1907, Mason and his COGIC body were making steps toward the development of a religious institution.

A question must also be raised about the sermon's timing. In earlier passages, Mason was in the federal jail in Jackson, Mississippi, around the June 21st to June 25th, 1918. If he were in jail during this time, how could he have preached a sermon for baptismal ceremonies in North Memphis? The other scenario is the possibility Secretary Elder Holt placed the current date on the sermon, but the sermon was preached at an earlier time, maybe in the spring of 1918, which served as another possible time for water baptism. If the sermon was preached at an earlier date, a problem of documentation arises. How could Holt remember the specific details of a sermon preached at an earlier date and how could the anti-Kaiser remarks of Bishop Mason be so contrary to his pro-Kaiser remarks recorded by the Bureaus of Investigations? The August 1917 files of the Bureau of Investigations documented Mason's sermon expressing to the listeners, "If you want to stay out of this war, you must get right with God, and join my church. There is no occasion for the negroes [sic] to go to war: -the Germans are the best friends the negroes [sic] have. Germany is going to whip the United States for the mistreatment accorded the negroes [sic], if for no other reason." "This is a rich man's war anyway.Wilson, before the election, was crying, peace, peace, peace, and now, since its war, war, war."[60]

The alleged inflammatory statements by Mason eventually landed him in front of a Paris, Texas grand jury of the federal court in October 1918.[61] According to Mason's testimony, "In 1918, I was called to appear before the judge of the Kangaroo Court [derogatory name for a biased court] in Paris, Texas. The presiding office looked at me and laid down his books and said, 'You all may try him; I will not have anything to do with him.' I will give God all the glory. Amen."[62] Despite the dramatics of Mason's testimony, the court decided not to prosecute him and others from his congregation. In reality, two key witnesses, one was deceased, and the other refused to testify against Mason, the government did not have a case. Also, since this court case took place in October 1918, the proximity to the war ending on November 11, 1918,[63] made the government's prosecution of the case insensible. Nevertheless, Mason and his church with interracial worship services continued to be viewed with suspicion across the South as Black-White relationships were characterized as being a platform for communism, socialism, and populism movements. After being under investigation, Mason's COGIC Holiness-Pentecostal Church proceeded to move into a transitional phase that was similar in growth to his former preaching partner, Charles P. Jones.

4.6. SIMILARITIES BETWEEN COGIC, INC. AND CHURCH OF CHRIST (HOLINESS)

As Mason's church marched toward being institutionalized, there were glaring similarities in the developments of the Church of God in Christ and the Church of Christ (Holiness). In 1899, Jones organized a Sunday School Convention, before he and Mason separated in 1907, in Jackson, Mississippi.[64] COGIC's Sunday School Department was organized in 1908 and the first convention was held in 1951 in Kansas City, Missouri at Bishop Virgil M. Barker's Church, Temple COGIC.[65]

Due to segregation and financial frugality, many of the COGIC Conventions, before the decade of the 1970s, convened at COGIC churches in the host city. In 1899, Charles Jones created a weekly paper called The Truth based on principles in the Book of Proverbs, it became a pioneering African-American publication at the time.[66] In 1907, Mason and his delegation of preachers raised money to establish a biweekly newspaper publication called The Whole Truth, which was the Pentecostal version that rivalled Jones' Truth. Mason claimed that Jones rejected the doctrine of "tongues" and did not preach the entire truth of the Gospel, but the gift of speaking in "tongues" allowed Mason to preach the whole truth.[67] Elder David J. Young was chosen as editor of the newspaper by Mason and the assembly due to his educational background that included enrolling at Morehouse College in Atlanta and Benedict College in Columbia, South Carolina. The paper served as the voice for COGIC, Inc.[68]

In 1909, Church of Christ Holiness had Christian Women Willing Workers (CWWW) and the women's meetings were called Prayer Bands and Bible Bands.[69] COGIC Inc. started a Women's Department in 1911 and the Prayer and Bible Bands were under the authority of the Women's Department. In 1914, the Willing Worker moniker was applied to the COGIC youth department, Young People Willing Workers.[70] In 1917, Church of Christ (Holiness) held its National Convention in Jackson, Mississippi, where Jones was a prominent pastor.[71] In 1925, COGIC, Inc. held its National Holy Convocation in Memphis, Tennessee, at the Tabernacle on 392 South Wellington Street.[72] Memphis became the home city for COGIC's Holy Convocation.

Another similarity in organization and development dealt with the title of overseer. Eventually, both denominations dropped the title of overseer and adopted the title of bishop. In 1927, an episcopal form of government was adopted in Church of Christ (Holiness). Charles Jones was elected as the first bishop and president, and four "junior" bishops were also elected.[73] The church was reorganized into four dioceses under the supervision of the four elected bishops. In the COGIC Church, Mason and his clergy changed their titles from overseers to bishops in 1933. In that year, the first five bishops were appointed in the Church of God in Christ in designated states. Mason became the Senior Bishop and Chief Apostle of the Church of God in Christ. One last similarity in development dealt with splinter groups.

As discussed above, Mason had one splinter group led by Elias D. Smith, forming Triumph the Church and Kingdom of God in Christ and another formed in 1914, when several White preachers under Mason left COGIC in order to support the formation and development of the Assemblies of God. Looking at the records, Jones only had one splinter group under his leadership. In 1920 at the Church of Christ (Holiness) Annual National Convention in Atlanta, Georgia, Elder K.H. Burruss withdrew his membership and founded Church of God (Holiness) with headquarters in Atlanta.[74] As COGIC and Church of Christ (Holiness) grew in membership and developed as institutions, the connection that Charles Jones and Mason had in the Holiness era was evident in their leadership over their particular denominations. Both leaders maintained strict lifestyles that were governed by the Bible and had an earnest desire to evangelize the world with a sanctified theology. Mason's COGIC Church surpassed Jones' Holiness Church in the numbers of converts and membership. The COGIC Church concentrated heavily on domestic evangelism and converted numerous people in the South and then quickly branched out to urban centers like Chicago, Detroit, New York City, St Louis, and Los Angeles. Mason's departments specifically targeted women and young people and gave them responsibilities of serving the church, making both groups take ownership into the Church of God in Christ. The people had "something" that they personally built with an obligation to God.

Mason's greatest traits were that he preached to people on their level with charisma and uplift as he equalized the pulpit, making a preacher qualified to minister the Gospel just by claiming that he had the Holy Ghost and spoke in tongues. The COGIC brand appealed to the poverty-stricken sections of the South with rural farmers and families, and in the North among areas of low-income and poverty. Many COGIC Churches started in buildings that were closed businesses. These churches became known as "storefronts", not providing many amenities. When the churches began to grow and multiply, Mason, with the help of his overseers, began to organize the states into districts with leading elders, and those leading elders answered to the state overseer. By the 1940s, the COGIC Church was entrenched in numerous cities across the nation with missions in Canada and the Caribbean, outpacing and out-converting the Church of Christ (Holiness). However, Mason soon faced another split in his COGIC Church, similar to the split he experienced with Charles P. Jones, and this time, Mason had to deal with an opposing faction within the COGIC ranks, led by one of his closest associates of Arkansas, Bishop Justus Bowe.

4.7. 1932: The Third Splinter Group and the Second Court Case

Another splinter group separated from Mason in 1932, and the group was led by one of Mason's original preachers who sided with him against Charles Price Jones. That leader was Justus Bowe, among one of the first overseers in Arkansas. Bowe decided that a congregational form of church government was better than the current episcopal form of government that Mason had endorsed while being a part of the Holiness-Pentecostal Movement. So, in 1932, those preachers who wanted a congregational form of government met in Hot Springs, Arkansas and formed Church of God in Christ, Congregational. Justus Bowe became the first Senior Bishop in October 1932 as he was forced to withdraw from COGIC, Inc. COGIC, Congregational headquarters was established at 103 Daisy Street, Hot Springs, Arkansas.[75] This separation was not amicable because Mason took Bowe to court to maintain the churches under the COGIC, Inc., banner. Despite Mason's background as a Baptist preacher, Mason had assimilated into the hierarchal Holiness ecclesiastical structure that gave a pastor and leader more power and control over the congregation than the Baptist counterparts. The Chicago Defender reported on the legal controversy involving COGIC, Inc. and COGIC, Congregational: Appendix C outlined the case between Mason and Bishop Bowe.

According to the court case in Appendix C, a Pine Bluff, Arkansas Church of God in Christ grew tired of their pastor, Noah Smith. As a result, the COGIC church elected Justus Bowe, the overseer of Arkansas, to be the pastor. Mason, Elder William Rogers, and Elder Noah Smith ordered Bowe to be arrested because the COGIC organization was an episcopal church that had to secure the approval of the state overseer/bishop, and, in many cases, the approval of senior bishop, Mason, in order for a pastor to be removed.[76] The COGIC Church in Pine Bluff had not consulted with Bishop Mason about changing leadership which showed disrespect to Mason's authority. Nevertheless, the Jefferson County Arkansas judge ruled in a landmark decision that a congregation with a majority vote had the right to select its own leader, and he scolded the Church leaders by stating that they should have prayed and let God handle their Church matters.[77] The judge upheld the power of the congregation, not the appointing authority of Senior Bishop Mason.

Bishop Bowe moved forward and led the new COGIC, Congregational. However, COGIC, Inc. leaders made a plea to Bowe for him to come back for he was considered one of the founding pioneers, and Bowe was confident that he would be considered as one of the leading officials, again.[78] Eventually, in 1946, Bowe left COGIC, Congregational, and went back to COGIC, Inc. to serve in the state of Arkansas. A meeting was called in East St. Louis, Illinois on January 11,1946, between the leaders of COGIC, Inc. and COGIC, Congregational. The COGIC, Congregational Board of Elders refused to reunite with COGIC, Inc., only Bishop Bowe reunited with the Church of God in Christ, Inc.[79]When Bowe left COGIC, Congregational, George Slack started his tenure as the senior bishop. Slack refused to go back to COGIC, Inc. because he was against COGIC, Inc. preachers who taught that if a person did not tithe (give 10% of their income to the Church), then that person was not saved. Slack led COGIC, Congregational from 1946 to 1970. [80]

4.8   1933: THE BEGINNING OF AN INSTITUTION; FROM OVERSEERS TO BISHOPS

One year after the departure of Bowe to form COGIC, Congregational, Mason decided to transform his leadership corps. At this juncture, the first phase of the Mason Era ended, leaning toward a more hierarchal and bureaucratic Church. In 1933, Mason ordained the first five bishops in COGIC, Inc. Looking back, Mason had used the title of overseer when he was preaching with Charles Price Jones in the Holiness Movement. The overseer title was biblical in nature and the title distinguished Holiness and Holiness-Pentecostal preachers from the Baptists and Methodist preachers. Now that a new era had begun for COGIC, Inc., and the title of bishop was also considered biblical and was more modern than the title overseer, Mason decided to drop the overseer leadership title in favor of the bishop title. Mason appointed five distinguished state leaders across the United States to assume the title of bishop.

One of the first five bishops was Emmett Morey Page of Dallas, Texas. Page was born to Richard and Polly Ann Page in Yazoo County, Mississippi, on May 19, 1871. His family was affiliated with the AME Church and Page stayed on the farm until he was twenty-three years old, and then moved to Jackson, Tennessee. In 1903, Page moved to Memphis, Tennessee and converted to Holiness under the preaching of Overseer Mason. Page joined Mason's church, Saints Home COGIC, and received the Baptism of the Holy Spirit in 1907. Later, he was called to preach, and he left his job to preach the Gospel in Mississippi. After many financial hardships for himself and his family, Page claimed that many people began to bless him and meet his needs. In 1914, Mason sent Page to Texas to oversee the establishment of COGIC churches in the area. Page worked diligently in the areas of Dallas and Houston, prompting Mason to make him one of the state's first overseers.[81] Page replaced David J. Young as Overseer of Texas, when Young chose to move to the state of Kansas.

Riley Felman Williams was also one of the first bishops appointed by Mason. Williams was born in St. Francisville, Louisiana and was one of Mason's prolific COGIC generals. According to the 1944 version of the COGIC Manual, Williams was the overseer of Georgia, Ohio, and Alabama, simultaneously. He was the first leader to create districts in Georgia. According to Pleas in Fifty Years Achievement, the concept of districts was created by a COGIC leadership committee in Texas. Districts were composed of local COGIC Churches in certain areas of the state. Districts were led by a superintendent, who was a leading pastor. Each superintendent reported to the state overseer, who became the state bishop.

Mason considered Overseer Williams one of his most faithful and dedicated administrators. In 1925, when Mason was having problems in Georgia with former Church of the First Born leader, John Q. Croom, Mason dispatched Overseer Williams to observe Croom's actions and to make sure that he was following the doctrines and regulations of the COGIC Church. Eventually Croom was replaced due to his adherence to First Born doctrines instead of adhering to COGIC doctrines.[82] After the blatant disregard for Mason's authority, Mason replaced Croom with Overseer Riley F. Williams.[83]

Another long-time bishop candidate and COGIC general was William Matthew Roberts. Roberts was a member of Mason's church in Memphis and was sent by Mason to evangelize the state of Illinois. Roberts testified in the Frank Avant v. C.H. Mason, court case, remaining faithful to Bishop Mason's new theology of speaking in tongues within the presence of the Holy Spirit. Roberts served as a deacon under Bishop Mason at Saints Home COGIC in Memphis, and he was eventually called to preach while serving under Mason's leadership. As the first overseer of Illinois, several ministries and Gospel music pioneers were affiliated with Roberts' church, Roberts Temple COGIC.[84] Moreover, the funeral services for young Emmett Till, who was slain because he was accused of not speaking properly to a White woman in Mississippi, were held at Roberts Temple COGIC.

Another leader in the ranks of the first appointed COGIC bishops was Israel S. Stafford of Detroit, Michigan. Stafford was a medical doctor and he served as the third overseer of the state of Michigan.[85] He succeeded Mack E. Jonas who had previously been the overseer of Georgia.

The final overseer to be promoted to the office of bishop was Ozro Thurston Jones. Overseer Jones was a pioneer and key developer of the COGIC Young People Willing Workers (YPWW) Department. O.T. Jones had the pulse of the youth in the COGIC denomination and due to his strong leadership skills within the department, many COGIC leaders were advanced to the office of bishop after leading the National YPWW Department. O.T. Jones was responsible for spreading the COGIC message of Pentecost in the state of Pennsylvania as his church was headquartered in Philadelphia. O.T. Jones, Sr. was born in Fort Smith, Arkansas on March 26, 1891. O.T. Jones graduated as a Latin scholar and valedictorian from Lincoln High School in Fort Smith.[86] He was also one of the early pastors of First COGIC in Fort Smith before moving to Philadelphia.

O.T. Jones' resume included the following COGIC achievements: 1) In 1914, he organized the Youth Department and was later appointed president; 2) In 1916, he authored and edited YPWW topics making the quarterlies one of the largest Pentecostal publications in the nation; 3) In 1928, Jones founded the International Youth Congress of COGIC which became one of the largest annual gatherings of Christian youth and youth workers in the country; 4) In 1925, he was appointed pastor of a Philadelphia congregation which became Holy Temple COGIC. O.T. Jones started with a handful of members and grew the church to more than 2,000 members. After the death of Bishop Mason in 1961, Jones became the second and last Senior Bishop of the COGIC Church.[87]

Also, a change occurred within the COGIC Women's Department in relation to the title of overseer. The national women's overseer title became National Supervisor of the COGIC Women's Department.

State female overseers' titles were changed to state supervisors. The transition from the title overseer of women's work appeared to have been permanently abandoned after the death of Mother Elizabeth Robinson, the first national overseer of women's work. Furthermore, the women ministry leaders had the titles of supervisor, mother, missionary, evangelist, and deaconess. Mother Lillian Brooks Coffey became the first female leader to be named the General Supervisor of the COGIC Women's Department. Eventually the title of overseer was officially abolished from COGIC leadership in 1954.[88]

The Mason Era faced many challenges on the American and world religious landscape. COGIC was viewed by many established religions as a cult that espoused "Spirit" possession along with the "babbling" of "tongues." Mason also faced an inward denominational threat posed by Elias D. Smith who challenged Mason with a theology of the Christian being able to live forever and never feel pain again after experiencing the Baptism of the Holy Ghost. Smith was able to persuade a significant amount of people to follow his doctrines, but he died in Africa, and the failure of his theology of living forever devastated the membership of Triumph the Church and Kingdom of God in Christ. Additionally, Mason went to court against a long-time friend, Bishop Justus Bowe, who formed COGIC, Congregational on the premise that the congregation had a right to select their pastor. Mason believed in episcopal authority, like the Methodist Church, when the bishop appointed the pastor to the church without any input from the congregation.

Nevertheless, Mason, with assistance, organized key departments in the COGIC Church. The YPWW Department focused heavily on recruiting the youth of America to live a lifestyle of holiness and sanctification. Several of those young people stayed with the COGIC Church and became bishops and leading missionaries. Young ministers of the YPWW Department like Chandler Owens, G.E. Patterson, and Charles Blake became presiding bishops of COGIC. Young missionaries like Mattie McGlothen and Willie Mae Rivers were appointed as the National General Supervisor of the COGIC Women's Department.

The COGIC Women's Department sustained COGIC's focus on missions in the United States and abroad. COGIC women greatly supported Mason's ministry during the convocations with hospitality and, the women raised a significant amount of funds to build the COGIC headquarters, Mason Temple in Memphis. Without a doubt, the female membership of COGIC, outnumbering the male members, sustained the spiritual growth and the financial strength of COGIC. Female missionaries recruited new members through missions and established churches all over the United States, and in places like Haiti, Jamaica, Africa. As the COGIC church membership grew with people joining from all over the world, Mason decided to revamp the leadership titles in COGIC. Utilizing the title of bishop, which was also used by established religions such as the Catholics and Methodists, Mason dropped the title of General Overseer of COGIC and then renamed himself Senior Bishop and Chief Apostle of the Churches of God in Christ. As senior bishop, Mason continued to serve as the face and persona of COGIC's and led its impact on the world of religions through Holiness and Pentecostalism.

CHAPTER 5

SECOND PHASE OF THE MASON ERA (1933-1961): COGIC INSTITUTION

During the late 1930s and 1940s, COGIC under Mason's authority captured the attention of people across the United States and globally. After the 1934 court case with Bishop Justus Bowe, Mason decided to codify the episcopal authority of COGIC, an authority characterized by Mason who appointed pastors and overseers nationally. Bowe was able to capitalize on the judge's ruling that a congregation could decide who it wanted as pastor. Bowe left Mason's COGIC, Inc., and led those preachers and members who believed in the congregational authority of church administration.

For the pastors and overseers who stayed under Mason's authority, the growth of COGIC churches on the state levels had problems in leadership that had to be addressed by Mason. For example, in Georgia, local congregations were growing, and growth necessitated more leadership and territorial expansion. In 1946, after the tenure of Bishop Riley F. Williams, the state of Georgia was divided into two jurisdictions with Northern Georgia covering territory north of Macon, and the Southern Georgia Jurisdiction conducted ministries south of Macon. The first state bishop of the Northern Georgia Jurisdiction was James J. Hinsley, while the first bishop of Southern Georgia Jurisdiction was Fred W. Winans.[1] Hinsley served for two years as bishop before vacating the position, and then Bishop J. Howard Dell assumed the mantle of leadership and greatly enhanced the COGIC ministries in Georgia by training many elders and missionaries.

In Arkansas, after Bishop Bowe left COGIC, Inc. in 1932, to form COGIC Congregational, Overseer J.E. Hightower took control of the COGIC ministries. Hightower oversaw the state for about ten years. Then Bishop Minor Jones took over as bishop of the Arkansas Northeast Jurisdiction. During the tenure of Minor Jones, an intra-territorial split occurred in 1950. The new jurisdiction was called Arkansas Southwest, and Bishop Walter Quincy Washington became the first bishop to cover the new jurisdictional territory. However, Bishop Washington only served one day as he suddenly died after assuming command. So, in 1951, Witt Henry Kendricks took control as bishop of Arkansas Southwest. Eventually, these two Arkansas Jurisdictions came to be known as Arkansas First Jurisdiction (Northeast) and Arkansas Second Jurisdiction (Southwest).[2]

Overall, COGIC infancy, proliferation, and legacy were berthed from the state of Arkansas. COGIC founders and leaders, Mason and Charles Price Jones, were initially trained as Baptist preachers at Centennial Baptist Church in Helena, Arkansas.[3] Then both preachers attended the Minister's Institute Program that was part of Arkansas Baptist College in Little Rock, Arkansas. In 1897, Mason received the name Church of God in Christ, according to COGIC's traditional claim, while walking down 8th and Gaines Streets in Little Rock, Arkansas. Other COGIC Arkansas pioneers included Bishop Justus Bowe, one of the original members of the Mason Faction who separated from Charles Price Jones, and founder of COGIC, Congregational Church; Elizabeth Robinson was one of COGIC's prolific women preachers who became the first National Overseer of Women's Work; Bishop Wyoming Wells became the state bishop of North Carolina and served on the first COGIC General Board of 1968; Bishop Frederick Douglass Washington was the son of Bishop Walter Washington, the first bishop of the Arkansas Southwest Jurisdiction, migrated to New York and established Washington Temple COGIC. Bishop F.D. Washington also ordained Alfred Sharpton, Jr. (Rev. Al Sharpton) as a COGIC Pentecostal minister at the age of ten. Senior Bishop Ozro T. Jones,

Sr. from Fort Smith, Arkansas became the National COGIC leader upon the death of Bishop Mason in 1961. Also, some megachurch COGIC pastors from Arkansas were Bishop William Goldsberry of Chicago, Illinois and the current Presiding Bishop Charles Blake, born in Little Rock, Arkansas, who pastors the world-renown West Angeles Church of God in Christ with members like Denzel Washington, Angela Bassett, Courtney Vance, George Wallace, Samuel L. Jackson, J. Anthony Brown, and Earvin "Magic" Johnson. Presiding Bishop Blake's father, Junious Augustus Blake, was a YPWW leader in Arkansas and served on the 1968 COGIC General Board. COGIC has many roots in the state of Arkansas which have branched out into every part of the United States and around the world.

Like Georgia and Arkansas, Texas also was divided along the territorial lines with new leaders. Emmett Page was carrying the state as the solo leader of COGIC evangelism. However, after the death of J.H. Galloway who had succeeded Bishop Page in 1944,[4] Texas proceeded through a territorial split in 1956 with four leaders who together evangelized the state more efficiently. John Elbert Alexander was appointed to lead the Texas Northwest Jurisdiction[5], while Texas Northeast Jurisdiction was led by Bishop F. L. Haynes. In the southern part of Texas, Raymond E. Ranger was appointed over Texas Southeast Jurisdiction and Texas Southwest Jurisdiction was headed by Thaddeus D. Iglehart. As the member rolls of the COGIC Church grew across the United States, many preachers ascended to the office of bishop based on growth of organized churches. During the 1930s and 1940s, many of the COGIC divisions within a particular state occurred because of the phenomenal growth of membership in the South, North, East and West. Mason, along with his staff of bishops, elders, mothers, and missionaries, were trying to organize and control the massive growth with programs focused on the Holiness-Pentecostal brand.

5.1. COGIC WOMEN BUILDING HOLINESS
AND CIVIC FOUNDATIONS

While Mason was handling the affairs of the male preaching corps and church administration, his counterpart, Mother Robinson, the General Overseer of the COGIC Women's Department, was handling the structure and administration of the Women's Department. Some of the first state female overseers appointed by Robinson served across the United States, as Mother Robinson supervised COGIC operations in Arkansas and Oklahoma: 1) Bennie Roberts of Arizona and New Mexico; 2) Emma Cotton of Northern California; 3) Millie Crawford of Southern California; 4) Lula Williams assisted Mother Robinson in Oklahoma; 5) Jessie T. Simons of New York; 6) Lizzie Jones of Colorado; 7) Mary Little of North Carolina; 8) Jennie Watson of Mississippi; 9) Margana Kelley of Georgia; 10) Eliza Hollins of Louisiana; 11) Lillie Early of Kansas; 12) Lucinda Bostic of Illinois and Missouri; 13) Catherine Hudson of Tennessee; 14) Hanna Chandler of Texas; and, 15) Rosa Vaughn of Virginia.[6] Mother Robinson saw a need for COGIC development in key areas such as biblical studies, domestic responsibility, and physical and spiritual cleanliness. She started the following COGIC auxiliaries under the guidance of the COGIC Women's Department: Bible Band, Sewing Circle, Home and Foreign Missions, Sunshine Band, and Purity Class. The Bible Band's purpose was to help women study and understand the Word of God so that they could live the life of a saint and rear their children properly.[7] The Sewing Circle helped women to utilize their artistic fingers to supply the needs of their homes, families, and themselves.[8] Since COGIC male preachers and female missionaries preached against women wearing pants, the Sewing Circle encouraged women to sew for the purpose of transforming their trousers into dresses. The Home and Foreign Mission Auxiliary under Mother Robinson provided outreach to spiritually hungry souls and naturally hungry people, both in countries overseas and in the United States of America.[9] The last two auxiliaries, the Sunshine Band and the Purity Class, focused on the Church's instruction for children and young female adults. The Sunshine Band's purpose was to train children between the ages of five and twelve on Biblical principles and how to obey the Word of God so that their minds would not be destroyed by the public elementary schools and broken homes; on the other hand, the Purity Class was specifically for young girls between the ages of twelve and sixteen so that the girls could develop into healthful, happy, and moral adults. Mother Robinson taught the concepts of living by the Holy Bible, utilizing the broom for performing the domestic duties in the home, and encouraging young ladies to keep physically clean with the bath.[10] Thus, the soul was cleansed by the Bible, the home cleansed by the broom, and the body cleansed by the bath.

Mother Robinson led the COGIC standards of morality and piety until her death in 1945. Her last contribution to the COGIC faith was her dedication in mobilizing the women to provide financial support in the construction of Mason's Temple. Over her thirty-four-year tenure as the national overseer of women's work, Mother Robinson utilized her influence in mobilizing every COGIC woman to obligate funds to build the National Tabernacle. In 1945, at the COGIC Holy Convocation in Memphis, the funds had been raised for the national headquarters, and Mother Robinson had personally allocated funds for the neon sign to be placed in front of the building that was later named Mason Temple.[11] Mother Robinson died during the services of the 1945 COGIC Holy Convocation.

After the death of Mother Robinson, Mother Lillian Brooks Coffey, born in Paris, Tennessee, assumed the mantle of leadership as the National Supervisor of the COGIC Women's Department. During the Coffey Era, some of the strict dress codes concerning holy women were revisited and changed. Coffey set the trend for the "modern" sanctified COGIC woman by allowing women to straighten and process their hair; to wear open-toed shoes, to wear dresses with hems down below the knee instead of draping the floor[12], and to participate in civic organizations.

Concerning the civic function and growth of COGIC Women ministries, one focal point was on higher education despite the early anti-education remarks by the founder during his short tenure at Arkansas Baptist College. By 1917, Saints Industrial and Literary School was established in the basement of St Paul COGIC, Mason's church in Lexington, Mississippi, by Sister Pinkey Duncan. The school was designed for the rural area of the Mississippi Delta, training students in home making, agriculture,[13] and mechanical skills. Professor James Courts was appointed head of the school in 1918 and oversaw the only formal COGIC educational institution until his death in 1926.[14] However, the Saints Industrial and Literary School later transformed into Saints Junior College under the leadership of Dr. Arenia Cornelia Mallory.

Mallory was educated in the public schools of Jacksonville, Illinois and studied how to become a concert pianist; however, she attended a Pentecostal revival tent service and was converted to Pentecostalism. She met General Overseer Mason in St. Louis and was asked to come to Lexington, Mississippi to take charge of the fledgling Saints Industrial Literary School.[15] With the assistance of the members of the Alpha Kappa Alpha Sorority and a friendship with Mary McLeod Bethune, Mallory transformed the rural downtrodden COGIC school into a viable operation by the 1930s. Saints Industrial and Literary School acquired 350 acres of land, buildings appraised at $50,000, hired fifteen teachers, and enrolled 400 students. The COGIC School eventually taught grades one through twelve, becoming the first high school for African-Americans in Holmes County, Mississippi.[16] The Mallory-Bethune relationship gained another member after the death of Mother Robinson in 1945. Mother Coffey became a great supporter of Mallory's educational mission, and Coffey entered this sanctified civic union that transformed COGIC women and their impact on society. COGIC women became exposed to the civic responsibility of the National Council of Negro Women(NCNW) which focused on equality for gender and race. The COGIC woman's focus under Mother Coffey emphasized sanctifying the world that existed outside of the realm of the Church, to go and bring Holiness, education, and welfare to people[17] in territories that were economically and spiritually impoverished.

Another key COGIC arena for women was mission work overseas. COGIC women established churches in Africa, Haiti, and Jamaica. Mother Lillian Brooks-Coffey focused on COGIC overseas missions in Liberia and Haiti. Coffey initiated fundraising campaigns to provide housing and education to needy people in both countries. Since the Home and Foreign Mission Auxiliary was placed under the supervision of the Women's Department, early COGIC foreign ministries were dominated by women. For example, in 1927, the first person who answered the call to travel to foreign lands was Mother Mattie McCauley of Tulsa, Oklahoma. Mother McCauley established missions in Trinidad, Cristobal in the Panama Canal Zone, and Costa Rica.[18] In 1929, Missionary Elizabeth White worked in Cape Palmas on the west coast of Africa and at Bonika Station. White was confronted by witch doctors who wanted her to stop teaching Christian principles, but White continued her work and later received assistance when Mother Willie C. Ragland of Columbus, Georgia joined her at Bonika Station. In Liberia, Sister Bernice Lott of Dallas, Texas and Sister Martha Baber of Chicago, Illinois established COGIC mission works, while Charles Pleas was appointed bishop of Liberia. Other missionaries and elders who served in Liberia included Naomi Lundy, Pearl Page, June Blackwell, Ozro T. Jones, Jr., Mary Kennedy, Charles Kenney, and Francis Wiggins.[19]

In 1922, Haiti, a major mission focus of COGIC was evangelized under the ministry of Mother Ann Pennington (who became the wife of Bishop John Seth Bailey of Detroit, Michigan). Elder Paulcius was saved under Mother Bailey's ministry and then he established the first Church of God in Christ church in Haiti in the home of Joseph and Mary St. Juste. Elder Paulcius became the first overseer of Haiti, but later resigned, and then Joseph St. Juste was appointed to the overseer position. One of the key female pioneers of Haiti was a native of Cleveland, Ohio, Sister Dorothy Webster-Exume'. In 1947, Exume' founded the Charles H. Mason School in Port Au Prince and with the help of Elsie Mason, Bishop Mason's third wife, and Bishop Samuel Crouch. The school was built and educated thousands of Haitian students.[20]Exume' began her work in missions in Haiti by assisting Mother Elizabeth Bracy, and she was assigned to mission work after the approval of Mother Coffey, Mother Lott, and Overseer St. Juste. Mother Exume' entered Haiti on July 2, 1947 accompanied by Mother Coffey and Bishop A. B. McEwen to attend to the needs of over 10,000 COGIC Haitian members. Mother Exume' operated at a primary site called Petionville where she helped to open new churches, orphanages, schools, housing projects, and feeding programs. For over three decades, Exume' improved the physical and spiritual well-being of the Haitians under COGIC's foreign mission work.[21] Her hard work and sacrifice were indicative of the plights experienced by the women of COGIC.

One of the overlooked contributions to America by COGIC female Pentecostals was their impact on the proliferation of American music which had strong ties to a Gospel foundation. COGIC's own songbird, Arizona Dranes, took secular ragtime music and substituted lyrics of praise and worship to God. In 1891, Arizona Dranes was born blind to Milton and Cora Drane of Sherman, Texas; nevertheless, when she attended school, she learned classical piano and voice at the Institute for the Deaf, Dumb, and Blind Colored Youth in Austin, Texas.[22] In 1926, she was invited to Chicago by Okeh Records to record some "test" records of her COGIC Pentecostal sound.[23] Dranes' music was not referred to as Gospel music because the genre had not been invented. Dranes' music was religious in nature, but was referred to as race music. All music created by Blacks during this era was considered race music, a designator by the record labels to segregate Black music from White music. Dranes was singing Gospel-styled music before the arrival of Thomas Dorsey, usually credited with being the "Father of Gospel Music." Arizona Dranes, not Thomas Dorsey, was responsible for creating the gospel beat, and Dorsey admitted, in an interview in 1961, that if he could mix Arizona's music with blues, then he would have created a gospel style. [24] Dranes did not attempt to embark on a career in music; instead, she continued working in COGIC ministries as a travelling evangelist, blessing COGIC members and leaders with religious songs that caused a "shouting" frenzy during services. Basically, she used her gift of song to edify God and her church.

Another COGIC musical legend was Rosetta Tharpe. Tharpe, a female, charismatic guitar playing songstress dazzled crowds with her melodious Gospel singing and her mastery of the stringed instrument. Recognized as the Godmother of Rock-N-Roll, Rosetta Tharpe was the harbinger for America's music known as Rock-N-Roll. Rock-N-Roll is a mixture of blues and Gospel music and Rock-N-Roll artists like "Little" Richard Penniman, Elvis Presley, Chuck Barry, and others were greatly influenced by the music of Rosetta Tharpe. Elvis Presley borrowed freely from sacred performers like Tharpe as he listened avidly to Black radio broadcasts and frequented local services of the Church of God in Christ[25] in Memphis. Tharpe was born in the Mississippi "Blues" Delta in Cotton Plant, Arkansas.

In, 1921, at the age of six, Rosetta Tharpe was taken to Chicago by her evangelist mother, Katie Bell, and they joined Roberts Temple Church of God in Christ, pastored by William M. Roberts. Arizona Dranes also routinely sang at Roberts Temple COGIC. Roberts had been under the tutelage of Bishop Mason before pastoring Roberts Temple. Also, Roberts Temple was founded through mission work completed by Mother Coffey.

In 1938, at the age of 23, Tharpe left her unhappy marriage and COGIC teachings, defying the preaching that secular music was a sin and the teachings that a COGIC woman should not leave her husband. Tharpe entered show business and performed music with sexual innuendoes in New York City's famed Cotton Club and Café Society where she was noticed by Cab Calloway and Duke Ellington. Another admirer, Elvis Presley, enjoyed Tharpe's melodious voice and her mastery of the guitar. Tharpe fused her religious themed singing with blues music, writing songs like Rock Me and Tall Skinny Papa. Yet, during the 1940s, Sister Tharpe returned to her COGIC-religious musical roots, singing spirituals[26] and performed in packed churches and theaters throughout America and Europe.[27]

Along with Rosetta Tharpe's indelible impact on sacred and secular music, in later years, COGIC music in the form of choirs dominated the Gospel music genre under the leadership of women. COGIC's music department, established in 1968, was led by Director Mattie Moss Clark. Sister Clark was the first state minister of music in the Church of God in Christ who had a choir to produce a Gospel album. She was the state choir director for the Southwest Michigan State Choir under the leadership of Bishop John Seth Bailey.[28] Under Mattie Moss Clark, COGIC choirs became national and international phenomenon. Also, Clark oversaw the formation and growth of the famous Gospel group, The Clark Sisters. The group was originally composed by five of Clark's daughters, but one daughter left the group during its infancy. The Clark Sisters' music transitioned the genre of Gospel music, as many of their songs had a crossover appeal. Their hit single, You Brought the Sunshine, was often played in secular venues such as night clubs.

As COGIC women contributed greatly to the success of COGIC missions and Gospel music, Mother Coffey was responsible for creating one of the greatest contributions of organized women in the Holiness-Pentecostal Movement. Mother Coffey approached Bishop Mason about the idea of a church women's conference. Bishop Mason conceded to her request and then she gathered a team to work on making her dream a reality.[29] In 1951, Mother Coffey chaired the organizational meeting of COGIC women around the world. In Los Angeles, California, more than 500 COGIC women delegates met at Emmanuel Temple COGIC pastored by Bishop Samuel M. Crouch to convene the first conference of COGIC women. The conference was composed of 60 divisions that represented every state in the nation with leading women like Mother Ann Bailey of Detroit, Mother Freeman of Joliet, Illinois, and Elsie Washington Mason, the third wife of Bishop Mason.[30] The COGIC Women's Convention became a successful venue for women to unite in designated cities across the United States to exemplify the beauty of Holiness. The Women's Convention received great accolades from the people in the host city. City leaders commented on the dignity and professionalism displayed by COGIC women. Hotel managers boasted that among COGIC women, there was no loud talking, no smoking, and no slouches. The women were well dressed with many smiles as they looked their best in public.[31] Additionally, the COGIC Women's Department greatly supported Mason' leadership and maintained the ideal that the assistant supervisor, upon the death of the supervisor, would take control and continue to lead.

5.2. The Creation of the Official COGIC Manual and the Building of the Temple

A decade before the Women's Convention, Mason oversaw the creation of a codified official manual for COGIC, Inc., in 1940, and a revised version in 1944. The appearance of one of the first versions of the COGIC manual was compiled by William B. Holt. Holt was one of the few White preachers that stayed under Mason's leadership and served as the General Secretary of COGIC. The first version of the COGIC Manual had an organization year of 1895. [32] The manual contained written passages to prove that male COGIC members were conscientious objectors during America's participation in World War I. The earliest version of this manual also listed the general overseers in different states along with an official list of women overseers. Alarmingly, the early manual did not specify that speaking in tongues was a mandatory sign of the Holy Spirit. In retrospect, the doctrine of Pentecostalism claimed that speaking in tongues was a mandatory sign of the Baptism of the Holy Spirit, preached by Charles Parham and William Seymour. However, under Mason's authority, the COGIC manual authored by William Holt did not make speaking in tongues a mandatory sign.

The early COGIC manual stated:

While we do not presume to teach that no one has the Spirit that does not speak in tongues, or that one is not saved that does speak in tongues. But we believed that a full baptism of the Holy Ghost as poured out on the Day of Pentecost is accompanied by speaking in tongues. And that the baptism of the Holy Ghost has the same effects and results upon every child of God that receives it; and results on everyone that is born of the Spirit. And we do not consider any one Pentecostal who teaches contrary to this doctrine.[33]

Again, the statement is borderline on speaking in tongues being a mandatory sign for a believer in receiving the Holy Ghost, and the statements posed a separation of any persons not agreeing with the Pentecostal doctrine of tongues.

The revised manual of 1944, edited by Bishop Ozro T. Jones and Bishop J. E. Bryant, had a similar interpretation on the possession of the Holy Spirit. The section is stated in the following passage:

Baptism of the Holy Ghost

We believe in the baptism of the Holy Ghost (Spirit) with the sign and seal of speaking with tongues as recorded in Acts 2:4, 'And they were all filled with the Holy Ghost, and began to speak with other tongues as the Spirit gave them utterance.'

We do not presume to teach that no one has the Spirit that does not speak with tongues, yet we believe that a full baptism of Holy Ghost as was poured out on the day of Pentecost, is accompanied by speaking with other tongues.[34]

Again, the revised manual, much like the first manual that appeared in 1917, is confusing about speaking in tongues as a mandatory sign of the Holy Spirit. The first part of the passage sends a mandatory message tone, while the second part of the passage is not as dogmatic on speaking in tongues being a definite sign of the Holy Ghost. Overall, the statements of the manual are confusing and not definitive about the ideal of tongues being a mandatory sign of receiving the Baptism of the Holy Spirit.[35]

In 1945, after the first manual was revised, Mason and his leaders focused on building a temple to house COGIC members during the Annual Holy Convocation held in November. In retrospect, the Holy Convocation was being held in Memphis as early as 1918, and beginning in 1925, the Holy Convocation was held at "The Tabernacle" at 392 Wellington Street. The Convocation was composed of prayer, fasting, preaching, and the conducting Church business. Under Mason's leadership, the Holy Convocation opened with three days and three nights of fasting and prayer[36] for the purpose of focusing on the Spirit of God. The "Tabernacle" burned down in 1936, then the Holy Convocation was moved to Mason's church, Temple COGIC located on 672 South Lauderdale Street.[37] Years earlier, Temple COGIC was the new name for the former Saints Home COGIC located on 392 Wellington Street, the church that was involved in the court case Frank Avant v. C.H. Mason in 1907. Temple COGIC was the temporary location for the COGIC Holy Convocation, as Mason initiated a project to build a permanent national meeting place in Memphis for the COGIC Saints' annual pilgrimage.

On April 12, 1940, Bishop Riley F. Williams was commissioned by Senior Bishop Mason to build a national temple on 958 South 5th Street in Memphis, Tennessee. Williams secured the services of Elder William Hershey Taylor as the lead architect for the project and Bishop Ulysses E. Miller as the superintendent for temple construction.[38] Obstacles in obtaining funds and building materials were met by Bishop Williams and his construction team. COGIC Inc. only had about $2,900 in the treasury and could only pay Elder Taylor's architectural fee, while others, including Bishop Williams, had to work on the project without pay and hope in good faith that COGIC would recompense the Temple Construction Team. Also, during this period, America was involved in World War II, and there was a shortage of steel for domestic building purposes. Nevertheless, Bishop Williams used Mason's influence and COGIC unity among members to raise funds that exceeded $300,000.[39]

Concerning the steel, COGIC had help from Elder James Logan

Delk, along with William Holt, two prominent White preachers in COGIC. Delk was born around 1887 in Pall Mall, Tennessee. Delk heard Mason preach to thousands of people in Conway, Arkansas and was inspired to write a biography on Mason called He Made Millions Happy. Delk also noted the melodious singing of Charles Jones, Mason's General Overseer, at the Conway meeting. Delk was licensed as a COGIC preacher and became pastor of the First Church of God in Christ in Hopkinsville, Kentucky and started a radio broadcast. Delk was a close confidant to Mason and was known as the "Kentucky Cyclone" evangelist that preached throughout Kentucky, Missouri, Ohio, and Pennsylvania. As a member of the COGIC clergy, Delk had some political allies and influences, even though he had unsuccessful bids as governor of Tennessee, Kentucky, and Missouri. Delk utilized his political influence with Senators Alben Barkley, Happy Chandler, and Harry Truman to secure about $48,000 worth of steel for COGIC to complete the construction of Mason's Temple.[40]

After Elder Delk helped to acquire the steel needed for the temple, Bishop Williams had problems acquiring windows and doors. Williams stated that he had called mills in the South and as far as California to buy doors for the temple. In the end, he went to Cleveland, Ohio, one of the states supervised by him, and bought one door, and three or four doors in another place. Finally, after much intense searching, Bishop Williams had accumulated forty doors and he carted the doors by truck back to Memphis. With great efforts in overcoming external and internal obstacles, COGIC opened Mason Temple for services on the Year of Jubilee[41] Holy Convocation on November 25 – December 3, 1945. Mason Temple would be the site for the Holy Convocation for the next twenty-eight years.

As the COGIC crowds could not be accommodated by Mason Temple, COGIC leaders and the Memphis Convention Bureau partnered with each other in a contract to host the Holy Convocation at the newly constructed Cook Convention Center in 1974.

5.3. Fourth and Fifth Splinter Groups:
1945, Church of God in Christ, Jesus Apostolic,
and 1947, Evangelist Temple House of Refuge
for all Nations COGIC

During the construction phase of Mason Temple, another splinter group developed on the grounds of water baptism. The background of this splinter COGIC group also began in a relationship with Bishop Mason. In the early 1930s, Mother Mayfield had started a COGIC church with five people in her house on Pressman Street in Baltimore, Maryland. Needing the help of a male preacher, Bishop Mason sent Elder Randolph A. Carr to pastor the new fledgling religious body.[42] However, Elder Carr had been baptized in "Jesus" name in New York, thus he was an advocate of the Unitarian doctrine of baptism, when a person is baptized in the name of "Jesus" only. This doctrine conflicted with Mason's Trinitarian doctrine of water baptism which believed a person had to be baptized in the name of the Father, Son, and Holy Ghost. The Oneness Doctrine preached by Elder Carr had caused the same dissension at the Azusa Street Revival. One group claimed to be correct for baptizing in "Jesus's" name only, and the other group proclaimed that one had to be baptized in the name of the Father, Son, and Holy Ghost. To this present-day, the argument yet prevails throughout Apostolic, Holiness, and Pentecostal Christendom. Several denominations have been formed on the baptismal disagreement and both sides argued that the Bible supported both baptismal practices.

So, in 1945, Elder Carr left the fellowship of Bishop Mason because of his conflicting stance on the Apostolic Doctrine of being baptized in Jesus' Name. With five church members, Elder Carr established Rehoboth Church of God in Christ, Jesus Apostolic (COGICJA) and the church grew in membership. In that same year, Elder Carr became Bishop Carr and he presided over the newly incorporated denomination with a Board of Bishops. Carr acquired several church properties as he expanded the membership of Rehoboth COGICJA. Bishop Carr presided over the administration and operations of COGICJA until he passed away in the fall of 1970.[43]

In 1947, Singleton R. Chambers left COGIC, Inc. and formed Evangelist Temple House of Refuge for all Nations Church of God in Christ with a headquarters in Kansas City, Missouri.[44] Chambers reason for leaving Mason's Church are unknown, with some rumors that he was displeased with not being appointed to the office of bishop. Chambers had a close relationship to Mason and served as a national evangelist for COGIC before he established his own movement by planting churches in Arkansas, Mississippi, Missouri, Kansas, Oklahoma, Illinois, Haiti, Jamaica, United Kingdom, Cuba, and Africa.[45]Chambers had the title of chief apostle and bishop, and he led the movement until his death on October 6, 1991.

5.4. The Third Court Case, Special Commission, and Civil Rights

About six years after the developing splinter group, COGICJA, Mason, being one person, could not fully lead the COGIC, Inc., denomination by himself any longer. Mason consented to the need for a commission of bishops to help and support the management and administration of COGIC, Inc., affairs. Two very important COGIC events occurred during the 1950s; first, Mason had to choose the bishops who would have to help him bear the responsibility of leading over two million COGIC Christians. Then, after choosing the bishops, the official COGIC manual had to be changed for administrative and accessional purposes upon the death of Bishop Mason.

A couple of years before choosing the members of the special commission to help Senior Bishop Mason, in 1949, James Delk filed a lawsuit against ten COGIC officials. The lawsuit alleged that COGIC officials had circulated a false rumor about Reverend Delk, and the rumor had stated that Delk had defrauded COGIC of $16,000. Delk claimed that the rumor had destroyed his future earning capacity, livelihood, and his profession in the ministry. Delk was suing for damages in the amount of $242,600, and one of the defendants was Bishop A.B. McEwen.[46]

However, in December of 1950 at the COGIC Elders' Council Meeting, Delk met a group of COGIC leaders, including Mason, Mother Coffey, and O.T. Jones, Sr., in Memphis at the COGIC Elder's Council meeting to apologize for the lawsuit. Delk stated that he had made the worst mistake in his life by suing the ten officials of COGIC, Inc. and he personally apologized to seven members and would have apologized to the other three if he had seen them. After Delk's apology, Elder J. E. Bryant made a motion and Elder G.W. McGlothen seconded the motion for the Elders' Council to forgive Elder Delk for his actions. After the unanimous vote to forgive Delk, Mason stated that when anyone does wrong that they should repent so that God could blot out all for that person to have a part in the glorious ministry.[47]

After the legal battle with Elder Delk, in 1951, Mason chose the first three bishops for the Special Commission to aide him in the handling the administration and legal matters of the Church. The first three bishops were A. B. McEwen of Memphis, Tennessee, John S. Bailey of Detroit, Michigan, and Otha M. Kelly of New York.[48] Bishop McEwen remained in close proximity to Bishop Mason because of his ministry and church being co-located in Memphis, near Mason's church and Mason Temple, the headquarters of COGIC, Inc. Bishop Bailey had established his church and ministry throughout the area of Detroit and Bishop Kelly made strides in the communities of New York City. In 1952, Bishop Ulysses E. Miller was added to the Special Commission and served as the secretary, and J.O. Patterson, Sr. was added as the assistant secretary. In 1955, O.T. Jones, Sr. and Samuel M. Crouch were added to the commission.[49] Earlier, Bishop Miller had supervised the construction of Mason Temple and was one of Mason's major supporters in ministry; he served as the leading bishop of Michigan, and then upon the death of Bishop Riley Williams, he became the bishop of Ohio and pastored Williams Temple COGIC. Bishop J.O. Patterson was closely tied to Mason by way of marriage. Patterson married Deborah Indiana Mason and they had two children that were reared in the COGIC Church, Bishop James Oglethorpe Patterson, Jr. and Janet Patterson, who, according to COGIC members, prayed like Bishop Mason. The other Special Commission members, Bishop O.T. Jones, Sr. and Bishop Crouch were COGIC ministry pioneers in Philadelphia and Los Angeles, respectively. Bishop Jones was the prominent COGIC leader of the Young People Willing Workers' Department. O.T. Jones had been responsible for the training of COGIC youth on the doctrines of Holiness and sanctification. Bishop Crouch, on the other hand, hosted the first COGIC Women's Convention at his church, Emmanuel Temple COGIC, in Los Angeles.

However, the only assignment defined for this Special Commission, which has also been named the Executive Commission, was to assist Bishop Mason with the general operations of the Church. Nevertheless, in the case of Bishop Mason's death, authority and supervision over the COGIC Church would be relegated to the Board of Bishops,[50] not the Special Commission. According to the 1957 COGIC Manual, the Special Commission did not have any defined powers to have authority or conduct Church operations upon the death of Bishop Mason. Moreover, no records existed of Mason designating the Special Commission to have authority over the Church of God in Christ, Inc. After the death of Mason in 1961, the Special Commission became the dominating force in changing the direction and leadership arm of the COGIC Church.

Also, during the last years of the Mason Era, COGIC was greatly impacted by the social and political climate of the American Civil Rights Movement. In 1955, Emmett Till and his mother, Mamie Till, were members of Bishop Louis Henry Ford's church in Chicago, Saint Paul COGIC. Mamie Till had been reared in Roberts Temple COGIC under the leadership of Bishop William Roberts. When she became an adult, Mamie Till decided to follow the progressive ministry of

Bishop Ford. In the summer of 1955, Emmett Till, a COGIC youth, became the martyr of the Civil Rights Movement. The heinous crime perpetrated on Emmett Till by two Money, Mississippi White men shocked the United States and the world displaying a brutality of racism that justified the killing of a child. Across the nation, Black and White Americans denounced the racist killing of Till as barbaric and inhumane. To entrench the crime in the minds of all people, Mamie Till decided to have an open casket funeral at Roberts Temple COGIC. Showing the extremely disfigured body of her son raised the consciousness and righteous indignation of America and the world that racist killings were morally and legally wrong. Emmett Till's murder marked the point in COGIC history of a church that could no longer just proclaim righteousness and Holiness for the soul, but had to address the moral and ethical decline of a society that promoted racism and segregation. Bishop Ford's stance with Mamie Till and his relationship with Mayor Richard Daley of Chicago became a catalytic example in transforming the office of COGIC bishop from an entirely religious position into a socio-religious-political position.[51] Bishop Ford's connection to the civil rights of African-Americans in Chicago served as an implication of changing times for COGIC involvement in the world as active participants instead of Christians on the sidelines waiting to die and go to heaven.

During the second phase of the Mason Era, COGIC male and female leaders were involved in movements for racial and gender equality. Despite the dominant atmosphere to only be concerned with "spiritual" matters, some COGIC members became concerned with their status on earth and wanted to fight against racial injustice. COGIC women, Dr. Arenia Mallory and Mother Lillian Brooks-Coffey worked with Mary McLeod Bethune on advancing the rights of African-American women breaking the mold of stereotypes that COGIC women were only concerned with praising God, supporting the preachers, and doing church work. Mallory and Coffey focused on providing educational opportunities for COGIC members with goals of providing economic empowerment to the COGIC and the African-

American community. As Mallory and Coffey became involved in civil affairs outside of the walls of the Church, Bishop Louis Henry Ford realized the need for his strong participation in the fight against racial injustice as the lynching of young Emmett Till, his church member, caused a great outrage among Black Americans. Bishop Ford extended his COGIC ministry into the fight for civil rights and economic opportunities for not only COGIC members, but also for African-Americans in Chicago and other urban areas across the United States. For the most part, there are no records showing that Mason supported or hindered the actions of Mallory, Coffey, and Ford, each COGIC leader changed the foundation of the isolated focus on "going to heaven" to improving the standard of living conditions of the people, especially African-Americans, on earth. The rights of Black men and women were being violated and Ford, Coffey, and Mallory decided to take civil action along with praying and preaching.

The early actions on civil rights gave COGIC members a foundation to take part in the demonstrations and marches in Memphis, Tennessee, and Mason Temple was designated as the make-shift headquarters for Martin L. King and other Black civil rights leaders and organizations.

CHAPTER 6

POST-MASON ERA:
THE ASCENSION AND OUSTING OF O.T. JONES, SR.

On November 17, 1961, Bishop Charles Harrison Mason died in a Detroit hospital, leaving a sustaining legacy as a grassroots prophet who operated under the power of the Holy Spirit. The funeral had all the dignitaries onboard to honor his founding and service to the Church he loved for over 53 years.[1] The Tennessee State COGIC choir provided music with soloists Pearl Hines, Ann Fletcher, Ruth Davis, and Mattie Wigley. The Old Testament Scripture was read by Bishop Raymond E. Ranger of Texas Southeast Jurisdiction and the New Testament was read by Bishop D. Lawrence Williams of Virginia, Chairman of the Board of Bishops. Remarks were given by all the leaders of COGIC Departments like Sunday School, YPWW, and the Women's Department. Bishop Charles Pleas, supposedly, Mason's second convert and author of Fifty Years Achievement, gave remarks about his pastor and friend. The eulogy was preached by Bishop O.T. Jones, Sr., the last surviving bishop of the five original bishops initially ordained by Bishop Mason. The program also noted that Jones was a member of the Executive Commission.[2] Bishop Jones gave a soul-stirring eulogy of Mason denoting how he was honored to serve with such a great and anointed preacher of the Gospel. Jones told how he connected with Mason's ministry in Arkansas and travelled extensively with him to save souls. In a sense, Jones' sermon established him as the obvious choice in assuming the role as the national leader of COGIC.

Before Jones could assume the position held by Mason, the Chairman of the Board of Bishops took control of the COGIC operations and administration. Bishop D. Lawrence Williams, Chairman of the Board of Bishops, along with the General Assembly of members agreed to leave the senior bishop position vacant for one year before selecting a national leader and senior bishop of COGIC. D. Lawrence Williams later supported the selection of Senior Bishop Jones as the leader to succeed Bishop Mason.

COGIC leadership accession controversy resulted due to Mason's lack of action to properly address the problem before his death. Battles over the right to lead COGIC in the Post-Mason Era illustrated examples of the harsh political realities within a Holiness-Pentecostal denomination that was expected not to have any political fights and battles. Firstly, Mason did not leave or clearly designate a successor. So COGIC was left with the task of choosing a leader after the death of a dominant original leader who had become a legend in the Pentecostal faith. The first choice was the man who had assisted Mason and who had the designation of being the senior leader among COGIC preachers. O.T. Jones, Sr. was the only surviving bishop personally ordained by Mason. By 1961, Bishops Roberts, Stafford, Page, and Williams were dead. Per seniority, and the COGIC ideology of senior spiritual succession, Jones was the obvious choice for leadership, and he had been chosen to lead the COGIC Church during the Holy Convocation in 1962. However, O. T. Jones, Sr.'s leadership was challenged after the Holy Convocation in 1964.

Another possible succession candidate to lead COGIC was Mother Coffey. She had several supporters who were willing to help her secure the national leadership position. Nevertheless, Mother Coffey declined the position stating the COGIC Church would not function well under female leadership,[3] because the male clergy leaders were not ready to accept a woman in the senior bishop position. The other candidate for the senior bishop position was Mason's son, Charles H. Mason, Jr. who was the pastor of Temple COGIC, Mason's first established church in Tennessee. Charles Mason, Jr. also declined to pursue the role of national leader as he began to support the candidacy of O. T. Jones, Sr. Another candidate with seniority was Bishop A. B. McEwen. McEwen had chaired the Special Commission that had supported Mason's efforts in providing administration and oversight of COGIC affairs.

At the death of Mason, the COGIC Board of Bishops oversaw COGIC affairs. The Board of Bishops granted the members of the Special Commission's authority to oversee the Church for one year. At the end of that year, the Commission was responsible for preparing the Church's General Assembly[4]to select a new Senior Bishop. At the end of the 1962 Holy Convocation, the election for a new Senior Bishop was postponed. The General Assembly rescheduled the selection of the Senior Bishop to take place during the April 1963 session in Memphis.[5] So in the Holy Convocation of November 1962, COGIC had two main candidates to lead the church into the sixties and beyond. The choices were Ozro T. Jones, Sr. and A. B. McEwen. However, the General Assembly that met in November 1962, changed course, and chose Ozro T. Jones, Sr. for the national position of Senior Bishop. In a surprising manner, Bishop Patterson stood up in the meeting of the General Assembly on the last night of the 1962 Holy Convocation and stated that he had a dream concerning the leadership of COGIC. J.O. Patterson's dream influenced the COGIC body to elect O.T. Jones to the office of Senior Bishop, as Patterson supported the election of O.T. Jones, Sr, stating that the COGIC Church should not operate another year without a national leader.[6]

6.1. 1962 - THE BEGINNING OF THE O.T. JONES, SR. ERA

Thus, O. T Jones, Sr. became responsible for continuing the Holiness-Pentecostal legacy of Mason and the Church of God in Christ, Inc. Jones had been a close protégé and advisor to Bishop Mason with leadership experience in church administration as one of the first five bishops ordained in COGIC, and he was also the premier leader of the YPWW Department. He served as one of COGIC's outstanding theologians and preachers, often delivering the annual sermon for Mason during the Holy Convocation. Overall, many COGIC members felt that Jones was qualified to help the Church remain true to Holiness and Pentecostalism; therefore, the members received him gladly.[7] Bishop Jones was congratulated on being selected as the new leader. Bishops Frederick D. Washington, Otha M. Kelly, B.H. Dabney and the Chairman of the Board of Bishops, D. Lawrence Williams, all congratulated Bishop O.T. Jones, Sr. on his ascension to the highest COGIC office.[8]

When Bishop Jones assumed his leadership role, he was accompanied by the selection of a newly formed Executive Board, once called the Special Commission. The Executive Board was composed of twelve bishops: A.B. McEwen of Memphis, Chairman; John S. Bailey of Detroit, Vice-Chairman, James O. Patterson of Memphis, Secretary, Wyoming Wells of North Carolina, Ulysses E. Miller of Ohio, Otha M. Kelly of New York City, Samuel M. Crouch of Los Angeles, Louis H. Ford of Chicago, W.G. Shipman of Detroit, John White of New Orleans, C.E. Bennett of Gary, Indiana, and B.S. Lyle of Clarksdale, Mississippi. Among the Executive Board, Board of Bishops, and the General Assembly of the 55th Holy Convocation, there seem to have been a consensus in the selection of Bishop O.T. Jones, Sr. to replace Bishop Mason.[9] Again, the Constitution of COGIC and its manual did not define or proclaim the existence of an Executive Commission. Later, many bishops stated that the Special Commission which morphed into an Executive Board was supposed to have been disbanded after the death of Bishop Mason; however, the Board received an extension for a one-year assignment to select a national leader, given by the Board of Bishops in 1961.

Bishop O. T. Jones, Sr. attempted to have the Church remain steadfast to true Holiness. Bishop Jones brought outstanding service to the office of Senior Bishop. He had organized churches in Arkansas, Oklahoma, and Kansas. He was sent to Philadelphia, Pennsylvania, by

Bishop Mason to establish COGIC churches. Under his leadership as Overseer of Pennsylvania, O. T. Jones, Sr. started with eleven church congregations and grew the jurisdiction to 200 churches. Most of all, he was the profound leader of the COGIC Youth Department (YPWW), establishing the first Youth Congress in 1928 which was the second largest national meeting of the Church of God in Christ. O. T. Jones, Sr. served the Church with distinction: president, National Board of Education, trustee, original corporation of COGIC, commissioner for Senior Bishop Mason, and co-author of the Official Manual of the Church of God in Christ which codified the Church's doctrines and practices.[10] Obviously, O.T. Jones, Sr. had the qualifications and acumen to assume the leadership of COGIC after Mason's death.

Upon his selection as the new COGIC national leader, O. T. Jones, Sr. appointed committees to do the following tasks: develop a survey of all Church property at the headquarters in Memphis; develop a complete survey of all Church finances and financial system, conduct a complete survey of all Church publications; and, to undertake a complete survey of all Church departments and auxiliaries. Once completed, the reports were to be presented to the General Assembly for the entire Church to study and to provide recommendations for action.[11] Also during the Jones Era, a census was taken in 1964 which reported 425,000 members and 4,100 congregations.[12]

The Holy Convocations of 1963 and 1964 occurred without incident under Jones' leadership. In 1964, Senior Bishop Jones appointed Bishop John Dale Husband to the Central Georgia Jurisdiction after the death of founding bishop James J. Hinsley. Jones also appointed Bishop R.S. Eure to the Maryland Eastern Shore Jurisdiction. Moreover, Mother Coffey, Supervisor of COGIC Women's Department, died in 1964. Senior Bishop Jones appointed Mother Anne L. Bailey, the wife of thirty years of Executive Board Member, Bishop John Seth Bailey, to replace Mother Coffey as the Supervisor of COGIC Women's Department. Mother Bailey had been groomed by Mother Coffey for succession. Again, Mother Bailey's appointment, like Mother Coffey's appointment, was not challenged by anyone in the Women's Department or by the male clergy in leadership. The COGIC Women's Department continued their legacy of senior spiritual succession despite the death of Senior Bishop Mason.

Mother Anne Lee Pennington Bailey was born in Texas around 1897. At a young age, Ann Pennington heard a Holiness message that changed her religious world and made her a zealot in the Pentecostal Movement,[13]that motivated her to serve the Lord and His people within the ministry of COGIC, Inc. Mother Bailey extended the responsibilities of the Women's Department by adding auxiliaries and she enhanced the traditional COGIC women auxiliaries. Mother Bailey added the Business and Professional Women's Rescue Squad, the National Sunday School Superintendents' Wives, National Sunday School Representatives Unit, United Sisters of Charity, National Secretaries Unit, and Junior Missionaries Unit. Additionally, Mother Bailey renewed the publication, The C.O.G.I.C Woman, and she appointed the first president to the Sewing Circle-Artistic Fingers Auxiliary. Mother Bailey had a background as a successful evangelist and missionary, evidenced by her work establishing COGIC churches in Washington, D.C., Maryland, New Jersey, and New York.[14] One of her renown churches was Wells Cathedral COGIC, which, in later years was led by Bishop Chandler D. Owens, the third presiding bishop of COGIC. Because of her nice demeanor, humble spirit, and loving heart toward people, COGIC members and leaders referred to Mother Bailey as the Sweetheart of the Church of God in Christ and the Darling to the Brotherhood.[15]

Senior Bishop Jones appointed his son, Elder O. T. Jones, Jr., to be the National President of the COGIC Youth Department on December 11, 1964. Elder O.T Jones, Jr. continued to teach Holiness and Pentecostalism to the younger generations of COGIC. In 1964 Holy Convocation, the younger Jones found himself in the middle of an intense battle as the leadership of his father was being challenged by members of the COGIC Executive Board. Elder O.T. Jones, Jr showed great support for his father's leadership, speaking highly of his father during the Youth Night of the Holy Convocation.[16]

Perhaps the most impactful feat conducted by Senior Bishop Jones in 1964 was the executive meeting with Harry V. Richardson, the president of the Interdenominational Theological Center in Atlanta, Georgia. Dr. Richardson was invited by Senior Bishop Jones to explain the requirements and procedures to COGIC board members and department leaders on establishing a COGIC seminary.[17] Years later, the COGIC seminary was established under the leadership of Presiding Bishop James Oglethorpe Patterson, Sr., who became COGIC's national leader in 1968.

Senior Bishop Jones had superb qualifications, keen administrative skills, and a desire to improve the quality of Holiness among all COGIC members. With such qualifications, the legitimacy of his leadership was, yet, challenged. Jones' term was not inclusive of scandals of immoral behavior or blatant character flaws that were observed by clergy or lay members. Yet, his leadership was challenged after the Holy Convocation of 1964 by the same man who had the dream that Jones was to assume the leadership of the COGIC Church.

On December 31, 1964, The General Secretary of the Executive Board, Bishop Patterson, with no prior consultation or authorization from Senior Bishop Jones, sent a letter extending an invitation to the church's ministers and laymen for progressive action to meet in Memphis at 12:00 noon at 229 South Wellington Street on February 3, 1965.[18] This special meeting was to address water leaks, the painting of the building, and general repairs to the building (Mason Temple). Patterson's letter stated: "The building [Mason Temple] needed painting, general repairs." On January 11, 1965, Senior Bishop Jones addressed the letter from Patterson to the entire Church and stated that the letter by Patterson was not properly authorized and completely out of order.[19] Jones responded because the letter by General Secretary Patterson disrespected the office of the Senior Bishop, who was the national leader of the COGIC Church. If this action had been taken under Mason's leadership, Patterson would have possibly received public rebuke and a harsh reprimand for disregarding the leadership and authority of the COGIC's national leader. This letter by Patterson tested the strength and sustainability of O.T. Jones, Sr's position as the senior spiritual leader of COGIC by invoking the principles of young, progressive leadership and ambition. According to Patterson, a new era had come to COGIC and no one, especially Bishop O.T. Jones, Sr. should have the same power and authority as Bishop Mason.

While the controversial letter circulated, COGIC officials witnessed the formation of another splinter group. Bishop Ralph L. Johnson decided to form the Church of God in Christ of America, Inc. (COGICA). Bishop Johnson's COGICA Church claimed that it was the original COGIC body since 1964 and was reorganized under his leadership in 1969.[20] Bishop Johnson also proclaimed that COGICA did not believe in wearing Catholic-like robes or regalia and that all the leadership positions were by appointment and not decided by an election and voting. Bishop Johnson's COGICA followed the legacy of leadership through the line of Bishop Mason and then Bishop O.T. Jones, Sr. The impact of Johnson's separation was minimal to COGIC, Inc., because only a few churches left to follow Bishop Johnson even though he claimed he had the original COGIC charter from Mississippi in his possession. Johnson did not have control of COGIC buildings and assets.

6.2. Patterson Challenges the Leadership of the Senior Bishop

Remaining defiant to the authority of Senior Bishop O.T. Jones, on January 16, 1965, General Secretary Patterson after receiving Jones' letter of rebuke about the unauthorized meeting, yet, affirmed the invitation to the general Church body to attend the special meeting in Memphis. Patterson alleged that the special meeting that he called the Church body to attend was authorized by the Executive Board.

Patterson proceeded to state that "Senior Bishops are not an elective office, one becomes that by status of being. Actually, after the passing of Bishop C.H. Mason there is definitely NO AUTHORITY vested in Senior Bishops."[21] Apparently, whether intentional or unintentional, General Secretary Patterson and the Executive Board had strategically declared the national leader of COGIC, Inc., illegitimate and powerless. Yet, the power and authority in the COGIC Church rested in the hands of the Executive Board as Patterson stated and the appointing authority of the Senior Bishop was now the authority of the Executive Board. On, January 20, 1965, John S. Bailey, Co-Chairman of the Executive Board, sent a letter affirming to the COGIC general body that a very important meeting was taking place at Memphis Headquarters on February 3rd and 4th, 1965. This action by Bishop Bailey supported the request issued by Patterson. Another rebuttal letter was sent on January 28, 1965, in support of Jones' rebuke of Patterson's letters by Chairman of the Board of Bishops, Bishop D. Lawrence Williams. The Chairman sent a letter asking for support for the honorable Senior Bishop Jones. Williams also stated that Jones was continuing the sound principles in governing the Church initiated by Bishop Mason and that Senior Bishop Jones requested a full and complete report from all departments for the executive conference scheduled to convene in Memphis on April 13-15, 1965. Williams further stated that the meeting called by General Secretary Patterson on February 2-3, 1965 had not been properly authorized.[22] Bishop D. Lawrence Williams was a strong supporter of the senior spiritual succession, the old guard, which rivalled the progressive leadership agenda of Patterson. Evidently, Patterson also sought to dismiss Williams' authority. On January 29, 1965, Patterson issued another letter to the general Church body to confirm his meeting in February and alleged that the Chairman of the Board of Bishops, D. Lawrence Williams, was wrong in referring to himself as the Chairman because the Board of Bishops had not elected a successor to its former Chairman, B.S. Lyle. Patterson also confirmed his meeting by stating that the majority of bishops and pastors had planned to attend the meeting, and they had already made reservations.[23] In four letters, Patterson had basically reassigned the authority of the COGIC Church from the office of the Senior Bishop and the Board of Bishops to the Executive Board. These first steps were crucial in annihilating the authority of Senior Bishop Jones, and uplifting the power of the Executive Board Members.

After the meeting called by Patterson, on or about February 8, 1965, a document was sent to the Senior Bishop written under the heading of "Executive Board, Church of God in Christ, Inc." The document officially notified Senior Bishop Jones of the following assertions: Under the constitution and by-laws of the Church of God in Christ, there is no provision for the office of Senior Bishop after the death of the late revered Bishop C.H. Mason; the constitution and by-laws state that on the death of Bishop Mason, the power, authority and government of the Church shall vest in the Executive Board; this Board was created by the late Bishop C. H. Mason; the Board's power and authority were recognized and ratified by the General Assembly on several occasions; Bishop O.T. Jones, Sr. has since 1962 usurped the power of the Executive Board and abrogated unto himself the authority to appoint bishops, overseers, and other officials of the Church; all Senior Bishop Jones' appointments were unlawful and without authority; the Executive Board was making six state bishops [appointing bishops over states] and two national officers who had been previously appointed by the Senior Bishop; the Senior Bishop was officially notified to cease and desist from making any appointments [officially choosing male and female leaders to take positions of leadership]; that from this time forward, the Executive Board will NOT recognize appointments made by the Senior Bishop and the Board also serves notice that he or any appointee he may name will act at their own risk and peril. [24]

In retrospect, many of Bishop Patterson's claims were misleading and incorrect. For example, the constitution and by-laws of COGIC plainly stated that upon the death of Bishop Mason that the power, authority, and government of the Church shall be vested in the Board of Bishops, composed of all state and international bishops, not the Executive Board led by Bishop A. B. McEwen. The Executive Board came into existence after the death of Mason, not before his death. Patterson's claim that Mason created the Executive Board is false and misleading. During Mason's waning years, a Special Commission was appointed to assist him in running the affairs of the church. The Executive Board was berthed after the selection of O.T. Jones, Sr. as Senior Bishop. Another misleading statement by Patterson charged that all appointments made by Senior Bishop Jones were not lawful. However, Patterson and the Executive Board recognized those bishops appointed by Senior Bishop Jones when they supported the agenda of Patterson and A.B. McEwen, the key leaders on the Executive Board. Moreover, the Executive Board reappointed the unauthorized appointments made by Senior Bishop Jones. Not only did Patterson and the Executive Board nullify the Senior Bishop position, but they also threatened anyone who supported the authority of O.T. Jones, Sr.[25]

This attack on Jones' leadership per the COGIC Constitution and handbook did not have strong foundation because O.T. Jones, Sr. had co-authored the COGIC handbook, helping to complete several versions of the COGIC Constitution. Senior Bishop Jones led the corps of COGIC clergy in establishing the rules and regulations into a codified structure, and Bishop Patterson and the Executive Board was attacking O.T. Jones, Sr, the said leader who developed and structured the COGIC by-laws. Jones responded to the accusations on February 18, 1965, in a letter to the general church. Jones stated that the General Secretary, in a letter written over his signature as General Secretary, [not the Executive Board], had called the entire Church to an extra meeting at the same time and place to a meeting, alleged in the document, to be a meeting of the Executive Board Church of God in Christ, Inc. [Jones established the idea that Patterson did not have the authority to call a meeting without the approval of the Senior Bishop]. Jones continued to state that this meeting was not properly authorized and that he gave notice to Patterson that the meeting was not properly authorized. The notice of the meeting not being properly authorized was given to the entire church by the Senior Bishop and the Chairman of the Board of Bishops. Senior Bishop Jones clarified that no actions or directives, attempted by any person or group, at any improperly called meeting can be considered law and order for the church, and such actions may be disregarded. O.T. Jones, Sr. stated that in the Church of God in Christ, the General Assembly is the only doctrine-expressing and law-making body of the Church; and, that if any person or group is permitted at will to call unauthorized meetings and attempt to enact laws which would be binding upon the entire Church, then we, as leaders in the church, would be permitting a direct violation of the spirit of our Church and of a fundamental principle of our Constitution. Jones asked, should the Church condone such improper procedure?[26] It would permit the existence of a pattern of conduct which would destroy the existence of COGIC as an organized body. Jones declared that the attack made in this document [by the Patterson and Executive Board]was not only upon the person and the office of Senior Bishop, but was also a blatant disregard for the authority given by the Constitution to the Board of Bishops and the General Assembly. Also, if this type of flagrant, irresponsible procedure became a pattern, then no one's position in the church was secure. Moreover, Senior Bishop Jones then supported his statements with scripture, stating that the attempted actions set forth in Patterson's letters presented a radical departure for the pattern (Book of Hebrews 8:5) which the Lord had revealed for the order and government of the church, and which, up until then, had served so well. With remorse, Jones as Senior Bishop stated that he was deeply saddened that this letter from him was necessary, and, that he would have preferred to have worked to resolve the differences between the leaders and whatever other differences may have existed. As the Senior Bishop, Jones said that his concern was for what was right in the sight of God; therefore he, the Senior Bishop, requested the prayers of everyone for the church and for himself, the one whom the Lord had chosen to serve in the office of Senior Bishop, that the church, may ever abide in the unity of the Spirit and in the bond of peace.[27]

After Jones observed the blatant disrespect and systematic attack on his top leadership position in the Church of God in Christ, he appealed to the spirituality and the Holiness tradition of the COGIC Church, calling for a person of high moral character to lead the church under the guidance of the Holy Spirit. The Executive Board called a meeting not authorized by the Senior Bishop and then falsely stated that the COGIC Constitution allowed the Executive Board to have authoritative power in COGIC upon the death of Bishop Mason. The Constitution plainly stated that if Mason died, the authoritative power in COGIC would belong to the Board of Bishops, not the Executive Board. Overall, Jones seemed to have wanted to reconcile with his preaching brothers to solve the problem at hand over power and authority.[28] Nevertheless, Jones was not given a chance as the Executive Board declared that the position of Senior Bishop was powerless and had no authority.

At the 1965 Holy Convocation in Memphis, the confusion of leadership and the battle between the COGIC Senior Bishop and the COGIC Executive Board continued. An invitation was sent out to the people to come to the 58th Annual Holy Convocation to honor Bishop O.T. Jones, Sr. on the Official Day.[29] On the contrary, the Executive Board invited COGIC members to a Founder's Day to commemorate the legacy of Bishop Mason, refuting the act of having an Official Day for Bishop Jones.[30] According to Lucille Cornelius's eyewitness account, the Executive Board took charge of the Holy Convocation as Bishop A.B. McEwen and Bishop John S. Bailey presided over the services. The Executive Board enforced its will and agenda on the program, and many members did not know that there was dissension among the leading members, as many people, according to Cornelius, continued to shout and praise the Lord in the Spirit, clueless to the takeover by the Executive Board.

On Sunday, November 14, 1965, the Executive Board clearly established a Founder's Day Service, overshadowing any suggestions of an Official Day for Bishop Jones. Many pictures of Bishop Mason decorated the pulpit podium as banners. Bishop Jones was in the pulpit during the services; however, Bishop John White, Bishop of Western Louisiana Jurisdiction and member of the Executive Board, preached the official Sunday sermon, not Bishop Jones. After the sermon, Jones was allowed to speak to the crowd, and he sang a song and announced that he would be addressing the COGIC saints at the 8:00 pm Sunday service. At the evening service, Jones spoke of the Church not being divided and that he did not want to humiliate Bishop McEwen and he was glad to hear that Bishop Louis H. Ford, member of the Executive Board, did not want to humiliate Bishop Jones. Bishop Jones continued his sermon on the greatness of the Church maintaining a high spiritual ground. Jones ended his sermon with a song, "Let us have a Little Talk with Jesus."[31] The meeting adjourned with confusion among the COGIC leadership corps and some of that confusion had an impact on the watchful attendees at the Convocation, leaving many to ponder who was in charge of the Church of God in Christ. Nevertheless, this feud carried the same problems of leadership into the 1966 Holy Convocation, with the total shutdown of the office of Senior Bishop.

After the systematic takedown of Senior Bishop Jones during the 1965 Convocation, the Executive Board began to target the supporters of O.T. Jones, Sr. in the year of 1966. Some of the Executive Board's victims included the following clergy: Bishop Raymond E. Ranger of Texas Southeast Jurisdiction and the leader of the Senior Bishop Advisory Committee; Bishop Chester A. Ashworth of the First Diocese of Alabama; Bishop D. Lawrence Williams, the Chairman of the Board of Bishops; and the son of the Senior Bishop, O.T. Jones, Jr. Bishop Ashworth was the first victim of the COGIC leadership battle as the fight spilled over into the courts in Birmingham, Alabama.[32]

On April 2, 1966, the Executive Board and advocates of the Senior Bishop entered Alabama's court system evidenced by The Chicago Defender article in Appendix D. The judge in the court case of April 1966, Emmitt Jackson v. John Key, decided that the legal authority of the Church rested with the Executive Board, subject solely to the General

Assembly. Judge William C. Barber, of the Tenth Judicial Court of Alabama, stated that Bishop Jones' title was purely honorary and that his governmental powers were that of an advisor. The Executive Board directed its effort in splitting Bishop Ashworth's Alabama's First Diocese and forming Alabama Second Diocese. The lawsuitwas filed by in the Alabama circuit court by Emmitt Jackson, a trustee of the East Birmingham COGIC who disagreed with the Executive Board's decision to allow their pastor, Elder John Key, to transfer from Bishop Ashworth's First Diocese to the newly formed the Second Diocese under the leadership of James M. Bailey. Elder John Key, a part of Bishop Ashworth's First Diocese, and his congregation had voted to leave and become affiliated with Second Diocese. Judge Barber declared that the election to leave the First Diocese, was "null and void", and he appointed a special master to supervise the new election among church members of the East Birmingham COGIC to declare their decision to transfer to the Second Diocese. The lawsuit against the Executive Board's actions was dismissed, and the Second Diocese remained intact under the leadership of James M. Bailey, the brother of Executive Board, Co-Chairman, John S. Bailey. The court case complainants consisted of O.T. Jones, Jr., Bishop R. E. Ranger, Bishop C. A. Ashworth, Bishop R. S. Eure, and Elder Samuel Nesbitt. The defendants were A.B. McEwen, J.S. Bailey, J.O. Patterson, L.H. Ford, John White, Charles H. Brewer, Sr., and Frederick D. Washington. The judge also rebuked COGIC officials for bringing this action to court. However, the Executive Board had gained another victory against the authority and power of the Senior Bishop and his supporting cast.[33]

The case did not end in April 1966. The article in The Chicago Defender, August 27, 1966 shed light upon Jones' team who asked a judge to reassess the case. COGIC Information and Communication Officer, Elder W.E. Greer, stated that Judge Barber's ruling of the Senior Bishop title being "honorary", was based on falsified documents and testimony by the so-called Executive Board that could have led to arrests, convictions, and possible confinement of certain national church figures. However, the damage was done by the Executive Board as it successfully split the Alabama Diocese. Also in the newspaper article, Elder Greer stated that the case was not resolved by Judge Barber's decision. Greer continued to add that the Executive Board was issuing false information to the people when it stated that the case was closed.

After the COGIC Alabama fiasco, Bishop R. E. Ranger wrote a scathing review of the whole situation involving the overthrow of Bishop Jones. Bishop Ranger was one of O.T. Jones, Sr.'s greatest supporters and believed in the sanctity of leadership proposed by the office of Senior Bishop. Ranger believed that the office of Senior Bishop had the same authority and power when it was held by Mason. Ranger also believed that the same power, authority, and respect should have been given to O.T. Jones, Sr. According to Appendix F, Bishop Ranger,gave many warnings and reprimanded all leaders in COGIC, focusing heavily on the actions of the Executive Board. Ranger basically called the Executive Board a crew of liars who raped and robbed Senior Bishop Jones, the COGIC leader, of his power and authority. Bishop Ranger appealed to the greater COGIC membership and clergy to warn of the overpowering Executive Board that imposed on the rights of everyone in COGIC. Ranger claimed that the Executive Board had "displayed hatred and evil purpose among the brethren", "seized the entire machinery and financial power and government of the Church of God in Christ", "destroyed the authority of the Board of Bishops, General Assembly, and the office of Senior Bishop", "developed a campaign of lies and intimidation through national media and the publication called The Evangelist Speaks", and "caused problems for state jurisdictional bishops who opposed their agenda."[34]

One of Ranger's major claims was that the Executive Board's existence was not approved by the Board of Bishops. The contradiction in the minds of Ranger and others was that the Board of Bishops was currently being put into subjection under the authority of the Executive Board, so Ranger's question was how did the Executive Board become more powerful than the Board of Bishops? While denying the legitimate authority of the Executive Board, Ranger iterated the rightful authority of the Senior Bishop who was elected to the office on December 7, 1962. Ranger greatly denounced the actions of Bishop J.O. Patterson, the Secretary of the Executive Board. Ranger called him a liar because Patterson perjured himself in the court in Birmingham, Alabama. Patterson had stated that O.T. Jones had not been elected as Senior Bishop of COGIC, but he was only elected as the Senior Bishop of the Executive Board. Ranger noted that a letter that bore Patterson's signature was produced in court with Patterson stating, "I threw my "great influence" behind O.T. Jones as Senior Bishop of the Church of God in Christ because Bishop A.B. McEwen had widely circulated certain scandals regarding my moral conduct."[35] The other falsehood that Ranger accused Bishop Patterson of perpetrating was concerning the statement Patterson made about not having signed any credentials under the leadership of Senior Bishop Jones. Bishop Eure of Maryland was asked to testify in court and to produce his credentials. Eure's credentials were signed by Bishop Patterson.

Bishop Ranger and Senior Bishop O.T. Jones, Sr. attempted to maintain the office of Senior Bishop against the greatest political coup in COGIC History. Even though Bishop Patterson was caught perjuring himself on two different events, the media machine behind the Executive Board was strong enough to cause many clergymen and members to side with Bishops McEwen and Patterson. The defining moment of the Executive Board's power occurred when Patterson and others were able to nullify the power and authority associated with the office of Senior Bishop. Patterson and the Board members, basically, deconstructed the administrative legacy of Bishop Mason who was the first Senior Bishop. Furthermore, this blatant challenge on the top COGIC leadership position, more than likely, would not have been successful while Mason was alive. The problem that Patterson and his political coup faced was the idea of "obeying leadership." When the Executive Board challenged the leadership of the Senior Bishop of COGIC, other preachers had justification to disobey the leadership of the Executive Board, and, some created splinter groups from the mother COGIC body.

6.3. THE EXECUTIVE BOARD NULLIFIED THE AUTHORITY OF RANGER AND O.T. JONES, JR.

After Ranger's scolding letter of rebuke upon the Executive Board, a systematic attempt to silence and remove him from his office and jurisdiction began in October 1966. Also, at the COGIC April Call Meeting of leaders in Memphis, the Executive Board stripped O.T. Jones, Jr. of the title of President of the Youth Department (YPWW),[36] and gave the position to Elder Chandler D. Owens (In 1996, Owens became the third Presiding Bishop of COGIC, Inc.). Since Ranger was one of the strongest supporters of O.T. Jones' leadership, many COGIC members respected and valued his theological intelligence and ministerial expertise. The Executive Board faced a stern opponent in its quest to lead COGIC into the next decade of the 1970s. After taking all power and authority from Senior Bishop Jones, Bishop Ranger became the next target to be legally removed from office by the Executive Board. Evidenced by the letter in Appendix G, in the case of Bishop Ranger, General Secretary Patterson sent a letter to Bishop Ranger on October 4, 1966. Patterson's letter outlined the charges against Bishop Ranger. The Executive Board charged Ranger with conduct unbecoming of a bishop of COGIC; that he opposed the Executive Board's authorized duties; and that he aided and supported Senior Bishop Jones in excommunicating pastors in Pennsylvania. Also in Appendix G, Bishop Ranger responded to Bishop Patterson's letter with great disdain for the actions of Patterson and the Executive Board. Ranger noted that Patterson had an extensive ego and stated that "like the airship "Hindenburg", Patterson will blow up."

The letters between Ranger and Patterson caused a greater rift between the Senior Bishop's supporters and the Executive Board. The two groups carried the animosity and grievances into the 59th

Holy Convocation from November 8-18,1966. As the 1966 Holy Convocation convened, the Executive Board was fully in control of the services and program. When the Convocation opened at 9:00 AM on Tuesday, November 8, 1966, the presiding officials were Bishops A.B. McEwen, J.S. Bailey, and W.G. Shipman.[37] Senior Bishop Jones, Bishop Ranger, Elder O.T. Jones, Jr., and Bishop C.A. Ashworth of Alabama were not placed on the program. More than likely, the Executive Board, with intention, did not place Jones and those who supported him on the Convocation Program. The Executive Board refused to recognize Jones' leadership and stayed with the theme of a Founder's Day celebration in honor of Bishop Mason. These early snubs by the Executive Board became commonplace in COGIC history, denying and erasing the existence of Jones' tenure of leadership.[38]

However, Bishop D. Lawrence Williams' name appeared on the program, even though, he, as the Chairman of the Board of Bishops, had supported the leadership of O.T. Jones. Earlier in 1966, before the Holy Convocation, Bishop Williams had a visit from the Executive Board at the church he pastored, C.H. Mason Memorial COGIC. The Executive Board confronted Bishop Williams about his outstanding support for Bishop Jones; and, according to an eyewitness account at the meeting, Bishop Williams was asked, pointedly, by the Executive Board, "Do you recognize the pattern of authority in the Church?"[39] To analyze the question, the Executive Board was insinuating that it was the new legal authority in the Church, and the Executive Board had power over the Board of Bishops and the General Assembly. The pattern of authority was controlled by the Executive Board and the Board was steering the COGIC Church into the direction of "progress", leadership without a Senior Bishop. After Williams saw that he was being crucified and forced to recognize the authority of the Executive Board that threatened his position as Chairman of the Board of Bishops (observed by an eyewitness at the meeting), he asked for mercy from the Executive Board and recanted his support for Senior Bishop Jones.[40] At this juncture, Jones and all his supporters had been neutralized in the battle for rightful authority in leading the COGIC Church.

Bishop D. Lawrence Williams' name appeared on the 1966 Convocation booklet after a clandestine meeting in Virginia at Williams' church. Williams was on the Sunday program services conducting the "Call to Worship." Despite Williams recanting his support for O.T. Jones, the Senior Bishop moved forward with the intention to appeal his case before the attendees at the 59th Holy Convocation with the hope that he could answer his accusers (the Executive Board) and allow the congregants to assess the charges that were being brought against him by the Executive Board.[41] Jones and his supporters made one last attempt to place the Church back under control of the Senior Bishop. During the 1966 Holy Convocation, Bishop Jones and Bishop Ranger attempted to mount the platform on Saturday, November 12, 1966, demanding to be heard. The police were called to the meeting and Bishops Jones and Ranger, with their supporters were escorted from the premises.[42] General Secretary Patterson gave a much more dramatic version of the events to bolster support for the Executive Board. Patterson stated his assessment of the situation, in his publication called the Official. He chronicled the event in the following paragraph:

> *Yes, he [Bishop Jones] believes in the Constitution but his conspirers sought to take advantage of the Convocation and General Assembly by appealing to mass psychology. In attempting to accomplish their objective, on Saturday, when the little children were in charge and participating in our National Convocation, the Jones faction of "strong arm" men staged a simulated Martin Luther King planned "march-in."[43] This of course, backfired, the people's sympathy went to the children and those seeking to employ such methods to gain the sympathy of the people were looked upon as worldly and ungodly men. The Bible says, a man's gift will make room for him. If God intends for you to have something, he will make room for you andplace you in the hearts of the people so that they will love and respect you.[44]*

So, the factional disagreements on leadership and authority of the Senior Bishop and the Executive Board were not settled by the administration and management of two Holy Convocations. On Sunday, November 13, 1966, Bishop McEwen gave the sermon for the Official Sunday services and the meeting closed on November 18, 1966.

After the Convocation, another court decision took place in Houston, Texas on December 31, 1966. Bishop Ranger brought an injunction against the Executive Board in his state of Texas to halt the seizure of his jurisdiction by the Executive Board. Dashing the last hopes of the Jones faction, Judge Warren P. Cunningham of the Harris County District Court ruled in favor of the Executive Board, supporting the action of how the Executive Board stripped Ranger of his position as Bishop of Texas Southeast Jurisdiction. The Executive Board decided to provide temporary supervision of the Texas Southeast Jurisdiction until another bishop could be appointed over the churches. An account of the court case in the Chicago Defender, shown in Appendix H, gave details of the events that neutralized the power and protest of Bishop Ranger. Judge Cunningham of Houston, Texas ruled against Bishop Ranger in his home state where he ministered and pastored for several years. Furthermore, Bishop Ranger did not receive support from the other COGIC Bishops of Texas jurisdictions. Bishops F.L. Haynes, T.D. Iglehart, J.E. Alexander, and C.H. Nelson supported the efforts of the Executive Board. Without support in his home state, Ranger's efforts to fight against the authority of the Executive Board was in vain.

The 1966 Convocation and the victory by the Executive Board pushed both parties into a landmark court case that attempted to settle the dispute of "which person or body was the official leadership and authority of the COGIC, Inc. Church?" No negotiations were successful up to this point, thus the only avenue to solve COGIC's problem of leadership was, yet, another court case, hearkening back to the 1907 court case that the Mason faction and C.P. Jones faction fought for control over churches due to a doctrinal dispute about "speaking in tongues."

The showdown for the most impactful, landmark court case in COGIC history took place in Memphis, Tennessee, the headquarters of COGIC. With all the confrontations looming throughout the COGIC denomination, an encompassing lawsuit was filed in the Chancery Court of Shelby County, Tennessee in 1967 to end the battle for authority in the Church: A.B. McEwen, et al, Complainants vs. O.T. Jones, Sr., R.E. Ranger, and O.T. Jones, Jr. In Appendix I, on October 10, 1967, the Chancery Court in Memphis gave the final ruling to all parties involved in the lawsuit over the question of what entity had power and authority in the Church of God in Christ. Basically, the Executive Board won the case and the office of Senior Bishop was abolished; however, the court decision also abolished the Executive Board and gave power back to the COGIC General Assembly to elect a new presiding bishop and general board for COGIC. The General Assembly was ordered by the court decision to revise or amend the church constitution to create a majority vote in determining the offices of leadership.

After about 3,000 plus pages on the battle to achieve authority over COGIC members, in short, the Chancery Court decided to allow the General Assembly members to decide COGIC leadership in a Constitutional Convention that would convene on January 30, 1968 in Memphis. According to the court decision on page 5, the General Assembly's certifiable members were listed in this order: All ordained elders, state bishops, Board of Bishop members, one state supervisor (female leader), and one lay delegate from each state jurisdiction (the person could be male or female). After the election for a new leader, the office of Senior Bishop and the Executive Board would no longer exist in the Church of God in Christ, Inc. Furthermore, before the election took place, the 60th Annual Holy Convocation convened November 7, 1967. Definitely, the Executive Board was still in charge of the administration and management of COGIC affairs. If a person viewed the 1967 Holy Convocation souvenir book, anyone could see, in big, bold lettering, the "EXECUTIVE BOARD OF BISHOPS

PRESIDING, November 7-17, 1967." The program focused on the legacy and pictures of Bishop Mason and had an acknowledgement of service letter from President Lyndon B. Johnson. Bishop O.T. Jones, Sr. and his supporters were not pictured or mentioned on the 1967 Holy Convocation Program.

Mason had led the COGIC Church since 1907, guiding it through the segregation, the Nadir period in African-American history, the Great Depression, World War I, World War II, and the Korean Conflict, and the Civil Rights Era. Mason, despite the several splinter groups that formed under his leadership, maintained stability for an organization that have several million members across America and the world. After his death, his power and influence as the senior bishop and leader faded, and he did not designate a particular person to succeed him. Therefore, Patterson, as the General Secretary of COGIC, took advantage of an opportunity to challenge the office of senior bishop held by O.T. Jones, Sr. Due to the political climate ripened after the death of Mason, O.T. Jones, Sr. was vulnerable to any challenge to his authority because he was not Charles Mason, the Father of COGIC. After two years as senior bishop, O.T. Jones' authority was nullified by the Executive Board led by the administrative onslaught of J.O. Patterson, Sr. The acts by the Executive Board and Bishop Patterson plunged the COGIC Church into an era of politics, where delegates voted for a leader. Voting caused factions to develop around certain leaders and was contrary to the established mandate preached by Bishop Mason, that each COGIC member should obey leadership, as the leader obeyed God. The voting process, created by the actions of Patterson, ended the concept of leadership chosen by the Holy Ghost or God and began a legacy of political leadership based on popularity and name recognition.

Nevertheless, after the ousting of O.T. Jones, Sr., Bishop Patterson restored some respect to the office of leadership as the new Presiding Bishop. Reason being, the majority of COGIC members did not know about the battle for authority between the Senior Bishop and the Executive Board. The senior bishop title created by Mason was removed from COGIC, Inc. as it transitioned into the post-modern era as an institutional church, yet, outwardly claimed its Holiness-Pentecostal legacy. Mason's vision was a church guided by the Holy Spirit, a spiritual church, while Patterson created a church based on a hierarchy of leadership that espoused both practical and spiritual guidance with a politically-charged process of leadership. While Mason was the face of COGIC from 1907-1961, J.O. Patterson, Mason's son-in-law, became the face of COGIC from 1968-1989.

O.T. Jones and Family

CHAPTER 7

THE END OF THE O.T. JONES ERA AND THE 1968 COGIC CONVENTION

On January 30, 1968, the election process began to nominate a leader for the embattled Post-Mason Era COGIC denomination. Bishop O.T. Jones, Sr. was not satisfied with the court decision based on his ideals of traditional COGIC doctrine and the Bible. Jones chose not to participate in the election, and some splinter groups developed from his departure as COGIC travelled down the path to electing a leader by the voting process, versus accepting the concept of senior spiritual succession. Senior spiritual succession took place when O.T. Jones, Sr. succeeded Bishop Mason. Jones was the most senior bishop with age and experience in COGIC. With seniority in age and ecclesiastical training, Jones appeared to be the most qualified person to lead COGIC. The groups who followed Jones' idea believed in the concept of leadership by a Senior Bishop, and that was the traditional COGIC standard of authority, established by the founder, Bishop Mason.[1]

Several committees and chairs were selected to carry out the process of creating a new COGIC Constitution. Bishop D. Lawrence Williams, the temporary Chairman of the Board of Bishops, appointed Bishop Levi Willis of Virginia to chair the Credentials Committee. Then Williams appointed Elder John Butler as Chairman of the Rules Committee to establish rules to govern the conduct and procedure of the convention. The Bishop T.D. Iglehart of Texas was voted Chairman of the COGIC Constitutional Convention and one of the most important committees to be appointed was the Constitutional Committee composed of these members: Bishop Wyoming Wells, Chairman, Elder J.C. Griffin, Elder O.T. Jones, Jr., Dr. M. McGregor Jones, Bishop C.W. Williams, Elder W. Jones, Mother Anne Bailey, Dr. T.L. Pleas, Elder C.E. Canon, and Clifton Williams. This committee was responsible for reviewing all forms of the COGIC Constitution and had the job of recommending changes to the convention for consideration.[2]

With many positive and negative reactions, delegates registered a vote of 1,085 for the amendments and 286 against the amendments. Seven recommendations to amend the Constitution and By-laws were passed by the convention:

1. That the General Assembly is the only doctrine-expressing and law-making authority in the Church of God in Christ;

2. That a General Board of twelve (12) bishops be elected for a term of four years by the General Assembly from the Board of Bishops to conduct the executive and administrative affairs of the church between meetings of the General Assembly;

3. That the General Assembly elect for a term of four years from the General Board a Presiding Bishop and First and Second Assistant Presiding Bishops. The Presiding Bishop shall be the Chief Executive Officer and would be empowered to conduct the executive affairs of the COGIC between meetings of the General Assembly and the General Board and the actions of the Presiding Bishop would be subject to the approval of the General Assembly and the General Board;

4. That neither the Presiding Bishop nor any other member of the General Board can serve at the same time as an officer of the General Assembly, General Council, or the Board of Bishops;

5. That all civil officers of the corporation known as the Church of God in Christ shall be elected by a majority vote of the General Assembly, and the heads of the departments of COGIC shall be appointed by the General Board for a term of four years, if the appointments are approved by the General Assembly;

6. That the Office of Senior Bishop and Executive Board of Bishops be abolished;

7. That any amendment in the Constitution of COGIC that is not consistent with the amendment herein is hereby repealed.[3]

In the next General Assembly meeting, Elder Chandler D. Owens recommended that the election of the General Board and the Presiding Bishop be deferred until a later date. The resolution unanimously passed along with the actions of selecting an Interim Board and deciding that the election would be held during the 61st Annual Holy Convocation in November 1968. Bishops A.B. McEwen, J.S. Bailey, J.O. Patterson, S.M. Crouch, O.M. Kelly, Wyoming Wells, and L.H. Ford were selected to serve on the Interim Board and perform the administrative functions of the Church until November 1968.[4]

7.1. COGIC Connections to Civil Rights During the 1960s

Before COGIC Inc.'s first historic election of a national leader, the leaders and members had a chance to host Martin Luther King, Jr. at Mason Temple on April 3, 1968 during the sanitation workers' strike in Memphis. COGIC's participation in the Civil Rights Movement occurred during the late 1960s in Memphis, the headquarters city of COGIC. During the Sanitation Workers Strike of 1968, two key COGIC preachers and cousins, J.O. Patterson, Jr., and Gilbert E. Patterson, were highly involved in the strike. J.O. Patterson, Jr., the son of Presiding Bishop J.O. Patterson, Sr., had served as a state representative and later was elected to the Memphis City Council in 1967. On February 23, 1968, Patterson, Jr. and other Black council members attempted to meet the demands of the striking sanitation workers during a meeting at the city auditorium with the workers and their supporters; but the other White council members voted against the workers' demands for union checkoffs and pay raises.[5] After the sanitation strikers' demands were not met, ministers in support of the strike encouraged everyone to march from the city auditorium to Mason Temple. During the march to Mason Temple, the Memphis police sprayed mace on many of the strikers and supporters; ministers and the marchers were outraged about the police harassment.[6] At that moment, Gilbert Patterson assisted Jesse Epps, the union leader, and Reverend James Lawson in developing a new civil rights organization called Community on the Move for Equality (COME). G.E. Patterson used his radio broadcasts to call for boycotts and encouraged the people to demonstrate and march for equality and justice.[7]

Bishop J.O. Patterson met with King, and he supported COGIC members who were involved in the sanitation strike. King had come to Memphis in March of 1968 to advance his "People's War on Poverty" campaign. The sanitation strike, King hoped, would be an opportunity to further the agenda of the war on poverty. The sanitation strike and the "People's War on Poverty" programs merged under the roof of Mason Temple, the headquarters of COGIC.[8] On March 28, 1968, a march was planned by King and the protesters; however, the city erupted in violence as the marchers clashed with the local police. The National Guard was called to the scene, and the courts issued an injunction that kept King from leading the planned march.[9]

After the failed attempt of a nonviolent march in Memphis, King left the city, but returned on April 3, 1968, tired and not feeling well. Mason Temple, again, served as the meeting center for King's planning and operations. On that fateful night, King had decided to rest and not speak to the crowd that had gathered at Mason Temple. Instead, Abernathy went to the meeting, and about two thousand people were greatly disappointed after not seeing King. Abernathy knew the importance of this Mason Temple gathering and immediately knew that King had to speak to this energized crowd. So, King arrived at 9:30 PM, and he delivered one of his most memorable civil sermons in history, "I've Been to the Mountain Top."[10]

Other COGIC Civil Rights Movement connections in the 1960s involved Medgar Evers and Malcolm X. Before Reverend Al Sharpton left COGIC for the Black Baptist Church, Medgar Evers had decided to do the same for he was unsatisfied with the "other world", heavenly preaching of the COGIC Church. Evers' mother was a dedicated COGIC member who made her children go to the COGIC church about three times a week. After Evers came of age, he rejected the COGIC ideals of having a majority focus on the after-life, and became involved with the Civil Rights Movement by joining the NAACP and becoming its field secretary in Mississippi.[11]

Concerning Malcolm X, on February 27, 1965, Ossie Davis eulogized the Muslim leader at Faith Temple COGIC, pastored by Bishop Alvin A. Childs. Bishop Childs was the only pastor to allow the controversial Muslim leader's family to hold the funeral at a place of worship.[12] Malcolm X had been a profound critic of Black Baptist preachers and other Black Christian preachers, and their lack of militancy to destroy the system of segregation and racism. For the most part, COGIC pastor, Alvin Childs, opened the church doors to all people in the community of Harlem, stepping outside the insular religious beliefs of COGIC members having no fellowship with other religions, especially Islam. Child's progressive actions allowed the family of Malcolm X to conduct Muslim funeral rites in a COGIC Christian Church, which was revolutionary for both Muslim and Christian faiths. The funeral displayed a unity among people regardless of religious affiliation.

7.2. THE FIRST COGIC ELECTION: PRESIDING BISHOP JAMES OGLETHORPE PATTERSON, SR.

As African-Americans lost two key national leaders due to racism and discrimination, King and Malcolm X, COGIC was engaged in its first election of a national religious leader in its sixty-one-year history. On November 13, 1968, Bishop S.C. Cole received the nominees to be elected to the General Board. Speeches were given by each candidate and then the General Assembly prepared to elect its first presiding bishop and general board of twelve. On November 14, 1968, the results of that election are included in the following table:[13]

GENERAL BOARD OF TWELVE

Member-Bishop	Votes
J.O. Patterson	828
J.S. Bailey	816
S.M. Crouch	810
Wyoming Wells	712
L.H. Ford	706
O.M. Kelly	700
C.E. Bennett	695
J.A. Blake	600
J. White	579
D.L. Williams	561
F.D. Washington	500
J.D. Husband	450

On November 15, 1968, the General Assembly met to elect the first Presiding Bishop of COGIC. Bishop Cole received the list of nominees and the Assembly voted for the designated candidates:[14]

Bishop J. O. Patterson	362 Votes
Bishop J. S. Bailey	264 Votes
Bishop S. M. Crouch	244 Votes
Bishop Wyoming Wells	51 Votes
Bishop O.M. Kelly	29 Votes

Thus, Bishop James Oglethorpe Patterson was elected the first Presiding Bishop in the COGIC Church, establishing a new foundation of leadership, based on a General Assembly election held every four years. The election was a departure from Mason's ideals of leadership succession.

As Bishop Patterson assumed the reigns of leadership, the COGIC splinter group, Church of God in Christ International was founded in Chicago, Illinois, by Bishop William David Charles Williams. Williams believed in the leadership concept of a Senior Bishop, and rejected the concept of a Presiding Bishop and General Board. This splinter group was an organized protest to the political election of a presiding bishop. Organized in 1969 in Evanston, Illinois, COGIC International had many claims; that the embattled former Senior Bishop Jones became a part of this organization after being ousted by the courts and the first COGIC election.[15] Furthermore, COGIC International would endure a splitting process in 1976. Bishop Carl Williams found COGIC, International[16] (the difference between the two churches is that one has a comma separating International while the other one does not have a comma). Currently, COGIC International is headquartered in Jonesboro, Arkansas.[17]COGIC, International is headquartered in Bridgeport, Connecticut.

Another splinter group that developed from the fall out of COGIC Inc.'s first election was Church of God in Christ, United. The founder of COGIC, United was Bishop James Feltus, Jr., the son of the pioneering overseer in Louisiana, James Feltus, Sr. Feltus, Sr. who was known for his stance against Elias Dempsey Smith's "Never Dying" doctrine, supported Bishop Mason's effortsto keep the COGIC members united against the new doctrine that claimed eternal life in the physical body. COGIC, United began to separate in the mid-1960s and officially organized in 1973 with headquarters located in New Orleans, Louisiana.[18] The other two splinter groups along with COGIC, United followed the original doctrine and concepts of leadership that was sanctioned by Bishop Mason. In a sense, the claims of these three splinter groupshad merit because Mason and Jones were Senior Bishops, not Presiding Bishops.

7.3. THE J.O. PATTERSON ERA: MODERNIZATION OF COGIC, INC.

COGIC's first Presiding Bishop, James Oglethorpe Patterson, was born in Derma, Calhoun County, Mississippi on July 21, 1912 to William and Mollie Patterson. He was reared in the COGIC Church and was ordained as an elder, in 1936, by Bishop A.B. McEwen, his fellow Executive Board Chairman. Also in that same year, Patterson pastored churches in Tennessee and in New Jersey.[19] J.O. Patterson married Deborah Indiana Mason, the daughter of the founder of COGIC, Inc, Bishop Mason. Deborah was a faithful worker and pioneer in the COGIC Music Department. Also, Patterson found and pastored Pentecostal Temple COGIC in Memphis, Tennessee. He was prominently known among COGIC members as a shrewd and keen businessman, owning several properties and businesses around Memphis, Tennessee.

From 1952 to 1953, J.O. Patterson had two great achievements as he advanced in COGIC's leadership. In 1952, he was appointed to the Special Commission with other senior leaders to assist Mason in the operation and administrative tasks of COGIC, Inc. In 1953, Bishop Mason appointed his son-in-law as bishop over the Second Jurisdiction of Tennessee,[20] elevating his position from a local elder to a state jurisdictional bishop. Another key milestone in Patterson's advancement occurred after the death of COGIC National General Secretary, Bishop Ulysses Ellis Miller, in 1963. After Miller's death, The COGIC Elders' Council and General Assembly elected J.O. Patterson to succeed Miller.[21] The General Secretary was a key position in COGIC, Inc. because the person holding this title had unlimited access to communication lines that connected every COGIC leader and member to the headquarters in Memphis. The General Secretary worked closely with Mason, and since Patterson was his son-in-law, he had a very close relationship due to family ties. With positions as a jurisdictional bishop, a Special Commission member, and the National General Secretary, Patterson created an almost perfect path to his ascension to becoming a COGIC national leader. His ambition paid off in 1968 when he was elected as the first presiding bishop of COGIC, Inc.

From 1968 to 1972, Patterson proposed financial goals that increased COGIC's budget and established a Department of Research and Survey to determine the numerical strength of COGIC, worldwide. Patterson was also credited with the C.H. Mason Memorial Scholarship Fund to help COGIC youth use their college education to support the administration and mission of the Church. Other modern implementations by Patterson included the following: COGIC Hospital and Health Plan; upgraded printing system and machinery for the Publishing House; created a new Constitution for a new age ecclesiastical structure to be codified in a revised COGIC handbook; completed one of the visions of the O.T. Jones Era in 1970 by establishing the Charles Harrison Mason Theological Seminary in Atlanta, offering a Masters' Degree in Divinity and a Masters' Degree in Religious Education; organized a system of Bible Colleges throughout the jurisdictions under the Church; and the greatest gift to COGIC was the Chisca Hotel in Memphis, Tennessee, donated by Robert Snowden; the hotel gift was valued at three million dollars.[22] Another landmark accomplishment of Bishop Patterson's administration occurred around 1976 when the COGIC Departments of Youth, Sunday School, Music, Evangelism, and Missions were combined for the purpose of having one annual convention meeting place. This annual meeting was called United National Auxiliaries Conference (UNAC),[23] saving expenses for COGIC members who participated in multiple departments.

In 1975, upon the death of National COGIC Women's Department Supervisor, Mother Anne Bailey, Bishop Patterson appointed Mother Mattie McGlothen, Mother Bailey's assistant, as the National

Supervisor. Mother McGlothen, formerly Mattie Mae Carter, was also born in Texas in 1901 in a town called Tehuacana.[24] Around the age of 20, McGlothen was recorded to have suffered from tuberculosis. So, she went to the Church of God in Christ to be healed from her disease. Mother Anna Powell of Arkansas, a COGIC prayer warrior, prayed for her healing. McGlothen remembered: "After a while, something got a hold of me, something I could feel it coming down.... like a tube down in me, and began to pump like they used to pump up a car.... And it pumped ... and.... pumped until my lungs began to swell.... they kept praying.... I could hear Mother Powell say, 'Come on God, come on God.' 'Do your work, do your work!' When the tube (spiritually) came out of my mouth...then the Holy Ghost came in! I jumped to my feet and jumped through a window that was broken out. On my way home, I ran and said, Daddy, I got it, Daddy, I got it, Daddy oh, Daddy, it's real, it's real!" Following the Holy Ghost experience and proclaimed miraculous healing from tuberculosis, McGlothen claimed salvation in May 1922. She married George McGlothen in 1933, and he became a COGIC Bishop of Nebraska and Iowa.[25] Mother McGlothen became the Supervisor of Women in the Northwest Jurisdiction of California, and she advanced to the position of COGIC National Supervisor while serving California. As the National Supervisor of the Women's Department, McGlothen founded the International Hospitality Group, Lavender Ladies, Bishop Wives' Scholarship Fund, Education and Scholarship Fund, and the Business and Professional Women's Federation.[26] McGlothen's vision for the Business and Professional Women's Federation gave COGIC women an opportunity to actively participate in civic endeavors while maintaining their relationship to COGIC's Holiness agenda. The Business and Professional Women's Federation created a network for COGIC women to support local businesses, especially COGIC female entrepreneurs. McGlothen's indelible trademark on COGIC ministries and services were profound in her focus on women in ministry and hospitality, a program that served COGIC members and church leaders during all conventions and conferences. Moreover, McGlothen focused on women serving the Lord and the people, and she created the "habit", the COGIC woman's ministerial uniform.[27] Like Mother Bailey's demeanor that earned her the "Sweetheart of COGIC" moniker, Mother McGlothen's work earned her the moniker of "Sister of Hospitality."

The Patterson Era was characterized by notable accomplishments by the presiding bishop and staff along with the many achievements of the Women's Department. Nevertheless, there were several challenges faced by Bishop Patterson during the early to mid-1980's that proved to be detrimental to COGIC unity and the credibility of financial accountability. First, in Georgia, Patterson and the General Board were petitioned by Superintendent George Briley, pastor of Jones Avenue COGIC in Atlanta, to become a bishop by establishing a new COGIC jurisdiction in the state of Georgia. Briley was under the leadership of Bishop J. Howard Dell of Northern Georgia Jurisdiction. If Patterson allowed Briley to establish another state jurisdiction, this would show disrespect to the leadership of Bishop Dell. Nevertheless, letters from Dell and Briley circulated back and forth between Atlanta and Memphis. Patterson and the General Board allowed Briley to become a bishop of a new state jurisdiction called Georgia Northwest in 1974 as he left from under the authority of Bishop Dell. Bishop Briley led the Georgia Northwest Jurisdiction until his death in 1976.[28] After the death of Bishop Briley, Patterson chose not to have a successor for the jurisdiction, so he told the pastors and elders under Briley's leadership to affiliate with another jurisdiction in Georgia. Superintendent Marshall Carter, the elder who was second in command under Bishop Briley, and others refused to accept the disintegration of Georgia Northwest and petitioned the Memphis headquarters to recognize their churches for a COGIC jurisdiction. Marshall Carter had organized the Churches of God in Christ Incorporated of Georgia. After about three years of Patterson's refusal to recognize the churches of the former Georgia Northwest Jurisdiction, the Churches of God in Christ Incorporated of Georgia was dissolved. Then Superintendent Marshall Carter became elevated as the first presiding bishop and chief apostle of the United Churches of God in Christ, Inc. on January 1, 1980.[29] Another

COGIC splinter group had formed in protest to Patterson's decision in not making the Georgia group an official COGIC, Inc., jurisdiction.

The other problem with Patterson's leadership dealt with financial accountability with a fundraiser that occurred around 1982. Bishop Patterson had proposed the concept and dream of building a four-year college called All Saints University. The university was to be located in Memphis, Tennessee near the area of the Chisca Hotel, the hotel that was donated to COGIC by Robert Snowden. A good reason for Patterson's desire to build another college was due to the closing of COGIC's Saints Academy in Lexington, Mississippi in 1976. For fiscal reasons, Saints Academy closed after being in operation for almost sixty years.

During the 1982 Holy Convocation in Memphis, the Church had a themed 75th Anniversary Diamond Jubilee Celebration to commemorate the date Mason established the first COGIC, Inc Assembly in 1907. The Diamond Jubilee Program had statements about following a dreamer's dream to make the following items a reality: tithing system, church extension, retirement, hospital, home for the aged, system of Bible Colleges, theological seminary, handicap program, and a worldwide evangelist system. The program also had a rendition of All Saints Center along with a proposed site for the university, land occupied by the Chisca Hotel. Also, a large picture of Presiding Bishop Patterson was placed beside both building concepts as the dreamer of making Saints Center and All Saints University. The 75th Diamond Jubilee Program was promoted as a one-time celebration and the program had several written goals: 1) open All Saints University in 1984; 2) complete the renovation of the old Chisca Hotel; 3) add 75,000 souls to the Church for Christ; 4) have 75,000 people in attendance at the Diamond Convocation Celebration, November 9-19, 1982 with the possibility of being a Diamond Card Delegate; and, 5) last goal, 75,000 members were to give $75.00 toward the projects; if a member gave $1,000, he would receive a diamond lapel pin. At this 75th Diamond Celebration, the COGIC General Board consisted of J.O. Patterson, Presiding Bishop, Otha M. Kelly of New York, Louis H.

Ford of Chicago, Frederick D. Washington of New York, Junious A. Blake of California (the father of the current Presiding Bishop Charles E. Blake), John S. Bailey of Detroit, John D. Husband of Georgia, John W. White of Louisiana, Cleveland L. Anderson of Michigan, Chandler D. Owens of New Jersey, Leroy Anderson of New York, and, Ozro T. Jones, Jr. of Philadelphia (the son of the ousted Senior Bishop O.T. Jones, Sr.).[30] O. T. Jones, Jr. had returned to COGIC Inc., and earned a spot on the General Board, about eight years after his father's death. O.T. Jones' presence was a sign that the great rift in COGIC in the 1960s had healed in a small degree, evidenced by the participation of the younger O.T. Jones, Jr. serving as a bishop under the leadership of the man, Presiding Bishop J.O. Patterson, who was responsible for ending O.T. Jones', Sr. tenure as senior bishop in COGIC.

From 1982-1984, global and national fundraisers took place to support the dream of All Saints University. Many Southern COGIC Churches held revivals during the summers; COGIC servicemen sent money from overseas, and many other members sold items to support the dream of a COGIC University. Nevertheless, at the end of 1984, no school was built, and no one was held accountable for the monies raised to build All Saints University and the Saints Center. The dream and idea just dissipated along with the money. Strangely, the atmosphere among COGIC members and leaders on the failed attempt to build All Saints University appeared to have been apathy as there was no demand for the proper accounting of the funds raised to build the university. Overall, many COGIC members acted like the idea of building Saints Center and All Saints University never existed. Furthermore, the author was in high school during this period and lived near Memphis, about sixty miles away in Helena, Arkansas. The author never saw any groundbreaking episodes, no construction equipment, or construction plans when visiting the city of Memphis to view the site of the university that he had planned to attend. So, by 1985, the whole idea of All Saints University ended on a sour note and led to a great level of distrust toward COGIC leadership, especially leadership of the Patterson Era. During the COGIC April Call Meeting of members of the General Assembly, Patterson talked about merging the All Saints University concept with an existing institution; however, he claimed that he was upset that the universities would not allow COGIC to use the name, "saints." Patterson also claimed that COGIC youth members had to have a sanctified environment of higher learning to continue the legacy[31] of Holiness-Pentecostalism. All Saints University was never constructed, and the monies raised for the project (some COGIC members estimated about 44 million dollars), supposedly, was placed in the Church's General Fund. However, no one has given a proper accounting record for the funds received toward All Saints University, and, for the most part, there was no public display of outrage after the "dream" university did not become a reality.

Even though All Saints University was a dismal failure connected to the leadership of Bishop Patterson, he remained as the presiding bishop until his death in 1989. He had the longest tenure as a COGIC national leader, only second to the founder, Bishop Mason. Patterson's popularity as the leader brought COGIC out of the turbulent years (incorrectly referred to as the Dark Ages or Years of Wilderness Wandering) of the 1960s and overhauled its administration and operations with business-like precision. A reason that Patterson remained in power for such an extended period was due to his COGIC popularity and he had religious influence and political power in Memphis, Tennessee. Patterson not only had a religious impact on COGIC, but he also had a civic impact in his home base of Memphis. Patterson and his family had influential businesses and his son, James O. Patterson, Jr. served as a city councilman for the city of Memphis, and had served as interim mayor in 1982. Basically, Patterson solidified his power base with the support of the clergy in the General Assembly and the support of the civic leaders in the community of Memphis. Not one bishop in COGIC ran for the position of presiding bishop against Patterson during a string of seven elections that occurred every four years in November during the National Convocation. He died in office as the Presiding Bishop and, in his waning years, he did reflect upon the lost "Holiness" theme of COGIC. Patterson ushered in the era of COGIC politics by being voted into power as the first presiding bishop. Patterson helped to create a political system that uplifted power and popularity instead of Holiness and sanctification. Depending on the individual's opinion, Bishop Patterson was considered a great leader who brought COGIC out of the "Dark Ages" into a modernized era; on the other hand, Patterson was a manipulative politician who orchestrated the ousting of O.T. Jones, Sr. and became the undisputed presiding bishop of COGIC. Also, many considered Patterson as a great orator and preacher who had mastered the homiletic feature of storytelling, while others believed he was not good at preaching or teaching. Nevertheless, he had a great impact on COGIC's direction after the death of Mason with a legacy that COGIC preachers not only had to be religious, but they also had to be political. Bishop James O. Patterson died on December 29, 1989 at the age of 77.

CHAPTER 8

BISHOP LOUIS FORD ERA, 1989-1995, AND SUCCESSIVE BISHOPS

After the death of Bishop J.O. Patterson, Sr., Bishop Louis H. Ford, who was also a key member of the Executive Board during the O.T. Jones Era, succeeded Bishop Patterson as the new presiding bishop of COGIC. Ford was born in Coahoma County, Mississippi on May 23, 1914[1] to a Baptist father, Cleveland Ford, and a COGIC mother, Chaney Ford. Chaney Ford influenced young Louis to follow the path of COGIC Holiness-Pentecostalism as he attended church and listened to sermons preached by Bishop Mason. Mason was a popular preacher in the Mississippi Delta as he evangelized in the states of Arkansas, Mississippi, and Tennessee. Young Ford eventually received the call to ministry in 1926 and attended Saints Industrial Academy in 1927, located in Lexington, Mississippi, under the direction of Dr. Arenia Mallory.

In the early 1930s, Ford moved to Chicago and was ordained an elder in the COGIC Church by Bishop William Roberts in 1935. After being ordained, Ford founded St. Paul COGIC in 1936, and became an outstanding radio minister in Chicago, who conducted many tent revivals.[2] He became a prominent "community" preacher that carried the Gospel message outside of the atmosphere of COGIC. His community involvement broke down the stereotypical barriers of COGIC doctrines that denounced being worldly or being involved in politics and community. Bishop Ford utilized his sacred and secular assets as he formed alliances with political organizations. Ford served on the NAACP national executive committee and served as a special advisor to Chicago's mayor Richard Daley. After forming alliances with the NAACP and the National Urban League, Ford assisted in feeding, clothing, and providing jobs to Blacks in the inner cities.[3]

Ford also climbed the COGIC's leadership ladder; in 1954, he was appointed bishop of the Central Illinois Jurisdiction and was on the Board of Education for Saints Industrial Academy, his alma mater. In 1955, he presided over the funeral of Emmett Till, the young lad and his mother, Mamie Till attended Ford's church. Ford advocated for justice and civil rights for the Till family and the African-American community across the nation, using his ties to Mayor Richard Daley in Chicago. He was also appointed as COGIC's National Public Relations Director and was Chairman of the National Founder's Day Program.[4]

Eventually, Ford became a member of the Executive Board that was instrumental in ousting Senior Bishop O.T. Jones, Sr. Like Patterson, Bishop Ford became one of the first members of the new COGIC General Board, finishing with votes that gave him fifth place as Patterson came in first place. Ford, like Patterson, was elected to the General Board consistently after 1968. Ford, in 1988, became the First Assistant to Presiding Bishop Patterson, making him second in charge.[5] In 1989, he succeeded Patterson and began his era which was filled with ideals about reconciling broken relationships and "getting back" to Holiness.

One of Ford's first actions in "getting back" to Holiness and focusing on the Baptism of the Holy Ghost like Bishop Mason, was calling for a Holy Ghost Conference, the first conference of this kind in the post-modern history of COGIC. The Holy Ghost Conference was held in January 16-18, 1990 in Birmingham, Alabama.[6] Bishop Ford's actions were strategical and offered spiritual healing to the past actions of the former administration. By holding the conference in Birmingham, some spiritual healing could be addressed that was never addressed during the turbulent 1960s. Looking back, Birmingham was the site of a great rift between the COGIC Senior Bishop Jones and the

COGIC Executive Board led by Bishop A.B. McEwen. The Executive Board split the Alabama First Diocese under the leadership of Bishop Ashworth, giving some churches to Alabama Second Diocese under the leadership of James M. Bailey, the brother of the Co-Chairman of the Executive Board, John Seth Bailey. The Holy Ghost Conference served as a spiritual ground of repentance for past actions as each nightly service opened with prayer and repentance.

Nevertheless, the Holy Ghost Conference Steering Committee gave credit to Bishop Patterson for creating the idea of this unique conference. Ford led the continuation of the conference with goals addressing the problems of America, specifically Black America, and to correct the misinterpretations of COGIC's history and practices. The goals of the Holy Ghost Conference were to focus on the legacy of the Azusa Street Revival with an emphasis on modern-day applications: 1) To equip and empower the Saints for ministry in the decades of the 1990s; 2) To broaden the understandings of both clergy and lay persons of the Church of God in Christ's historic vision and to explore how that vision given to the fathers and mothers in the first decade of the 20th century, could provide focus on the mission and ministry in the last decade of the 20th century; 3) To correct the misreading of COGIC history and misinterpretations of COGIC practices; 4) To lead serious seekers of the Baptism of the Holy Ghost to an authentic experience; 5) To put into the hands of the bishops, pastors, teachers, evangelists, male and female workers, the materials to assist them in leading persons to a blessed empowering by the Spirit of God; 6) To provide for the COGIC constituency a clear and comprehensive statement of the priorities, mission, and ministry of the Church in the 1990s; and, 7) To celebrate and thank God for the leadership of Bishop J.O. Patterson over the last 20 years.[7] Overall, the Holy Ghost Conference defined the mission of Ford's administration, a retreat to the spiritual legacy of Bishop Mason and the Azusa Street Revival.

Furthermore, Bishop Ford tested the pulse of the Church through personal visits to many COGIC state jurisdictions. After considerations from the visits and a focus on getting back to Mason's leadership standards, Ford disbanded his predecessor's UNAC concept. Instead of having one meeting for all the COGIC Departments (Youth, Sunday School, Music, Mission, and Evangelism), Ford separated the departments into three entities and the new departments had three separate annual meetings. Also, while he conducted his visits, he gained support as he re-opened his alma mater, Saints Academy in Lexington, in September of 1993, after closing in 1976. Bishop Ford revived the campus as he ordered the construction of a multi-million-dollar facility that featured modern upgrades.[8] With much support around the country as he advocated a "back" to Holiness mission, Bishop Ford paid a visit to Bishop J. Howard Dell's church, Christ Temple COGIC, in Atlanta. Ford mended the relationship between the national COGIC administration and the state administration under Bishop Dell. About fourteen years earlier, Patterson's decision to make one of Dell's superintendents a bishop without the support and recommendation of Bishop Dell had caused a rift in Georgia, and eventually berthed another COGIC splinter group, the United Churches of God in Christ.[9]

Ironically, one of the nadir points of Ford's administration occurred in the state of Georgia. On September 30, 1992, Bishop Dell died after serving forty-four years as the bishop of the Northern Georgia Jurisdiction. Bishop Dell had certified letters dated September 4, 1991, empowering his first administrative assistant, Superintendent Mark Walden of Thomson, Georgia, as co-pastor of Northern Georgia Headquarters Church, Christ Temple COGIC. In the position of co-pastor, Dell had made his intentions known about Walden being his successor. However, at the funeral on October 6, 1992, Bishop Ford announced, "All papers originated by Bishop Dell, died with Bishop Dell." That statement was a testament to the fact that Presiding Bishop Ford had no intentions of abiding by the letter that made Superintendent Walden the co-pastor of Christ Temple COGIC.[10] After the funeral, Bishop Ford presided over an election of a new bishop of the Northern Georgia Jurisdiction. Four candidates were running for the position, and all four men had served as superintendents under the later Bishop Dell: Elder Mark Walden of Thomson, Elder Leroy James of Augusta,

Elder Benjamin Collins of Atlanta, and Elder Adrian Williams of Albany. After a first vote and a run-off vote, Bishop Ford announced that Superintendent Adrian Williams had won the election and was the new bishop of Northern Georgia.

The election results did not fare well among the voting clergy of Northern Georgia. Many felt that Elder Walden was more seasoned and qualified and did not want to be under the authority of the newly elected Bishop Adrian Williams. So, several pastors left the jurisdiction of Northern Georgia and formed a fellowship (a group of churches that petitioned the National COGIC Church to become a jurisdiction) under Superintendent Walden. Eventually, after many headaches for Presiding Bishop Ford, Elder Walden became Bishop Walden of Northern Georgia Second Jurisdiction in 1995. According to Elder James, Bishop Ford had regretted his decision that had caused an internal rift in the state of Georgia.[11] Looking on the bright side, at least another COGIC splinter group did not form because of the incident.

Overall, Ford's tenure forced COGIC leadership to look back to its roots and focus on soul winning as a top priority. Bishop Ford oversaw the first Holy Ghost Conference and desired to provide religious-themed academics for Church youth who attended Saints Academy. After taking the reins of leadership in 1989, he always appeared to be in a rush to complete his goals. One uncommon act of selflessness on his part, during one of the National Holy Convocations in the 1990s, Ford told his administration that he did not want an official offering, so he told the officials to take the monies and help the COGIC members. He also opened the Mattie McGlothen Home of Love and the Hope Shelter for the homeless in Memphis. The Ford Era had many highlights of Mason's original vision which focused on being filled with the Holy Spirit and helping the poor. However, one of the greatest highlights of his administration was when 1992 presidential candidate and governor of Arkansas, Bill Clinton spoke at the 1991 Annual Holy Convocation in Memphis, asking COGIC members and leadership for their blessing and support.[12]

Ford's political ties with the mayors of Chicago and the president of the United States made him a great COGIC political figure. Moreover, Ford used his political connections to help the poor and needy in his urban area of Chicago and other urban areas across the United States. His vision of Holiness included a platform that reached far outside the walls of COGIC, and into the world of distressed people and politics. Nevertheless, displaying that his time was short as he always appeared to be in a rush, Bishop Louis Henry Ford died on March 31, 1995. Ford, in his waning years, provided a leadership example on how a presiding bishop could be more concerned about the spiritual life and legacy of the COGIC Church, instead of focusing on the power, politics, and popularity connected to being a national leader.

8.1. ANOTHER COGIC SPLINTER GROUP AND THE ASCENSION OF MOTHER CROUCH

During Ford's tenure, another COGIC splinter group developed, not in the United States, but in Canada. Vinnel T. Channer left COGIC, Inc. in 1991 to form Lighthouse Church of the Apostle of Canada. According to his son, Bishop Wayne Channer, COGIC leadership did not support the ministries in Canada, and there was general resentment dating back to the 1930s against the non-support by COGIC headquarters. Dating back to one of the pioneer COGIC bishops of Canada, Clarence L. Morton, Sr., tensions grew from the lack of support and funds by COGIC headquarters in supporting mission work in Canada. Even though, in Bishop Morton's case, Canada was close to his home in Detroit, Michigan; however, in other cases, COGIC bishops of foreign lands resided several hundreds of miles away from their assigned mission. Years later, one bishop of Canada resided in California. Moreover, Bishop Clarence Morton's son, Paul Sylvester Morton who would also leave his COGIC Inc., roots and found the Full Gospel Baptist Church Fellowship International in 1994. Bishop Paul Morton's fellowship fused the foundations of African-

American Baptist and COGIC Holiness-Pentecostal traditions which created another revival-like movement that was characterized by demonstrative worship services and charismatic preaching.[13]

Nevertheless, Vinnel Channer decided to expand the work of his newly developing church by obtaining a credentialing granting status from the government of Ontario in 2000. Bishop Channer ordained several ministers providing them with guidance and leadership. In 2004, after being diagnosed with a terminal illness, Bishop Vinnel Channer called on his son to take the leadership reins of the Lighthouse Church of the Apostle. His son, Wayne Channer, was also serving in COGIC, Inc. at the time of his father's request. Bishop Vinnel Channer died in 2005, and then Wayne Channer took control of the denomination. To secure his father's legacy, Bishop Wayne Channer decided to change the name of the church in 2006. Bishop Wayne Channer renamed the organization, Lighthouse Churches of God in Christ of Canada, Inc. in honor of the church his father started in Scarborough, Canada as a COGIC, Inc. pastor.[14]

Another key event in 1994 for COGIC was the death of Mother Mattie McGlothen. McGlothen, COGIC, Inc.'s fourth Supervisor of the Women's Department died on May 4, 1994. Her assistant was Mother Emma Crouch, and she assumed the position as National Supervisor on May 24, 1994 in Jackson, Mississippi.[15] Mother Crouch had COGIC family ties in connection with Bishop Samuel Crouch, a pioneering minister in California and Reverend Andrae Crouch, a renown Gospel Music artist. Before she assumed leadership in 1994, like others, Mother Crouch testified of a miraculous healing experience in 1993. Mother Crouch was sick for several days, but she believed in God and that God would heal her to lead the women. She was healed and led the COGIC Women's Department from 1994-1997.[16]

Mother Emma Frances Searcy Crouch was born to Mr. and Mrs. Robert Searcy in Morris County, Texas on February 14, 1911. She graduated from Booker T. Washington High School in Mount

Pleasant, Texas in May 1932, and in 1934 she graduated from Page Normal Industrial and Bible Institute. In 1938, she married Elder B.J. Crouch of Dallas, Texas, and they were married for twenty-two years until his death in 1960. Mother Crouch continued her education by receiving a certificate from the Madam C.J. Walker School of Beauty Culture, and she attended Bishop College in 1963.

Her contributions to the COGIC movement in Texas began with her serving as the first female chair of YPWW in her state's jurisdiction. She assisted State Supervisor, Mother Bertha Polk, and served as a district missionary for twelve years. Mother Crouch also served as the Chairperson of the Jurisdiction Finance Department for sixteen years and was selected as the second state jurisdiction president of the Sunshine Band, a department dedicated to teaching the young children about Holiness. Finally, in 1956, Mother Crouch was appointed supervisor of the Texas Southwest Jurisdiction under the leadership of Bishop T.D. Iglehart. Mother Crouch continued her service to COGIC on the national scene when she became a member of the Trustee Board, Saints Academy Board of Directors, Usher Board, and, in 1976, she was appointed as the First Assistant General Supervisor to Mother Mattie McGlothen, Supervisor of COGIC's Women's Department.[17] This appointment assured Mother Crouch's accession to the position of National Supervisor upon the death of Mother McGlothen.

When Mother McGlothen died in 1994, Mother Crouch became motivated to lead COGIC women after her health recovered. Mother Crouch, as the fifth Supervisor of the COGIC Women's Department, implemented some key programs for the development of ministries. First, she complemented the Young Women's Christian Council (YWCC) with a Christian Women's Council, which included women who were forty and over. For administrative purposes, she divided the Board of Supervisors among the women into two groups: Circle One and Circle Two. Another administrative move under Crouch was that she appointed state supervisors to serve as the national supervisor's representatives, establishing a chain of command for the organization of COGIC women. Additionally, Mother Crouch reestablished the National Pastor's Aide Department to focus on pastoral care and support. Other key departments that were created under Crouch's leadership were the General Board of Bishops' Wives Circle and the National Deaconess Board. Other visions were solidified in her appointments. She appointed a leading historian and an executive secretary, specifically for the Department of Women. Mother Crouch has been recognized for her leadership by the C.H. Mason Seminary, the COGIC Religious Guild, and the city of Memphis gave her the corporate salute in 1996.[18]Accomplishing many goals during her short tenure, Mother Crouch died on January 6, 1997 bequeathing a legacy to the next supervisor, Mother Willie Mae Rivers.

8.2. BISHOP CHANDLER DAVID OWENS ERA: 1995-2000

Before Mother Rivers succeeded Mother Crouch as the Supervisor of the Women's Department, the first administrative assistant, Bishop Chandler David Owens took control of COGIC, Inc., upon the death of Bishop Ford. Thestandard procedure of COGIC leadership upon the death of the presiding bishop during an incomplete term was to allow the first administrative assistant of the presiding bishop to serve the remainder term. So, in 1995, Bishop Chandler Owens succeeded Bishop Ford.

Chandler David Owens was born in Birmingham, Alabama to Reverend William Owens and Martha Owens on October 31, 1931. He was saved at Smithfield COGIC under Pastor Shepherd Skanes, at the age of five years old.[19] Being saved at this age, also ushered him into the ministry as he became known as the "boy" preacher. At the age of seventeen, the "boy" preacher was called to Chicago by Bishop Ford to lead a revival. As Ford mentored him, Owens served faithfully in the Department of Evangelism and the Youth Department.[20] He served as a shining example for COGIC ministry in advocating a holy lifestyle among young people. Owens graduated from A. H. Parker

High School in Birmingham, Alabama, but his parents could not afford to send him to college. So, young Owens began to spend long hours in the library studying and reading dictionaries, encyclopedias, thesauruses, and many other books on various subjects. His intense library experience became a major part of his preaching style as he ministered with a plethora of words during many of his trademark sermons. He became a junior pastor at his father's church, Power View COGIC. Later, as a young man, he became an adjutant to the founder of COGIC, Bishop Mason. [21]After high school, he relocated to Detroit, Michigan to work at the Henry Ford Auto Plant. While preaching in Detroit under the tutelage of Bishop John S. Bailey, he married Shirley Jeanette Hardy. Afterwards, Bishop Bailey appointed Owens to be the pastor of Wells Cathedral COGIC in Newark, New Jersey in 1965.[22]

Owens deep bass voice, extensive vocabulary, and homiletical skills, impressed the founder, Bishop Mason and other leaders in COGIC like Bishop Ford, Bishop Riley Williams, and Bishop James O. Patterson, Sr. Owen's alliance with Bishop Ford and Bishop Bailey placed him on the side of the Executive Board in 1965-1968. Looking back, Elder Chandler Owens replaced the ousted COGIC Youth Department (YPWW) President, Elder O.T. Jones, Jr., in 1966. Elder Owens held the position until 1972.

With his popularity as a youth evangelist and impressive revivalist, Owens ascended quickly to the office of bishop in the Church. As pastor of Wells Cathedral COGIC, Owens became a COGIC bishop. Owens became the state bishop of the New Jersey Third Ecclesiastical Jurisdiction. In 1976, Bishop Owens became a member of the General Board of COGIC and he was one of the youngest bishops ever elected to the General Board. In 1988, he became the second assistant to Presiding Bishop Patterson, and in 1990, he became the first assistant to Presiding Bishop Ford, his mentor.[23] Furthermore, in 1990, Presiding Bishop Ford and Bishop Owens had to handle another problem in Georgia. In the Central Georgia Jurisdiction under Bishop John D. Husband, who was headquartered in Marietta, there were accusations of mishandling church funds and conduct unbecoming of a bishop. Husband's financial woes included the foreclosure of his church, Hinsley Chapel COGIC, though many members thought that the church was mortgage-free. Eventually, Bishop Husband was stripped of his jurisdictional leadership and Bishop Owens moved from his jurisdiction in New Jersey to become, at first, the interim bishop of the Central Georgia Jurisdiction. After the loss of Hinsley Chapel COGIC, Owens purchased another building for the members of Hinsley Chapel. The new church was named Greater Community COGIC and is currently located at 406 Roswell Street in Marietta, Georgia. Furthermore, Bishop Husband died in 1991, and in 1992, Bishop Owens was officially appointed as the bishop of Central Georgia Jurisdiction. For the first time, the seat of power in COGIC national leadership resided in the state of Georgia, as Owens became the third presiding bishop of COGIC.

In 1995, Bishop Owens succeeded his mentor in becoming the third presiding bishop of the COGIC Church. However, to keep the position, he had to win the election in 1996. One of his opponents and closest friends in the preaching of the Gospel was Bishop Gilbert Earl Patterson, the nephew of the first Presiding Bishop James O. Patterson, Sr. The presiding bishop election of 1996 proved to be a political firestorm that shook the foundation of COGIC leadership like the years of the 1960s during the O.T. Jones Era.

Before the election of 1996, Bishop Owens and Bishop Gilbert E. Patterson had been long-time friends in the COGIC church. However, the 1996 election placed a strain on the long-time friendship. These two close friends entered a contentious political struggle over the top leadership position in COGIC, with two opposing groups, one led by Bishop Owens and the other group spearheaded by the alliance of Bishop G.E. Patterson and Bishop Charles E. Blake of California. In Detroit, both Owens and Patterson had served as young preachers under Bishop Bailey. Owens and Patterson had been GOGIC preachers and friends since their twenties. However, in 1974, Gilbert Patterson left COGIC, Inc., due to a dispute over his father's, William A. Patterson, church in Memphis. The battle over the church involved his uncle, James O. Patterson, Sr., the brother of William A. Patterson. Gilbert Patterson served as the co-pastor of Holy Temple COGIC in Memphis, and was instrumental in the growth of the church from 1964-1974.[24] The dispute caused Gilbert to leave COGIC, Inc. and Holy Temple COGIC on December 30, 1974. In 1975, G.E. Patterson purchased and remodeled the former Mount Vernon Baptist Church on 547 Mississippi Boulevard. With a new clergy title, Apostle G.E. Patterson's new church was named Temple of Deliverance, the Cathedral of Bountiful Blessings. Basically, he had formed his own organization of ministry in Memphis and in the same area as the COGIC headquarters.[25] Also, not far from Apostle G.E. Patterson's church, stood Pentecostal Institutional Temple COGIC pastored by his uncle and Presiding Bishop, James O. Patterson, Sr.

During Apostle Patterson's separation from COGIC, Inc., Bishop Owens maintained a relationship with the apostle and considered him a close friend. In November 1986, the COGIC General Board, which included Bishop Owens, voted 11 to 0 to invite Gilbert Patterson back into the active ministry of COGIC as a state jurisdictional bishop in Memphis, Tennessee. The action to allow G.E. Patterson back in to COGIC was not executed by Presiding Bishop J.O. Patterson, Sr. until January 29, 1988.[26] With the help of his friend, Bishop Owens and other General Board members, Apostle G.E. Patterson became Bishop G.E. Patterson, the state bishop of the Tennessee Fourth Ecclesiastical Jurisdiction, during the 1988 Holy Convocation. Then in 1992, during the Holy Convocation in Memphis, Bishop G.E. Patterson was elected to the General Board to serve with his long-time friend, Bishop Chandler Owens. In 1995, after Owens became the Presiding Bishop, he appointed G.E. Patterson as Chief Operating Officer for COGIC National Headquarters to oversee church property, financial operations, subsidiary corporations, personnel, and housing programs of the National Church. Owens noted G.E. Patterson's awesome talents and God-given leadership abilities.[27] Bishop G.E. Patterson's popularity as a charismatic preacher and speaker caused him to receive many invitations to conferences inside and outside of the COGIC denomination.

During the 1996 Holy Convocation, the presiding bishop position was highly contested. Owens, even though he was the first assistant to Bishop Ford, was not assured the position of presiding bishop. The 1996 election results showed the vulnerability of Bishop Owens' bid to become the presiding bishop with strong opponents like Bishop Charles E. Blake of California and Bishop G.E Patterson of Tennessee. Even though G.E. Patterson had only been on the General Board for four years, he had a strong following strategically located in Memphis, Tennessee. If delegates wanted to vote, the delegates had to attend the General Assembly sessions that occurred on Tuesday after the official Sunday services of the Holy Convocation. G.E. Patterson had a definite hometown advantage as his supporters were not subjected to the constraints of travel.

At the November 1996 COGIC election for presiding bishop, Bishop G.E. Patterson and Bishop Owens were the two main focal points of leadership. The election results can be seen in the following list:

Member-Bishop	**Votes**
G.E. Patterson	2,924
C.E. Blake	2,583
C.D. Owens	2,443
R. L. Winbush	2,221
O.T. Jones, Jr.	2,194
P.A. Brooks	2,086
I.C. Clemmons	1,995
J.N. Haynes	1,994
C.L. Anderson	1,847
L. Anderson	1,739
S. Green	1,580
L. Willis	1,477

PRESIDING BISHOP RUN-OFF ELECTION

C. D. Owens   1,429

G.E. Patterson   1,428[28]

Bishop Owens had won the election by a controversial one vote. Many members wanted Bishop G.E. Patterson to contest the vote. On the contrary, G.E. Patterson decided to let the results stand and wait until the next quadrennial election to run against Bishop Owens again. Bishop G.E. Patterson stated that he wanted to become presiding bishop without politics trumping the long-term friendship between Owens and himself. Regardless of the near feud that almost occurred over the one vote scenario between Owens supporters and G.E. Patterson supporters, Owens assumed the role as the third presiding bishop of COGIC, Inc.

During the era of Bishop Owens, he proposed a COGIC program called Vision 2000 and Beyond. Bishop Owens' platform had fifteen points that focused on a transformational Church of the future in keeping with a foundation of Holiness from the past. The vision of the future for COGIC, Inc. included these focal points: 1) The beauty of Holiness, Owens wanted to continue lifting the doctrine of Holiness among God's people; 2) Evangelism: The expression of love, Owens wanted to maintain the spiritual power of the Church; 3) Church growth; the leader wanted to provide local churches with support to grow membership; 4) C.H. Mason Bible Institute, the leader expressed need to have COGIC Bible schools for training across the country; 5) Financial Solvency, Owens wanted to be fiscally wise in spending Church funds; 6) Strengthen the National Auxiliaries, Owens wanted to adequately fund the Auxiliaries' programs and assist personnel; 7) The affirmation of women in ministry, the presiding bishop wanted to continue to confirm the necessity of women participating in ministry; 8) Memphis: An educational opportunity; Bishop Owens wanted to discuss the establishment of a COGIC educational institution in

Memphis; 9) A national ministry of care, Owens wanted to establish a COGIC Health Plan Program; 10) A special school for the disadvantage, Owens proposed a special school for the disadvantaged supported by the government, foundations, and charities; 11) Charles Harrison Mason Theological Seminary, Owens wanted the seminary to include students from foreign lands for the purpose of world outreach; 12) Jurisdictions: Hands of the national church, Owens wanted to redefine the roles of jurisdictions in evangelism, church growth, training, and missions; 13) Youth: They are worthy of being included, Owens was a former national leader of the COGIC Youth Department and desired to develop ethical and spiritual program designs to meet the needs of COGIC youth; 14) The General Board, the presiding bishop vowed to involve the General Board in all deliberations and actions dealing with COGIC, and Owens also claimed that for the past twenty-five years, the General Board had been marginalized when dealing with significant Church business; and, 15) One: The Church of God in Christ, Owens wanted all local congregations, departments, and auxiliaries in COGIC to be and act as "one" unit in the Spirit of God.[29]

With Vision 2000, Bishop Owens was attempting to modernize COGIC's financial state with accountability and streamline the administration and management of COGIC on three levels: national, state, and local community. Learning from the fiasco of All Saints University, Owens wanted to be financially astute in the accounting practices of handling all church funds. Furthermore, COGIC had not seen an extensive church assessment plan like Vision 2000, since the days of Senior Bishop O.T. Jones, Sr. in 1962. Owens' plan was proposed to maintain COGIC's tradition of being a Holiness-Pentecostal church and spiritual entity that focused on church growth without compromising the vision of its founder, Bishop Mason. Under Vision 2000, COGIC women and youth were encouraged to support COGIC ministries and Owens introduced a health care plan for the workers in ministry. Mainly, Owens vision focused on training and education for COGIC members and clergy in ministry with a focus on national and global outreach.[30]

Continuing the political-religious affiliation of Bishop Ford, Owens, in 1996, hosted President Bill Clinton in New Orleans. President Clinton was the keynote speaker for the COGIC International Women's Convention. In 1997, President Clinton invited Bishop Owens to deliver the official prayer for the 53rd Presidential Inauguration.[31] Also in 1997, Mother Emma Crouch, the Supervisor of the COGIC Women's Department, died on January 6, 1997. In her place, Bishop Owens appointed Mother Willie Mae Rivers as the sixth National Supervisor of the COGIC Women's Department.

Mother Willie Mae Smalls Rivers was born on February 20, 1926 to Robert and Anna Mitchell Smalls in Charleston County, South Carolina. Mother Rivers received a formal education in the Berkeley and Charleston County School Systems. Mother Rivers was serving in the Sunday School Department of Mount Zion AME Church, until she became a proselyte to COGIC, Inc. During a revival, she heard the Gospel preached by Superintendent Jacob and Francena Dantzler. She confessed receiving the Baptism of the Holy Ghost in 1946, and she became a hardworking member of Mason's COGIC denomination. She became a church mother at Calvary COGIC at the age of 20, and has been a church mother for over 70 years. Mother Rivers had served the National Church as a Marshall of the Women's Convention, member of the General Church Program Committee, member of the Executive Board, coordinator of the Leadership Conference, and assistant to the Supervisor of the Women's Department. Mother Rivers continues to serve in her community and she spreads the Gospel through the Evangelist Speaks ministry on WTUA 106.1 FM in North Charleston, South Carolina. Furthermore, Mother Rivers is the founder and president of the Community Christian and Women and Men Fellowship. This organization reaches people from all walks of life.[32] Mother Rivers led COGIC women in the foundation of Holiness with emphasis on maintaining moral discipline and serving others. She served under three Presiding Bishops of COGIC: Chandler Owens, Gilbert Patterson, and, the current presiding bishop, Charles Blake.

Bishop Owens made a wise decision to continue the process

of senior spiritual succession in the COGIC Women's Department. Mother Rivers maintained a great and positive influence upon the Women's Department, specifically, and the Church of God in Christ, Inc., generally. Another great decision by Bishop Owens was to reorganize five main departments of COGIC. Bishop Ford had separated the main departments into three groups, having three separate conventions. However, Owens decided to follow the old format that had been established by Bishop J.O. Patterson. So, Owens combined all departments: Youth, Music, Mission, Evangelism, and Sunday School. The departments had one convention called AIM (Auxiliaries in Ministry), which met annually around the months of June and July.

The greatest accomplishment of the Bishop Owens Era dealt with COGIC fiscal responsibility. At Bishop Owens funeral in 2011, Presiding Bishop Charles Blake testified that Bishop Owens ordered the General Board Members, composed of state jurisdictional bishops who were in the top twelve candidates during the quadrennial election, not to take a Church salary for one year to acquire and sustain monies for the General Fund of the church. Bishop Blake also stated that Bishop Owens' proposal had caused the COGIC Church's budget to increase to a surplus of 8 to 10 million dollars. COGIC was finally not operating in a deficit.

Despite Owen's accomplishments, his era would become overshadowed by a decision he made concerning a COGIC pastor named Derrick Hutchins. Hutchins had three churches, one in South Carolina, one in Tennessee, and one in Florida. Bishop Owens gave a proclamation to Hutchins to give up the church in South Carolina, and let Bishop H. Jenkins Bell pastor the church. Well, Elder Hutchins refused to obey the proclamation and a firestorm began under Owens' leadership.[33] Firsthand, Hutchins was the Chairman of the COGIC Pastors' and Elders' Council, the largest voting bloc for Presiding Bishop in the General Assembly. Secondhand, Elder Hutchins and Bishop Owens went to court in Florida, the site of Hutchins' 800-member church, and

Bishop Charles Blake of California, a member of the COGIC General Board of Bishops who served under the leadership of Presiding Bishop Owens, decided to fly to Florida to testify against his leader, Bishop Owens, and for Elder Hutchins. Bishop Blake stated that Presiding Bishop Owens did not have the right to order Elder Hutchins to give up the church in South Carolina. Bishop Blake gave a detailed outline of his support for Elder Hutchins in his pamphlet called Why I Stood for the Defense in Orlando: How Long This Madness? Thirdly, Bishop Gilbert Patterson of Memphis, Tennessee sided with Bishop Blake and Elder Hutchins against their National church leader. These actions signified another leadership rift in COGIC hearkening back to the O.T. Jones Era. The different parties involved in this dispute organized during the 2000 election for the Presiding Bishop position of COGIC, Inc.

Before the quadrennial election of 2000, Circuit Judge William C. Gridley ruled in favor of Presiding Bishop Owens. The judge's decision stated that Owens had the authority to remove Hutchins as pastor of the Orlando Institutional COGIC and replace him with Bishop H. Jenkins Bell.[34] Nevertheless, Hutchins took his 800-member church and formed a private corporation to prevent further legal proceedings. Even though Bishop Owens won the court case, Hutchins claimed that Owens turned against him because of his support for Bishop Blake in becoming the next presiding bishop.[35] Along with Bishop Blake's support, Hutchins received support from another ally, Bishop Gilbert Earl Patterson of Memphis, Tennessee. Both Blake and Patterson were seeking to run against Presiding Bishop Owen during the 2000 election. During the Elder Derrick Hutchins fiasco, Bishop Owens had lost a significant amount of leadership support among key benefactors in COGIC.

8.3. COGIC Election Year 2000 with C.D. Owens versus G.E. Patterson

The General Assembly of the Church of God in Christ, Inc. convened on November 13, 2000 at the Cook Convention Center in Memphis, Tennessee. At 5:40 PM, Elder Fluker opened the session with prayer, scripture, and a song. Then the session was turned over to the Chairman, Bishop James O. Patterson, Jr., the son of Presiding Bishop J.O. Patterson, Sr. and the first cousin to 2000 presiding bishop candidate, Bishop Gilbert E. Patterson. Chairman Patterson claimed that the 2000 General Assembly had the largest attendance in COGIC history. At about 3:30 PM, the certified delegate count of the General Assembly was at 5,550.[36] Afterwards, speeches were given by all the bishops running for a coveted spot on the General Board, and the bishops came to the podium in alphabetical order. Focusing on the three main characters, Blake, Owens, and G.E. Patterson, the speeches carried remnants of the leadership confrontations among the three bishops. Blake's spoke against dictatorial practices in COGIC, which might have been a jab at Owens' leadership. Owens spoke about how he did not have a famous COGIC father or mother, stating that he came to leadership from the ranks of the common folk, and that he had worked with prior bishops and leaders without fighting against them (a jab at G.E. Patterson and Blake).[37] Then Owens boasted how his administration had acquired a surplus of 7.5 million dollars for the general fund. G.E. Patterson spoke about how he loved the Church and having many connections to the Church, and he wanted to complete the mission of Charles H. Mason, the founder (G. E. Patterson never mentioned the period in which he left COGIC and became independent.)[38]

The next day, on November 14, 2000, the voting process started about 1:43 PM, after speeches were given by candidates running for the Trustee Board and the office of COGIC General Secretary. After the ballots were issued to members of the General Assembly, the voting process lasted from 2:00 PM to 2:21 PM.

The results of the first election for presiding bishop proved to be an uphill battle for Bishop Owens, looking at the following general board of twelve results:[39]

Member-Bishop	Votes
G.E. Patterson	3,471
C.E Blake	3,388
P.A. Brooks	3,144
W.W. Hamilton	3,049
R. L. Winbush	2,987
C.D. Owens	2,918
J. N. Haynes	2,766
S. Green	2,411
L. Anderson	2,279
G.D. McKinney	1,972
L. Willis	1,806
N. Wells	1,792

Then, at 2:42 PM, a run-off election for presiding bishop took place with four candidates: G.E. Patterson, Blake, Owens, and Winbush. The first run-off election for presiding bishop began at 3:30 PM and lasted until 4:34 PM. The results had G.E. Patterson leading, but he did not capture the requirement of 50% of the voting delegation. 2,748 was the vote count needed to secure the win for presiding bishop.

Member-Bishop	Votes
G. E. Patterson	2,105
C. D. Owens	1,739
C. E. Blake	709
R. L. Winbush	257[40]

So, another run-off election had to take place between G.E. Patterson and Owens. Before the second run-off election, Bishop Blake was allowed to give a speech which went against the protocol of the Chairman of the General Assembly's order. Earlier at 1:43 PM, Chairman J.O. Patterson, Jr stated plainly that there would be no more speeches given during the assembly. Yet, he allowed Bishop Blake to have a voice at the microphone, in which, Blake stated that the election should be settled without another vote, and that the victory should be awarded to Bishop G.E. Patterson. Chairman J.O. Patterson, Jr. explained that the act would be against parliamentary procedures and the process of amending the procedures and rules had not taken place during the current meeting of the General Assembly.[41] Nevertheless, in the audience, many of the Blake supporters were signaled to cast their votes in the last run-off election for Bishop G.E. Patterson, as Blake verbally gave his support to Patterson. The last round of voting began at 5:10 PM and lasted to 5:46 PM. The final tally sealed the defeat of Bishop Owens. G.E. Patterson had 2,619 votes and Owens had 1,786 votes. The new presiding bishop was G.E. Patterson, and the Patterson family name was once again back into the highest office of COGIC leadership.[42] Bishop Owens and Bishop Patterson shook hands afterwards in a gesture of good will; however, there was much sorrow and tension in the auditorium. Derick Hutchins, the elder that prompted resistance against Owens, was, again, elected as Chairman of the COGIC Pastor's and Elder's Council. Furthermore, Bishop G.E. Patterson chose Bishop J. Neaul Haynes as his First Administrative Assistant, the same bishop who was Owen's First Administrative Assistant. Then, of course, G.E. Patterson chose Bishop Charles Blake as the Second Administrative Assistant, which would advance Blake, eventually, to the office of presiding bishop.[43]

8.4. BISHOP GILBERT EARL PATTERSON ERA, 2000-2007

Bishop Gilbert Earl Patterson was born September 22, 1939, in Humboldt, Tennessee to Bishop William Archie Patterson, Sr. and Mary Louise Patterson. Gilbert was saved in May 1951 at the age of eleven at Holy Temple COGIC in Memphis, where his father was the pastor. In 1952, the Patterson family moved to Detroit where Gilbert graduated from Hutchins Intermediate and Central High School. In September 1956, he received his calling from God to preach the Gospel at the age of sixteen. He preached his first sermon on January 22, 1957, and in that same year he was licensed by his father and ordained as an elder by Bishop John S. Bailey in August 1958. In 1967, he married Louise Dowdy who was saved and filled with the Holy Ghost under his ministry.[44]

After G.E. Patterson's exit from COGIC, Inc. because of a three-way dispute between his father, his uncle, and himself, in 1975, he established the Temple of Deliverance along with a nationwide appeal and following. Patterson built a 1.2-million-dollar edifice and eventually had more than 17,000 members on the church's roll. G.E. Patterson was the Founder/President of Bountiful Blessings Ministries which had nationwide and international viewers on the B.E.T. and TBN television networks. G.E. Patterson also managed a radio station, WBBP Radio, and he was president of Podium Records. One of Podium Record's projects was nominated for a 1999 Grammy Award. His popularity in Memphis, around the nation, and around the world gave him a great advantage in defeating Owens for the position of COGIC presiding bishop.

As the fourth presiding bishop of COGIC, G.E. Patterson established COGIC Charities, Inc. This nonprofit corporation of COGIC, Inc. assisted victims of foreign and domestic natural disasters and put forth efforts to uplift humanity around the globe. Patterson also spearheaded the renovation of Mason Temple, having the church headquarters outfitted with air conditioning, fortified some structural defects, and retrofitted the church's audio-visual equipment.[45]   In 2004, Bishop Owens and Bishop Patterson were involved in another election for the office of presiding bishop; however, Patterson's support had grown over the years and Owens could not overcome Patterson's nationwide influence. Thus, G.E. Patterson was re-elected as presiding bishop.

From a laymen's perspective, Bishop G. E. Patterson had advanced the agenda and ministries of Temple of Deliverance and Bountiful Blessings more than the agenda of COGIC, Inc. For the most part, Patterson did not propose a visionary program for COGIC on a large scale in comparison to the ambitious 15-points of Vision 2000 established by Bishop Owens. There were no major themes that promoted getting back to Holiness and Pentecostalism, and there were no major meetings like the Holy Ghost Conference. Also, the surplus of funds under the Owens Administration dwindled, and COGIC, Inc. was again operating at a deficit. Evidenced by most of his biography, G.E. Patterson was well-known and prominent "outside" of the sphere of COGIC, Inc.

During the 2006 Holy Convocation, Presiding Bishop Patterson made a gesture to Bishop Owens. Patterson placed a ceremonial garb upon Owens. Many COGIC members who witnessed this impromptu ceremony believed that Bishop Patterson was passing the torch of COGIC leadership back to Bishop Owens.   Many people thought that Bishop Owens had another chance to become presiding bishop during the 2008 election. The 2008 presiding bishop election featured a showdown between Bishop Owens and the First Administrative Assistant to Bishop G.E. Patterson, Bishop Charles Blake. Bishop G.E. Patterson died on March 20, 2007 while serving his second term. Bishop Blake took charge as presiding bishop until the election of 2008.

8.5. BISHOP CHARLES EDWARD BLAKE ERA, 2007-PRESENT

The years of 2007 and 2008 in COGIC saw the end of the era of G.E. Patterson and some hope for a renewed candidacy of Bishop Owens. In 2008, Bishop Charles Blake had secured a commanding lead in votes that made the situation futile for Bishop Owens to return to office. So, in November 2008, Bishop Charles E. Blake was installed as the fifth presiding bishop and seventh national leader of COGIC, Inc.

Bishop Charles Edward Blake was born in Little Rock, Arkansas on August 5, 1940, to Bishop Junious Augustus Blake, Sr. and Lula Champion Blake. Bishop J.A. Blake, Sr. served in the state of Arkansas before being assigned to southern California. Bishop J.A. Blake, Sr. also was one of the first twelve bishops selected in 1968 to serve on COGIC's new General Board. Bishop Blake's father had greatly impacted the COGIC movement in the state of California and on the national scene, so he followed in his father's footsteps. He married Mae Lawrence and he currently pastors West Angeles COGIC in Los Angeles. West Angeles COGIC has an estimated 25,000 members, including celebrities like Earvin "Magic" Johnson, Denzel Washington, Courtney Vance and Angela Bassett, George Wallace, and Samuel L. Jackson. Also, on April 6, 2009, Bishop Blake was chosen by President Barack Obama to serve on the twenty-five-person White House Advisory Council on Faith-Based and Neighborhood Partnerships.[46]

Additional accomplishments of Bishop Blake include the following:

1) Founded the program of Save Africa's Children in 2001, which helped over 90,000 children affected by AIDS; 2) Served as the founding Chairman of the Board of Directors for the C. H. Mason Theological Seminary; 3) Served as an Advisory Committee Member for the Pentecostal World Conference; and, 4) Received several awards for his humanitarian works such as the Distinguished Leadership Award from the African Presidential Archives and Research Center in Boston, the Salvation Army's William F. Booth Award, and the Harvard Foundation Humanitarian Medal.[47]

However, there is one feat by Bishop Blake that had been received as a notable accomplishment by some and a notorious action by others. In the year of 2010, the Blake Administration moved the COGIC Annual Holy Convocation from the city of Memphis to the city of St. Louis, Missouri. The Holy Convocation had been in Memphis since 1907, over 100 years. Many COGIC purists were outraged and claimed that Memphis was COGIC's Holy Land, like Jerusalem to the Jews and like Mecca to the Muslims. The move took place in 2010 and the Holy Convocation, by the direction of Blake's leadership, have had no plans of returning the mass meeting to Memphis. Despite the controversial locality change to the Holy Convocation, other issues have been formidable challenges for the Blake Administration. The administration dealt with the problem of immoral allegations against ministers by instituting mandatory background checks for leaders and aspiring leaders in COGIC, Inc.

Additionally, one splinter group emerged under Blake's leadership. The Church of God in Christ America Incorporated was founded by Bishop Ray A. Lee in 2011. Bishop Lee left COGIC, Inc., per his electronic message, because he felt that COGIC, Inc. had left the foundation of Holiness which had been established by Bishop Mason. Bishop Lee desired to maintain the doctrines of the Holiness-Pentecostal traditions of Mason, so he started the COGIC America Incorporated movement with headquarters located in Hammond, Indiana.

Despite the challenges faced by the Blake Administration, the COGIC Women's Department continued to maintain the course of Holiness without bitter fights of politics and doctrine. Supervisor Willie Mae Rivers served under the leadership of a third presiding bishop. Mother Rivers maintained an example of Holiness and righteous leadership through the administrations of Owens, G.E. Patterson, and Blake. During the early years of Blake's administration, some rumors had circulated that the presiding bishop wanted to replace Mother Rivers as COGIC General Supervisor of Women. However, the rumors were soon dismissed as many COGIC women maintained a strong and united front against any notions of replacing the saintly Mother Rivers. Like all the Supervisors of the Women's Department before her tenure, Mother Rivers appeared to have solidified her position with the notion that a successor would be appointed upon her death. Keeping in line with the concept of senior spiritual succession, the successor had always been the first assistant to the General Supervisor of the COGIC Women's Department.

On an interesting note, the First Assistant General Supervisor under Mother Rivers was Mother Barbara McCoo Lewis. Mother McCoo Lewis had become the First Assistant General Supervisor because Mother Rivers' original assistant, appointed under her leadership, had died. Mother McCoo Lewis had served under the leadership of Bishop Blake when he was the state bishop of COGIC Southern California First Jurisdiction. Under Bishop Blake, Mother McCoo Lewis was chosen as his State Supervisor of Women in 1988. She had become the next successor to be the General Supervisor of COGIC's Women Department under the leadership of Presiding Bishop G.E. Patterson. Most recently, another historic event occurred during the Blake administration. On February 8, 2017, Presiding Bishop Blake decided to remove Mother Willie Mae Rivers from the position of COGIC General Supervisor of Women and appointed Mother Barbara McCoo Lewis to lead the national COGIC Women's Department.[48] For the first time in COGIC history, the general supervisor of the COGIC Women's Department did not die in her office. All mothers before Mother Rivers, died in office, and their appointed successor replaced them. The era of Mother Barbara McCoo Lewis began with speculations around the presiding bishop's actions to remove the faithful, long-serving, nonagenarian, Mother Willie Mae Rivers.

Nevertheless, despite moving the Holy Convocation to St. Louis, Missouri and replacing the general supervisor of COGIC women, with great support from Mother McCoo Lewis and other COGIC delegates from California and around the nation, Bishop Blake was consistently voted into leadership by the General Assembly. The General Assembly returned Blake to the position of presiding bishop in

2012, and, recently, 2016. Much like Bishop G.E. Patterson, Presiding Bishop Blake continued the trend of influencing COGIC, Inc. polity with a mega-church mentality and focus. Like Patterson's Temple of Deliverance COGIC and Bountiful Blessings Ministries, Blake's West Angeles COGIC not only had a local impact on the community but also had a global impact around the world outside the walls of COGIC, Inc. Presiding Bishop Blake enhanced and extended the COGIC Church with a focus on global evangelism with concrete humanitarian efforts. Bishop Blake also emphasized COGIC's Pentecostal heritage by releasing a nation-wide program mandate for all COGIC Churches to remember and have services that focused on The Pilgrimage to Pentecost. The purpose of the program was to commemorate Mason's journey to the Azusa Street Revival and how he received the Baptism of the Holy Ghost with evidence of speaking in tongues. Furthermore, Bishop Blake was instrumental in the COGIC's purchase of the house at 214 Bonnie Brae Street in Los Angeles.[49] The house was the meeting place of Elder William J. Seymour, the preacher who started the Azusa Street Revival with the emphasis on the Baptism of the Holy Ghost accompanied by glossolalia. While connecting directly to the past of COGIC Holiness-Pentecostal roots, Bishop Blake faced the challenges of promoting the strict moralities espoused by the founder, Bishop Mason, in the wake of a post-modern era of people that frown upon, what they consider outdated traditions of being holy and sanctified. The answers to those problems will rest upon the direction of COGIC leadership under the current administration.

Ever since the fight over leadership between Senior Bishop O.T. Jones and the Executive Board, COGIC leadership has been mired in the elements of power and politics owing this phenomenon to the election of the first presiding bishop, J.O. Patterson. Even though membership rolls have been estimated to be between three million to six million, much of the spiritual focus and actions established by Bishop Mason have disappeared. Bishops Ford, Owens, G.E. Patterson, and Blake tried to bring back the elements of Pentecost in attempts to recapture the Spirit of Azusa and Mason. However, the new generation of COGIC do not have a connection to or know about the history of Mason and Azusa. Many Pentecostal traits espoused by Mason have disappeared over time. For example, many COGIC Churches no longer have testimony services, a designated part at the beginning of worship services in which the people stood up and gave a testimony ranging from how God had blessed their lives economically to healing their bodies. Old-time spiritual singing, "speaking in tongues", and revivals have almost disappeared from the COGIC landscape; mainly, because the younger generation were not kept abreast of Mason's Pentecostal impact on worship services. Instead of conducting testimony services, COGIC opening services are led by a group of praise singers. The Holy Convocation, with Mason, started with three days of fasting and prayer in Memphis. The Holy Convocation has been moved from Memphis to St. Louis, away from the city that Mason had established as the "Jerusalem" for COGIC members. Bishop Blake made attempts to shed light on Mason's journey to Azusa; however, many members of COGIC are not familiar with the historical significance of Azusa, and many members and clergy are not aware of who founded the Church of God in Christ, Inc. The youth of this present generation of COGIC members need an extensive history lesson on the life of Mason, the doctrines of COGIC, and the lifestyle of being a Holiness-Pentecostal Christian.

EPILOGUE

Works about COGIC history have been incomplete and lacking critical analysis and objective viewpoints. For this project, I tried, with utmost professionalism and intense fact finding, to present a history free of legends, myths, and personal biases. From the beginning of COGIC's name to the global impact of the Blake era, no one had completed an official and certified, comprehensive history on the only major African-American Christian denomination founded and organized by African-Americans. Battling and deciphering all of the previous works done by several historical writers was a monumental task in interpreting the difference between unverifiable claims and facts. For the most part, I acted as a revisionist historian who tried to debunk myths and document actual events without the emphasis on faith and beliefs. The actual event and the exact actions of the persons involved in the events needed an unadulterated perspective without any personal slant. This research focused primarily on Mason, "the man", not Mason "the legend." With this completed project, COGIC members have a verifiable historic work, and future researchers have the opportunity and foundation to build extensive archives of COGIC historical accomplishments.

COGIC in its Holiness-Pentecostal fervor greatly impacted religion in America and around the world. COGIC's leader, Charles H. Mason challenged the notion of a mediocre Christian lifestyle by radically claiming that ordinary people could be "saints" and the people could live a sanctified, holy lifestyle just like the early Christians in biblical times. COGIC belief systems heavily stressed that a person could live like Jesus Christ and be free from the bondage of sin. These claims shook the religious establishment and the responses to Mason's Holiness-Pentecostal doctrines were met with claims that no one is "perfect" and that modern-day Christians could not live up to the standards of the people in the Bible.

Furthermore, Mason's preaching levelled the religious field for all Christians to be equal regardless of race, gender, or socio-economic status, taking a cue from the Bible in the Book of Acts which expounded on God pouring out His Spirit upon "all" flesh. Unlike the specialized category of sainthood in the Catholic Church, Mason preached that everyone had the chance to be a "saint" just by confessing and believing in Jesus. His preaching uplifted and empowered members in rural communities, especially African-Americans, in the segregated South. Mason's Pentecostal message gave hope to those who were bound by the system of sharecropping, giving them an outlet to praise God and believe in a better day. The hope for a better day was about going to heaven, if a person lived righteously.

Mason's leadership example also encouraged the equalization of the pulpit. According to Mason's early theological experience at Arkansas Baptist College in 1893, a preacher only needed the Holy Ghost to preach, not education. This stance on education encouraged other candidates who were "called"[1] to preach, to not worry about having a formal education or attending a seminary to be trained in homiletics, hermeneutics, and pastoring a church. Equalizing the pulpit was a double-edged sword because even though many who claimed to be "called" to preach had an earnest desire to serve God, other candidates who claimed to be "called" sought to take advantage of unsuspecting worshippers through exploitation and financial manipulation. As a man of the people, or as he claimed, God's people, Mason's preaching had several reports of signs and miracles like divine healing, and the wonder of "speaking in tongues", COGIC membership grew dramatically in the rural South and gained many converts in the North as COGIC missionaries and preachers began to evangelize urban centers in Detroit, New York City, Philadelphia, and Chicago.

Beginning with the first mythical reference to how Mason started the COGIC Church, the story of Mason had always been complicated and full of claims that he had started the COGIC Church by the Spirit of God via the Holy Ghost. Basically, God gave Mason the name "Church of God in Christ" and God was leading COGIC to evangelize the world. However, evidence showed that Mason obtained the COGIC name and the COGIC Churches by way of a court case decision in 1909. A court case had decided in Mason's favor, not Divine direction. Now for some COGIC writers, the court decision won by Mason was because of an act of God showing good favor to Mason. Nevertheless, the court case victory launched Mason's long tenure as COGIC, Inc.'s sole leader from 1907 to 1961. The court case, Frank Avant v. C.H. Mason, displayed COGIC's first leadership fight, pitting Mason against the leader, Charles Price Jones. Ironically, Mason and others claimed the importance of obeying leadership; however, some splinter groups formed under Mason's leadership dispelled the myth that everyone in COGIC, Inc. was unified and satisfied under the leadership of Mason. These early forms of political alliances, during a time when everyone was claiming to be in Holiness, provided contradictory reactions to a Christian lifestyle that was based on unadulterated unity and love. Like in every sector of society, power and politics also disrupted Christian unity.

Another point of discovery during this research was the fact that Mason's birthdate had been changed many times during COGIC Inc.'s existence. The U.S. Census data could not verify Mason's birth year and family members were not able to verify the year. I have concluded that Mason did not know his birthdate and that an official panel of

COGIC scholars and other academic professionals are needed to settle the controversy surrounding the different birth years of Mason. The main reason for the meeting would be to have a consensus on the year of Mason's birth for future researchers and advocates of the Holiness-Pentecostal Movement. If an official meeting does not occur, COGIC research and researchers will continue to be without an official birth date for the founder.

Another glaring historical contradiction was Mason's sermon against the Kaiser of Germany during World War I. The sermon needs to be verified as a legitimate sermon preached by Mason or a document attributed to Mason, written by him or a ghost writer. Glaring contradictions existed with the sermon. The date of the sermon and the place that Mason, supposedly, had preached the sermon are inconsistent with the files from the Bureau of Investigation. The Bureau's files appeared to have Mason in federal prison in Jackson, Mississippi, while at the same time, Mason was preaching the sermon on the banks of the Mississippi in North Memphis. The sermon appeared, first, in the historical writings of Professor James Courts and Mary Mason, the daughter of Bishop Mason. However, the sermon did not appear in the historical writings of Bishop Charles Pleas in Fifty Years Achievement, 1906-1956. The events need immediate attention and verification.

Hopefully, with the evidence presented, the legend of the Dark Ages or the Years of Wilderness Wanderings, will be extracted from the writings of COGIC history. The years of 1961-1968 show a plethora of events and people shaping those events. The era is renamed by the author as the O.T. Jones Era. The court cases and letters during the years show many confrontations which were basically kept secretive from the general population of COGIC members, even national leaders. Many of the leaders who I interviewed about the period could only say one thing, "I was there!" As many people attended the convocation during that time, the people did not have inside information about the fights that occurred among COGIC leaders. Tragically, many members and leaders witnessed an outward appearance of normalcy, not knowing that the senior bishop was about to be ousted, making way for another title of leadership, the presiding bishop. Immediately after the ousting of the Senior Bishop, the successors erased Jones' legacy and contributions to the COGIC Church. So many members thought that the lineage of leadership in COGIC, Inc. was passed from Mason to his son-in-law, J.O. Patterson, Sr. More analysis and information about this period are needed to obtain facts of the actual events that changed the course of a Holiness-Pentecostal Movement with a Senior Bishop to a Holiness-political organization with a Presiding Bishop.

Furthermore, this work highlights the contribution of COGIC's sustaining and supporting force known as the Women's Department. Mother Lizzie Robinson, the first General Overseer of Women's Work, establishes the holy standards of dress and conduct for women in the Church. Mother Robinson had several teachings against COGIC women wearing pants, make-up, and dresses that did not come down to the floor. Present-day COGIC women have viewed these regulations as extreme and outdated; however, for that period, Mother Robinson was attempting to separate holy women from unholy women in every facet of life. Basically, Mother Robinson and the Women's Department established themselves as the moral standard bearers of the African-American Holiness-Pentecostal Movement. Moreover, COGIC women like Mother Lillian Brooks-Coffey and Missionary Arenia Mallory were successful in joining Mary McLeod Bethune in promoting gender and racial equality, along with encouraging some educational foundations among COGIC leaders and members. Mallory led the growth of Saints Industrial Academy from a secondary school to a two-year college. Also, to this date, Mallory, who succeeded Professor James Courts, was the only female leader of an established COGIC College. Most of all, the prominent facet of leadership among COGIC women dealt with the succession of women as the General Overseer of Women's Work, with the title changing to the General Supervisor of the Women's Department. Each COGIC female leader was groomed for the position and had seniority which prevented fighting, court cases, and rampant ambition. Except for the year 2017, each general supervisor of COGIC women had died in office. Mother Willie Mae Rivers was the first supervisor who did not die in office and was appointed general supervisor emeritus by Presiding Bishop Blake. According to Presiding Bishop Blake's letter, Mother Rivers had served the church faithfully for many years, and he felt that the time was ripe for the Women's Department to have a new leader, Mother Barbara McCoo Lewis, who had served faithfully under his leadership in the state of California. COGIC male leadership could have learned from the early examples of transitioning female leadership, in which, no one ever went to court.

Another great impact on COGIC History was the constant creation of splinter groups. The splinter groups, for the most part, came about for two different reasons and during two different eras. The first splinter groups occurred during the Mason Era from 1912 to 1961. Those splinter groups differed with Mason on the grounds of biblical or theological doctrines. For example, Elias Dempsey Smith of Triumph the Church and Kingdom of God in Christ believed that the physical body could live forever after transformation occurred during a Holy Ghost spiritual trance. Mason disagreed with this doctrine citing scripture about people dying and going to heaven after death. COGIC Congregational started by Bishop Justus Bowe disagreed with Mason on whether the Church congregation could appoint the pastor or if the pastor should be appointed by the bishop. Mason disagreed with Bowe and this feud landed both parties in court in Pine Bluff, Arkansas.

Another disagreement over doctrine occurred with Bishop Randolph A. Carr in 1947. Mason and Carr disagreed over the age-old fight of the proper baptismal formula that pitched the Apostolic denominations against Holiness-Pentecostal denominations. Mason believed that a person should be baptized in the name of the Father, Son, and Holy Ghost, the Trinitarian formula. Bishop Carr did not concur and believed that a person should be baptize in Jesus' name only, the Unitarian formula.

During the Post-Mason Era in 1961, most COGIC splinter groups formed over the issue of proper or godly inspired leadership and succession. During the tumultuous years of the 1960s, many COGIC splinter groups like COGIC of America, Inc., COGIC, United, and COGIC International, did not agree with the ousting of Mason's successor, Senior Bishop O.T. Jones, Sr. They also wanted to keep the title of Senior Bishop as the national head of the Church. So, these splinter groups refused to remain under the transitioning leadership of the COGIC, Inc. Presiding Bishop. Many of the splinter group leaders felt that the legacy of Mason was being disrespected and dismantled with the acceptance of the title Presiding Bishop because Mason had chosen to be called Senior Bishop. After viewing all the splinter groups from Mason to the current time, for unification purposes, these groups could be contacted for reconciliation. Reconciliation could occur if COGIC, Inc. leadership offered to extend a hand of fellowship and consider bringing the splinter groups back under the COGIC, Inc. umbrella. COGIC, Inc. and the splinter groups could benefit from the unification and resources available in each organization. Bishop Willie Harris of COGIC Congregational was considering the proposal of being under the leadership of COGIC, Inc. However, many obstacles of pride and ambition may stand in the way of the consideration of a unification proposal.

Overall, researching and discovering the different facets of the only major Christian denomination in the United States founded, solely, by African-Americans has been a monumental task, specifically dealing with the revision of its comprehensive history. At the beginning of COGIC history, several persons did historical writings but not historical research and verification. Specific works conducted by Professor James Courts, Mary Mason, and Bishop Charles Pleas were not analytical in nature, but, mostly celebratory. Later works conducted by Bishop Ithiel Clemmons and Dr. Bobby Bean attempted to provide scholarship in COGIC history, but, again, the history celebrations can easily be seen in their writings about the legend of Bishop Mason. However, Bean and Clemmons gave sketches of a COGIC historical timeline to show how the denomination progressed from a religious movement under Mason to a political-religious organization under a presiding bishop. Additionally, studies conducted by Calvin White and Anthea Butler provided specific looks at two COGIC aspects: civil involvement and the contribution of COGIC women, respectively. Calvin White, along with the dissertation by Jonathan Chism, dispelled the longtime notions that the COGIC Church only cared about "jumping and shouting" and going to heaven. White documented how COGIC played a major role during the death of Emmitt Till and how Medgar Evers was reared in the COGIC Church by his mother. Chism provided evidence of how several COGIC preachers in Memphis, like G.E. and J.O. Patterson, participated in the Sanitation Worker's Strike. Also, Mason Temple served as the meeting site for the strikers, supporters, and civil rights leaders. Additionally, Butler documented the COGIC leadership in the Women's Department by displaying the lasting friendship between Mother Coffey, Dr. Mallory, and Mary McLeod Bethune. Coffey and Mallory served on the National Council of Negro Women. COGIC was involved in civil rights, gender rights, and racial equality as it preached a message of living sanctified and holy.

My research and analysis covered the history of COGIC, Inc. from three main eras that focused around the life of Bishop Mason, starting with a will to promote the Baptism of the Holy Ghost to the political battles for power and leadership within the institution. This research presented more participants with the idea of a third phase of salvation, the Baptism of the Holy Ghost, and displayed how several groups were berthed from that idea. Splinter groups helped to proliferate the COGIC name and legacy, reaching areas of Canada, the Caribbean, and other nations around the world. On the most important note, the narrative of an extensive historical documentation of COGIC events was conducted without accepting legends as facts and challenging all other historic works completed on the COGIC faith. Hopefully, in the future, COGIC researchers can finally provide concrete answers to the controversies surrounding the founder's birthdate, Mason's sermon on the Kaiser in 1918, and the troublesome years of 1961-1968.

At the beginning of the Black Holiness Movement that started with Charles Price Jones, Mason and other preachers sought a higher standard of Christian living. The early Holiness preachers re-focused on a renewed belief that the Bible was the supreme authority for a Christian to obey and live by, despite living in a sinful world. Jones and Mason started a church with emphasis on African legacies of dancing, Spirit-possession, and a call-and-response type style. Even though both men had noble efforts in trying to establish a church led by God, relationships became strained after Mason returned from Azusa with a new Pentecostal mindset, adding the requirement that all Christians not only had to live holy, but they also had to "speak in tongues" to provide evidence that they had been baptized with the Holy Ghost.

Azusa was a turning point for Mason and other preachers who proclaimed that they had direct communication with God, created mass followings, oversaw demonstrative worship services, and claimed acts of unexplained wonders and biblical miracles. Mason was a charismatic leader who was often viewed by his huge number of followers as God's prophet. Mason had several contemporaries in America from the early to mid-1900s. Father Divine, another charismatic prophet, was an attendee at Azusa in 1906, a year before Mason came to the revival. Divine founded the Peace Mission Movement and the members who followed his ministry considered him to be God.[2] Divine's Movement was initially based in Harlem, New York with Pentecostal-like services of people shouting, dancing, and "speaking in tongues." Also, in Harlem, Charles Grace, known as Sweet Daddy Grace, developed a movement of people who espoused Holiness and Pentecostalism. Grace was notoriously known as the preacher who evicted God (Father Divine) from his Number One Heaven building in Harlem in 1938.[3] Another contemporary of Mason was Prophet James "Papa" Jones out of Detroit, Michigan. Prophet Jones was a product of Elias Smith's movement, Triumph the Church and Kingdom of God in Christ. Like Father Divine and Daddy Grace, Prophet Jones was often called God by his followers or considered the exclusive messenger of God because he claimed that he was the only true prophet in the world. Unlike Father Divine, Daddy Grace, and Prophet Jones, Mason built an organization with a servant mentality, not allowing himself to be considered God, but only a common servant of God who had been anointed by the Holy Spirit. Mason's COGIC Church faced many challenges after his death, however, the bulk of the membership remained faithful to the COGIC brand of Holiness-Pentecostalism. Mason and his contemporaries were prime examples of how post-modern day Christian preachers launched the mega-church movement.

The mega-church movement, with examples of the Potter's House in Dallas, Texas with Pastor T.D. Jakes, the World Changers Church in Atlanta, Georgia with Pastor Creflo Dollar, and Lakewood Church in Houston, Texas with Pastor Joel Osteen, are offsprings of the Holiness-Pentecostal Movement once dominated by the COGIC Church. Mainly, the mega-church movement capitalized on the examples of mass gatherings of Christians accomplished by Mason's Holy Convocation and departmental conferences. Also, mega-churches have one central leader who has a claim that he is anointed by God to bring the Gospel of Jesus Christ to the people in order to make their spiritual and economic situations prosperous. Like Mason's leadership, the mega-church pastor's leadership is not to be questioned, but followed. From the 1900s to the 1960s, Mason's goal focused heavily on saving souls for Christ; however, the mega-church movement has focused on prosperity and the preachers have morphed into motivational speakers, not particularly preaching about sin and salvation. Many of the church services have become impersonal and commercialized as the practice of live streaming begins to be a popular venue of attending church without leaving the confinement of one's home.

Despite the trend from the spiritual legacy of Mason to church entertainment and commercialization, COGIC members can be proud of the fact that their faith had legacies connected to the Civil Rights Movement concerning the death of Emmett Till, the early influences of Reverend Al Sharpton and Medgar Evers, to the involvement of clergy and members in the Memphis Sanitation Workers' Strike. Moreover, with an unlikely service to the Black Muslim community, Bishop Alvin A. Childs allowed the funeral rites of Malcolm X to be conducted in Faith Temple COGIC. Childs refused to succumb to religious prejudice against the Black Muslin faith, but showed Christian compassion in its greatest form of love and mercy.

Without a doubt, the greatest contribution from COGIC to the United States and the world has been the proliferation of music that was formed in the African-American community, especially the mainstreaming of gospel music. Musical legends connected to the COGIC faith include the following entertainers: Rosetta Tharpe, Sam Cooke, Billy Preston, KC and the Sunshine Band, Sylvester, The Hawkins Singers, The Weather Girls, Maurice White of Earth, Wind, and Fire, The Winans, The Clark Sisters, and Kelly Price. Plus, COGIC Gospel Choirs gained a reputation for being superb in song and musicianship, and this reputation has continued into the postmodern era.

After researching the contributions of COGIC to the world and Christendom, the general membership of COGIC have an official reference of scholarly work on the founding and development of the church formed by Bishop Charles Mason. Also, followers in the COGIC denomination now have an historical body of work, not based primarily on legend and hearsay. Furthermore, COGIC members have a church that has survived challenges and setbacks for about 120 years. COGIC survived the first split among the leadership, Mason and Charles Price Jones, in 1907 and the court case that followed, with a victory for Mason. COGIC survived years of segregation in the Deep South and conducted interracial services during the upstart era of Jim Crow when Mason led a group of White COGIC preachers. Mason and COGIC persevered through several intra-denominational splits from Triumph the Church and Kingdom of God in Christ in

1912, from the Assemblies of God in 1914, from United Church of God in Christ in 1980, and from Church of God in Christ America, Incorporated in 2011. The Church endured over fifteen documented intra-denominational splinter groups, and maintained a strong membership standing with the second largest church membership in the African-American religious sector behind the National Baptist Convention, USA. Through the World War I persecution for being conscientious objectors and through the harsh economic downturn of the Great Depression, the COGIC Church survived political persecution and severe financial challenges, but still planted churches throughout the United States and the world. There was COGIC participation in the era of Civil Rights, from the funeral of Emmitt Till in 1955 to organizational meetings at Mason Temple in 1968. Also, COGIC leaders have hosted several US Presidents: Lyndon Johnson, James Earl Carter, Bill Clinton, George W. Bush, and Barack Obama. The Church incredibly advanced from an old cotton gin house in Lexington, Mississippi to a national institution hosting several dignitaries and participating in presidential initiatives.

Moreover, this Church served as a beacon of hope for the poor and rural Black communities of the South and urban areas of the North. Many African-American males had an outlet for leadership as they advanced from lay members to clergy in COGIC. In leadership roles, COGIC preachers were, for the most part, receiving ample funds as pastors to operate their local church and provide the necessities for their families. The COGIC Church provided leadership opportunities for women to help and train members to be ambassadors for Christ through the Home and Foreign Mission Department. If the tradition of Mason's Holiness-Pentecostalism message was to survive and thrive in this present age, the COGIC Church will have to maintain its foundation in helping the poor, continue to promote racial diversity and inter-gender leadership, recruit and educate the younger generation, and develop spiritual strategies to address the social problems of this post-modern society.

ENDNOTES

List of Key Terms Definitions

1. "Megachurch Definition," Hartford Institute for Religion Research, accesse September 27, 2017, http://hirr.hartsem.edu/megachurch/definition.html

Introduction

1. Albert J. Raboteau, *Slave Religion* (New York: Oxford University Press, 1978), 8.
2. C. Eric Lincoln and Lawrence Mamiya, *The Black Church in the African-American Experience* (Durham, NC: Duke University Press, 1990), 23.
3. E. Franklin Frazier, *The Negro Church in America* (New York: Shocken Books, 1975), 33.
4. National Baptist Convention, USA, Inc., "About Us," http://nationalbaptist.com/about-us/index.html(accessed March 15, 2016).
5. Allan Anderson, *An Introduction to Pentecostalism* (New York: Cambridge University Press, 2004), 40.
6. C. Vann Woodward, *The Strange Career of Jim Crow* (New York: Oxford University Press, 2002), 67.
7. Nikolai Bukharin & Evgeny Preobrazhensky, *The ABC of Communism: A Popular Explanation of the Program of the Communist Party of Russia* (Ann Arbor, MI: University of Michigan Press, 1966), 218.
8. J.O. Patterson, German Ross, and Julia Atkins, History and the Formative Years of the Church of God in Christ (Memphis, TN: Church of God in Christ Publishing House, 1969), 23.
9. The first dispensation(work) of grace was called confession. At the point of confession, the converted sinner accepted Jesus Christ as their Savior and becomes a Christian. In the Christian denominations like the Baptists and Methodists, and later Oneness Pentecostalism, the first dispensation(work) of grace included confession, sanctification/holiness, and the Baptism of the Holy Ghost. With Jones and Mason, confession and sanctification/holiness are two separated phases of salvation.
10. Vinson Synan, *The Holiness-Pentecostal Tradition: Charismatic Movements of the Twentieth Century* (Grand Rapids, MI: William B. Eerdmans, 1997), 36.
11. Ithiel Clemmons, *Bishop C.H. Mason and the Roots of the Church of God in Christ* (Bakersfield, CA: Pneuma Life Publishing, 1996), 37.
12. Ibid., 52.
13. Bobby Bean, *This is the Church of God in Christ* (Atlanta, GA: Underground Epics Publishing, 2001), 39.
14. German Ross, *History and the Formative Years of the Church of God in Christ,* 41.

15. Bean, 10.

16. Charles H. Pleas, *Fifty Years Achievement: A Period of History of the Church of God in Christ from 1906-1956* (1956, repr., Memphis, TN: Church of God in Christ, 1991), 103.

17. The Black Baptist Church was established in 1733 when the White slave owner of the Bryan Plantation allowed the slaves to have a church in Silver Bluff, South Carolina. The Black Methodists Churches, AME (African Methodist Episcopal) and AME Zion, started as a protest movement when White congregants barred Black parishioners from praying at the altar, at the front of the church. After Slavery, the CME (Colored Methodist Episcopal, now called Christian Methodist Episcopal) group separated in 1870 from the White Methodist Episcopal, South Church during Reconstruction.

18. Larry E. Martin, *The Life and Ministry of William J. Seymour and a History of the Azusa Street Revival* (Pensacola, FL: Christian Life Books, 2006), 198.

19. Ithiel C. Clemmons, *Bishop C. H. Mason and the Roots of the Church of God in Christ*, 25.

20. Bobby Bean, *This is the Church of God in Christ,* 10.

21. Ithiel C. Clemmons, *Bishop C. H. Mason and the Roots of the Church of God in Christ*, 61. Under Charles Jones' leadership, the movement would morph into the Church of God in Christ, an unincorporated religious body from 1897 to 1907.

22. Calvin McBride, *Walking into a New Spirituality: Chronicling the Life, Ministry, and Contributions of Elder Robert E. Hart* (Lincoln, NE: iUniverse, 2007), 138.

23. Calvin McBride, *Frank Avant vs C.H. Mason: Mason and the Holy Ghost on Trial* (Bloomington, IN: iUniverse, 2009), 27.

24. Ithiel Clemmons, *Bishop C.H. Mason and the Roots of the Church of God in Christ*, 61.

25. Calvin White, Jr., *The Rise to Respectability: Race, Religion, and the Church of God in Christ* (Fayetteville, AR: University of Arkansas Press, 2012), 39.

26. Calvin McBride, *Frank Avant v. C H Mason*, 5.

27. Surely, if Mason and his COGIC opponents had adhered to the Biblical mandate of spirituality, he would have been faced with the Scripture about "not taking your brother before the courts." First Corinthians, Chapter 6 chastised Christians who go to the law before the unjust instead of going before the saints.

28. Larry E. Martin, *The Life and Ministry of William J. Seymour and a History of the Azusa Street Revival*, 217.

29. Charles H. Pleas, *Fifty Years Achievement*, 6.

30. Calvin McBride, *Frank Avant vs C.H. Mason*, 53.

31. Calvin White, Jr, *The Rise to Respectability: Race, Religion, and the Church of God in Christ*, 97.

32. Cheryl Townsend Gilkes, *If it Wasn't for the Women* (New York: Orbis Books, 2001), 83.

33. Anthea Butler, *Women in the Church of God in Christ: Making a Sanctified*

World (Chapel Hill, NC: University of North Carolina Press, 2007), 44.

34.   Ibid., 76.

35.   COGICC, *Manual of the Church of God in Christ Congregational* (East St. Louis, IL: COGICC, 1946), 3.

36.   First Corinthians 6:1-7, forbade Christians to take church matters before an ungodly judge. The disputes should be judged by other Christians.

37.   Calvin White, Jr, *The Rise to Respectability: Race, Religion, and the Church of God in Christ*, 138.

38.   The period called the "Dark Ages of the Church of God in Christ" was used in COGIC Historical works by Bishop J. O. Patterson, Sr. and Bishop German Ross, *History and Formative Years of Church of God in Christ*, written in 1969. The COGIC Official Manual of 1973 also listed the same period as the Dark Ages. In 2001, COGIC history instructor, Dr. Bobby Bean, referenced the Dark Age Period in his book, *This is the Church of God in Christ*. Even though Dr. Robert R. Owens challenged the interpretation of the period and gave different conclusions, yet he referenced the period in his book, *Never Forget: The Dark Years of COGIC History.*

39.   Bobby Bean, *This is the Church of God in Christ*, 98.

40.   Ibid., 99.

41.   Ithiel Clemmons, *Bishop C.H. Mason and the Roots of the Church of God in Christ, 135.*

42.   Vinson Synan, *The Holiness-Pentecostal Tradition: Charismatic Movements in the Twentieth Century,* 2nd ed. (Grand Rapids, MI: William B. Eerdmans, 1997), 289.

Chapter 1
Baptist and Holiness foundations of COGIC

1.   Paul Harvey, *Freedom's Coming: Religious Culture and the Shaping of the South from the Civil War Through the Civil Rights Era* (Chapel Hill, NC: University of North Carolina Press, 2005), 146.

2.   E. Franklin Frazier, *The Negro Church in America* (New York: Schocken Books, 1974), 24.

3.   Eugene D. Genovese, *Roll, Jordan, Roll* (New York: Vintage Books, 1976), 263-264.

4.   C. Eric Lincoln & Lawrence H. Mamiya, *The Black Church in the African-American Experience*, 25.

5.   Eugene D. Genovese, *Roll, Jordan, Roll*, 263.

6.   C. Eric Lincoln & Lawrence H. Mamiya, *The Black Church in the African-American Experience*, 28.

7.   Ibid., 26.

8.   Synan, *The Holiness-Pentecostal Tradition*, xi.

9.   Ibid.

10. Ithiel C. Clemmons, *Bishop C.H. Mason and the Roots of the Church of God in Christ*, 5.

11. Vinson Synan, *The Holiness-Pentecostal Tradition*, 42-46.

12. Randall J. Stephens, The Fire Spreads: Holiness and Pentecostalism in the American South (Cambridge, MA: Harvard University Press, 2008), 17.

13. Bobby Bean, This is the Church of God in Christ, 38.

14. Randall J. Stephens, The Fire Spreads, 62.

15. Ibid.

16. Allan Anderson, An Introduction to Pentecostalism, 39.

17. C.F. Range and Clyde Young, eds., Church of God in Christ Official Manual (Memphis, TN: Board of Publications of COGIC, Inc., 1973), XXVII-XXVIII.

18. Bobby Bean, This is the Church of God in Christ, 20.

19. Larry E. Martin, The Life and Ministry of William J. Seymour, 72.

20. Iain MacRobert, The Black Roots and White Racism of Early Pentecostalism in the USA (Eugene, OR: Wipf and Stock Publishers, 2003), 51.

21. Ibid., 52.

22. Bishop Charles E. Blake, interview by *The Whole Truth*, Los Angeles, California, September 1, 2014.

23. Larry E. Martin, *The Life and Ministry of William J. Seymour and a History of the Azusa Street Revival*, 197.

24. Ithiel C. Clemmons, Bishop C. H. Mason and the Roots of the Church of God in Christ, 62.

25. Anita Bingham Jefferson, Charles Price Jones: First Black Holiness Reformer (Florence, MS: Stephens Printing, 2011), 68.

26. German Ross, *History and the Formative Years of the Church of God in Christ*, 22.

27. Elias C. Morris, Sermons, Addresses and Reminiscences of Important Correspondence, With a Picture Gallery of Eminent Ministers and Scholars (Nashville, TN: National Baptist Publishing Board, 1901), 32, accessed June 22, 2017, http://docsouth.unc.edu/church/morris/morris.html.

28. Ibid.

29. Paul Harvey, Freedom's Coming, 147.

30. C.F. Range and Clyde Young, eds., *Church of God in Christ Official Manual*, 146.

Chapter 2
The Pre-Mason Era: Jones and Mason Proclaimed Holiness

1. Anita B. Jefferson, *Charles Price Jones: First Black Holiness Reformer* (Jackson, MS: Jefferson, 2011), 8.

2. Ibid., 8,9.

3. Mary Peak Patterson, telephone conversation with the author, June 21, 2017. Ms. Patterson is the widow and second wife of Presiding Bishop J.O. Patterson, Sr.

She coordinates tours of COGIC holy sites in Lexington, Mississippi and Memphis, Tennessee.

4.   For example, for about thirty plus years, Bishop Mason's birth had been documented as September 8, 1866. Writers such as Bishop Ithiel Clemmons, Dr. Bobby Bean, Dr. Anthea Butler, Dr. Calvin White, and others have used the date of September 8, 1866. However, unknown to the publishers and others in the Pentecostal COGIC field of study, the date was changed by a panel as of 2014 to September 8, 1864. The panel led by a COGIC scholar named Dr. David Daniels found an 1870 census that showed that Charles Mason was five years old marking his birth date in the year of 1864. The controversy does not stop with the 1870 census. Further research has yielded other conflicting birth dates. Mason's obituary had the date of September 8, 1862 and one of his daughters, Leila Mason Byas, stated that he was born September 8, 1863. For the most part, these inconsistencies have warned this researcher of the precautionary measures to be undertaken for the verification of accurate information. Here are the following results of my research on of US Census records on Mason's birthdate:

1860 Census—Found a Charles Mason, not sure if its Bishop Mason. More research needed.

1870 Census—Mason is 5 years old, born in Tennessee, birth year 1864

1880 Census—Mason is 14 years old, born in Tennessee, birth year 1865

1890 Census—records were burned during the fire at the Washington DC depositories

1900 Census—Mason was not found in the census records for this year

1910 Census—Mason is 44 years old, born in Tennessee, birth year 1865

1920 Census—Mason is 50 years old, born in Arkansas, birth year 1869

1930 Census—Mason is 55 years old, born in Tennessee, birth year 1874

1940 Census—Mason is 74 years old, born in Arkansas, birth year 1865

5.   Ithiel C. Clemmons, *Bishop C H Mason and the Roots of the Church of God in Christ*, 5.

6.   A "calling" in the American religious experience upon one's life was defined as a spiritual appointment from God to go around the world and preach the Gospel of Jesus Christ so that people could be saved from their sins.

7   Ithiel C. Clemmons, Bishop C.H. Mason and the Roots of the Church of God in Christ, 5

8.   German Ross, *History and the Formative Years of the Church of God in Christ*, 22.

9.   Ibid., 16.

10. Iain Macrobert, *The Black Roots and White Racism of Early Pentecostalism in the USA*, 39.

11. Anita Bingham Jefferson, *Charles Price Jones: First Black Holiness Reformer*, 41.

12   Ibid., 51.

13   Ibid., 55.

14. Bobby Bean, *This is the Church of God in Christ*, 10.

15. Charles H. Pleas, *Fifty Years Achievement*, 5.

16. Calvin McBride, *Frank Avant v. C H Mason*: Mason, 9.

17. Church of God in Christ, Mennonite, "Who We Are," Church of God in Christ, Mennonite, accessed July 14, 2016, http://churchofgodinchristmennonite.net/en/who_we_are.

18. Ibid.

19. Calvin McBride, *Frank Avant v. C.H. Mason: Mason and the Holy Ghost on Trial*, 10.

20. German R. Ross, *History and Formative Years of the Church of God in Christ*, 15.

21. Ibid., 16.

22. Anita B. Jefferson, *Charles Price Jones: First Black Holiness Reformer,* 9.

23. Ithiel C. Clemmons, *Bishop C.H. Mason and the Roots of the Church of God in Christ*, 23.

24. Ibid., 24.

25. German R. Ross, *History and Formative Years of the Church of God in Christ*, 16.

Chapter 3
The Turmoil Around Tongues and the First Court Case

1. Estrelda Y. Alexander, *Limited Liberty: The Legacy of Four Pentecostal Women Pioneers* (Cleveland, OH: Pilgrim Press, 2008), 38.

2. Larry Martin, *The Life and Ministry of William J. Seymour*, 183.

3. Ibid., 181.

4. C.F. Range and Clyde Young, eds., *Church of God in Christ Official Manual*, xxvi.

5. Larry E. Martin, *The Life and Ministry of William J. Seymour*, 216.

6. German Ross, *History and the Formative Years of the Church of God in Christ*, 19.

7. Elsie Mason, *The Man, Charles Harrison Mason* (1866-1961) (Memphis, TN: COGIC Publishing House, 1979), 15-19.

8. C.F. Range and Clyde Young, eds., *Church of God in Christ Official Manual*, xxvii-xxviii.

9. Larry E. Martin, *The Life and Ministry of William J. Seymour*, 91.

10. Ibid., 269-270.

11. Ithiel C. Clemmons, *Bishop C.H. Mason and the Roots of the Church of God in Christ*, 49.

12. Ibid., 50.

13. Ibid., 48-49.

14. Larry E. Martin, *The Life and Ministry of William J. Seymour*, 287.

15. Ibid., 287-288.

16. Robert R. Owens, *Never Forget: The Dark Years of COGIC History* (Fairfax, VA: Xulon Press, 2002), 28-29.

17. C.F Range, *Church of God in Christ Official Manual*, XXVIII-XXIX.

18. In Bobby Bean's work, there were several white COGIC preachers. Leonard P. Adams was the overseer of the White COGIC. This White COGIC Church was complying with the segregation laws of the South. Another white COGIC overseer was William Holt. Holt became the first COGIC general secretary under Mason's leadership. Eudorus N. Bell was one of the key founders of the Assemblies of God Pentecostal denomination.

19. Calvin McBride, *Frank Avant v. C.H. Mason: Mason and the Holy Ghost on Trial*, 20.

20. Ibid., 21.

21. Calvin McBride, *Frank Avant v. C.H. Mason: Mason and the Holy Ghost on Trial*, 30-33.

22. Ibid.

23. Ibid., 90.

24. Ibid., 103.

25. Ibid., 230.

26. Ibid., 236.

Mason's justification for tongues was found in Saint Mark, chapter 16 and First Corinthians, chapter 12.

27. Ibid., 321.

28. Ibid., 329.

29. Ibid.

30. Ibid., 259.

31. Ibid., 37.

32. Ibid., iv.

33. Ibid.

34. Ibid., vi.

35. Robert R. Owens, *Never Forget: The Dark Years of COGIC History*, 31.

36. Ithiel C. Clemmons, *Bishop C. H. Mason and the Roots of the Church of God in Christ*, 66.

37. Anita Bingham Jefferson, *Charles Price Jones: First Black Holiness Reformer,* 72-73.

38. Ibid., 69.

39. Ithiel C. Clemmons, *Bishop C.H. Mason and the Roots of the Church of God in Christ*, 65.

40. Anita Bingham Jefferson, *Charles Price Jones: First Black Holiness Reformer*, 69.

41. Ibid., 72.

42. The years 1895, 1896, and 1897 have been used in conjunction with Mason's spiritual experience walking down Gaines Street in Little Rock, Arkansas. The date of 1897 has been finalized for that year of Mason's walk down Gaines Street with a supporting Scripture of First Thessalonians 2:14; however, Mason was under the leadership of General Overseer Charles Jones making Charles Jones the main leader and head founder of the movement. So, the year of 1897 could not be appropriated

for the Church of God in Christ under Mason's leadership. As of this current day, the founding year has been 1907. The year 1907 corresponded with the event of Mason being banished from the Holiness Assembly by Jones and then calling an assembly to bring preachers together who believed in the evidence of "tongues" being a sign of the Holy Ghost. The problem with the founding year of 1907 is the fact that all COGIC members and property were locked in a court case from 1907-1909, and further litigation over the COGIC name lasted until 1926. Another interesting observation was that Mason's COGIC body was registered in Mississippi as the Church of God in Christ of America. So, the year 1907 as a founding year of Mason's COGIC Church could be challenged with supporting documentation from court cases.

43. (COGICA) Churches of God in Christ of America, Inc., International, accessed January 22, 2014, http://bishopdrralphljohnson.webs.com/.

Chapter 4
First Phase of The Mason Era (1907-1933): COGIC Departments

1. Anthea Butler, *Women in the Church of God in Christ: Making a Sanctified World* (Chapel Hill, NC: University of North Carolina Press, 2007), 78.

2. Ibid., 55.

3. German Ross, *History and the Formative Years of the Church of God in Christ*, 16.

4. Bobby Bean, This is the Church of God in Christ, 124.

5. Ibid.

6. German Ross, *History and the Formative Years of the Church of God in Christ*, 126.

7. Anthea D. Butler, *Women in the Church of God in Christ: Making a Sanctified World*, 12-13.

8. Ibid., 13, 48.

9. German Ross, *History and the Formative Years of the Church of God in Christ*, 126-127.

10. Bobby Bean, *This is the Church of God in Christ*, 155.

11. "Women's Page," *The Whole Truth*, February 1968, 3.

12. Ibid.

13. Anthea D. Butler, *Women in the Church of God in Christ: Making a Sanctified World*, 15.

14. Ibid., 40.

15. Leonard M. Payne, *My People Yesterday, Today and Forever: History of the Glorious Church of God in Christ* (St. Clairsville, OH: Xlibris Corporation, 2008), 29.

16. Ibid., 26.

17. Mary Mason, *The History and Life Work of Bishop C. H. Mason* (Memphis, TN: Church of God in Christ, Inc, 1924), 13.

18. Mary Mason, *The History and Life Work of Bishop C. H. Mason*, 5.

19. Leonard M. Payne, *My People Yesterday, Today and Forever: History of the*

Glorious Church of God in Christ, 40.

20. Ibid., 44.

21. John Kobler, "Prophet Jones: Messiah in Mink," Saturday Evening Post, March 5, 1955, accessed June 21, 2017, http://eds.b.ebscohost.com.ezproxy.gsu.edu/

22. Ibid.

23. Ibid.

24. Ibid.

25. Bobby Bean, *This is the Church of God in Christ*, 126.

26. Ibid.

27. Charles H. Pleas, *Fifty Years Achievement,* 23.

28. Robert E. Coleman, Jr., ed., "The General Board Members of the Church of God in Christ, Inc.," The Whole Truth, July 2014, 9.

29. The Assemblies of God, "History," The Assemblies of God Faith, http://ag.org/top/About/History/index.cfm (accessed March 3, 2014).

30. Bobby Bean, *This is the Church of God in Christ*, 133.

31. Church of God in Christ, Inc., *From the Beginning of Bishop C.H. Mason and the Early Pioneers of the Church of God in Christ* (Memphis, TN: COGIC Publishing House, 1991), 127.

32. In 1955, Roberts Temple COGIC was the site of Emmett Till's funeral; he was murdered in Money, Mississippi for not talking "properly in deference" to a White woman.

33. Anthea Butler, *Women in the Church of God in Christ: Making as Sanctified World*, 58.

34. Charles Pleas, *Fifty Years Achievement*, 64.

35. C. F. Range, *Church of God in Christ Official Manual*, XXIX.

36. First Church of God in Christ, "Our History," The First Church of God in Christ, Fort Smith, Arkansas, http://www.first-cogic.org/history.html (accessed November 25, 2014).

37. Northern Mississippi Ecclesiastical Jurisdiction Church of God in Christ, "History," Northern Mississippi Ecclesiastical Jurisdiction Church of God in Christ, http://nmcogic.org/about-us/history (accessed July 30, 2016).

38. Ibid.

39. Larry E. Martin, *The Life and Ministry of William J. Seymour,* 183.

40. Marthene Talley Penn, *The Early Years C.O.G.I.C. North Georgia: Before there were Jurisdictions* (Columbus, GA: Brentwood Christian Press, 2003), 15.

41. Southern California Second Jurisdiction Church of God in Christ, "About Southern California Second," Southern California Second Jurisdiction Church of God in Christ, http://socal2nd.org/about/ (accessed July 25, 2016).

42. Charles H. Pleas, *Fifty Years Achievement*, 15.

43. Church of God in Christ, Inc., *From the Beginning of Bishop C.H. Mason and the Early Pioneers of the Church of God in Christ*, 49.

44. Bobby Bean, *This is the Church of God in Christ,* 129

45. Church of God in Christ, *Church of God in Christ Official Manual*, XXIX-XXX.
46. Ithiel Clemmons, *Bishop C. H. Mason and the Roots of the Church of God in Christ*, 76.
47. Church of God in Christ, *Church of God in Christ Official Manual*, XXX.
48. Ithiel Clemmons, *Bishop C.H. Mason and the Roots of the Church of God in Christ*, 77.
49. Church of God in Christ, Inc., *"Minutes of the 12th General Convocation,"* Memphis, TN, December 10, 1919.
50. Church of God in Christ, Inc., *"Minutes of the 13th General Convocation,"* Memphis, TN, December 8, 1920.
51. Calvin White, Jr., *The Rise to Respectability: Race, Religion, and the Church of God in Christ* (Fayetteville, AR: University of Arkansas Press, 2012), 59.
52. Bureau of Investigation, *Mason-Colored Preacher Alleged Openly Advised Against Registering.........., Treasonable & Seditious Remarks Against United States Government*, by Agent Schaumburger. Investigation. Lexington, MS. 1917.
53. Ibid.
54. Calvin White, Jr., *The Rise to Respectability: Race, Religion, and the Church of God in Christ*, 66-67.
55. Church of God in Christ, Inc., *From the Beginning of Bishop C.H. Mason and the Early Pioneers of the Church of God in Christ*, 7.
56. Charles H. Mason, "The Kaiser in the Light of the Scriptures," (sermon, COGIC baptismal ceremony, Memphis, TN, June 23, 1918). Sermon was recorded by Elder William B. Holt, Secretary to General Overseer Mason.
57. On a side note, the appearance of a discrepancy with the date of this sermon causes for some concern. The sermon was supposedly preached on June 23. On June 25, a letter from Major J.E. Spingarn stated that the mobile register on June 21st announced that from its Jackson, Mississippi Bureau that a colored pastor named Charles Mason of Lexington had been arrested for distributing large amounts of disloyal literature. On June 29, a letter from the Office of the United States Attorney in Jackson, Mississippi to Major Spingarn's letter on June 21st stated that Mason was in custody in Jackson, Mississippi. Around June 23-24 or earlier, Mason was being arrested in Lexington, Mississippi on charges of obstructing the draft. So, if he was being arrested in Lexington, how could he have been preaching a sermon in Memphis? In my hypothesis, Holt may have written the sermon to show the US government the patriotic stance of Mason and the COGIC Church, attempting to rid the COGIC Church of accusations of being German sympathizers.
58. Calvin White, *The Rise to Respectability: Race, Religion, and the Church of God in Christ*, 69.
59. War Department. Office of Chief of Staff. *Re: In Case of C.H. Mason, Henry Kervin, and Other Suspects*, by Colonel Churchill. Investigation of Violation of Section 37 and Section 32 of Penal Code US Statutes. Paris, Texas. 1918.
60. Bureau of Investigation, *Re: Rev. Charles Harris Mason, Lexington, Holmes

County, Miss., by Agent Palmer. Investigation. Jackson, MS, 1918.

61. Calvin White, Jr., *The Rise to Respectability: Race, Religion, and the Church of God in Christ*, 75.

62. German Ross, *History and the Formative Years of the Church of God in Christ*, 23.

63. Calvin White, Jr., *The Rise to Respectability: Race, Religion, and the Church of God in Christ*, 75.

64. Anita Bingham Jefferson, *Charles Price Jones: First Holiness Black Reformer*, 198.

65. Bobby Bean, *This is the Church of God in Christ*, 49, 125.

66. Anita Bingham Jefferson, *Charles Price Jones: First Black Holiness Reformer*, 208.

67. Calvin White, Jr, *The Rise to Respectability: Race, Religion, and the Church of God in Christ*, 40.

68. Church of God in Christ, *From the Beginning of Bishop C.H. Mason and he Early Pioneers of the Church of God in Christ*, 58.

69. Anita Bingham Jefferson, *Charles Price Jones: First Black Holiness Reformer*, 212.

70. Charles H. Pleas, *Fifty Years Achievement,* 23.

71. Anita Bingham Jefferson, *Charles Price Jones: First Black Holiness Reformer*, 217.

72. Bobby Bean, This is the Church of God in Christ, 48.

73. Anita Bingham Jefferson, *Charles Price Jones: First Black Holiness Reformer*, 223.

74. Ibid., 219.

75. COGICC, *Manual of the Church of God in Christ Congregational* (East St. Louis, IL: COGIC, Congregational, 1980), 3.

76. "Bishop and Pastor Lose Court Fight," *Chicago Defender,* March 31, 1934.

77. "Ibid.

78. COGICC, *The Manual of the Church of God in Christ Congregational*, 6.

79. COGICC, *The Manual of the Church of God in Christ Congregational*, 6.

80. Ibid.

81. Calvin S. McBride, *Walking Into a new Spirituality* (New York: iUniverse, Inc., 2007), 36.

82. Croom specifically utilized water for Communion instead of using the standard grape juice according to rules in COGIC. Also, Croom refused to conduct his state convocations in July or August. Instead, Croom kept the First Born Church tradition of having the convocation in December.

83. Bishop John Howard Dell, Northern Georgia Jurisdiction, interview by author, Atlanta, GA, October 4, 1991.

84. Mack C. Mason, *Saints in the Land of Lincoln* (Hazel Crest, IL: Faithday Press, 2004), 28.

85. The Historical First Ecclesiastical Jurisdiction of Michigan, "Our History," Northeast Michigan COGIC Jurisdiction, accessed March 23, 2015, http://www.nemichigan.org/nemhistory.htm.

86. James Whitehead, ed., "COGIC History Series," *COGIC YPWW Quarterly 33* (December 1996): 40.

87. Ibid., 40-41.

88. Pleas, *Fifty Years Achievement,* 81.

Chapter 5
Second Phase of the Mason Era (1933-1961): COGIC Institution

1. Dell, Interview.
2. Elder Ronald Kimbrew, Arkansas First Jurisdiction Researcher, interview by author, Little Rock, AR, August 21, 2016.
3. Ithiel C. Clemmons, *Bishop C.H. Mason and the Roots of the Church of God in Christ*, 6-7.
4. Charles Pleas, *Fifty Years Achievement,* 74.
5. Texas Northwest Ecclesiastical Jurisdiction COGIC, "History," Texas Northwest Ecclesiastical Jurisdiction, accessed October 13, 2016, http://www.texasnw-cogic.org/history.htm.
6. Charles Pleas, *Fifty Years Achievement*, 17.
7. Pearl Roberts McCullom, *Historical Sketches of Pioneer Women of the Church of God in Christ*, Inc. (Memphis, TN: COGIC Publishing House, 1975), 5.
8. Ibid.
9. Ibid.
10. Ibid.
11. Ithiel C. Clemmons, *Bishop C.H. Mason and the Roots of the Church of God in Christ*, 118.
12. Anthea Butler, *Women in the Church of God in Christ: Making a Sanctified World*, 144.
13. Ibid., 100.
14. Church of God in Christ, *From the Beginning of Bishop C.H. Mason and the Early Pioneers of the Church of God in Christ*, 65.
15. Anthea Butler, *Women in the Church of God in Christ: Masking a Sanctified World*, 103.
16. Ibid., 112.
17. Ibid., 136.
18. Church of God in Christ, *From the Beginning of Bishop C.H. Mason and the Early Pioneers of the Church of God in Christ*, 49.
19. Ibid.
20. Ibid., 52.
21. Obituary of Mother Dorothy Mae Webster Exume', January 15, 2011.
22. Sonya D. Bradford, "Highlights of Arizona Juanita Dranes: COGIC's Music Ministry," The Whole Truth, September 1, 2014, 37.
23. Ibid., 39.
24. Ibid.
25. Paul Harvey, *Freedom's Coming*, 167.
26. Rosetta Tharpe was singing Spirituals (also called Negro Spirituals), distinguishing between the definition of Gospel music invented by Thomas Dorsey around 1932 with a song called *Precious Lord, Take my Hand.* Spirituals were

mainly songs descended from the era of Slavery, while Gospel music was a mixture of Jazz, Blues, and Spirituals.

27. PBS, "Sister Rosetta Tharpe: The Godmother of Rock and Roll," PBS American Masters website, accessed November 1, 2016, http://ww.pbs.org/wnet/americanmasters/sisterrosetta-tharpe-full-episode/2516/

28. Bobby Bean, *This is the Church of God in Christ*, 135.

29. Ibid., 157.

30. "500 Church of God in Christ Women Gather for First National Meet", *Chicago Tribune*, May 5, 1951.

31. Lucille J. Cornelius, *The Pioneer: History of the Church of God in Christ,* 26.

32. Elijah L. Hill, *The 1917 FBI Files of Bishop Charles Harrison Mason,* 25-26. NOTE: The organization year of 1895 contradicts the 1909 Tennessee State Supreme Court decision in favor of Overseer Mason and the members that followed his leadership. The Tennessee State Supreme Court reversed the decision of Frank Avant v. C.H. Mason. The Chancery Court in Shelby County, Memphis, Tennessee had ruled in favor of Frank Avant, the Charles Price Jones group. The State Supreme Court in Jackson, Tennessee ruled that the Chancery Court had made a mistake because the Church of God in Christ religious body did not have any status as an organization with oversight that subjected local pastors and preachers under an authority. The years of the court case was between 1907-1909. The COGIC manual claiming an organization year of 1895 is problematic. Furthermore, other founding years for COGIC include 1896, 1897 (the year Mason received the named spiritually while walking down Gaines Street in Little Rock, Arkansas), and 1907 (the year Mason and his group separated from Charles Price Jones).

33. Church of God in Christ of America, *Official Manual of the Church of God in Christ*, ed. William Holt (Memphis, TN: self-published, n.d.).

34. O.T. Jones and J.E. Bryant, ed., *Manual of the Church of God in Christ* (Memphis, TN: Church of God in Christ, 1944), 17,18.

35. For several years in the COGIC faith, speaking in tongues had been taught as a mandatory sign of receiving the Baptism of the Holy Spirit. In rural areas, male and female clergy claimed that a person was not saved and did not have the Holy Spirit if that person did not speak in tongues or utter in tongues under the influence of the Holy Spirit. Nevertheless, in the present day COGIC era, the mandatory speaking in tongues doctrine is not preached in many COGIC Churches. This doctrine, as a whole, has been left to the interpretations of the local members, and, thus, is almost nonexistent.

36. Ithiel C. Clemmons, *Bishop C.H. Mason and the Roots of the Church of God in Christ*, 77.

37. Bobby Bean, *This is the Church of God in Christ*, 49.

38. German Ross, *History and the Formative Years of the Church of God in Christ*, 110-111.

39. Ibid., 112.

40. RootWeb.com, Inc., "James Logan Delk," RootWeb.com, accessed October 11,

2016, http://wc.rootsweb.ancestry.com/cgi-bin/igm.cgi?.op/ .
41. The 1945 Year of Jubilee Convocation represented 50 years of COGIC being organized. The organization date and seal had the year of 1895. From 1895 to 1945, COGIC was celebrating 50 years of being in Christian ministry. To note, the problem with that year is that it is verifying that COGIC was organized under the leadership of Charles Price Jones. The 1909 court cased stated that COGIC was not organized prior to 1907.
42. Rehoboth Church of God in Christ, Jesus Apostolic, "History of Rehoboth," Rehoboth COGIC, Jesus Apostolic, accessed October 2, 2016, http://www.rehoboth1.com/history-of-rehoboth.html.
43. Ibid.
44. Evangelist Temple House of Refuge for all Nations C.O.G.I.C., "Brief Biography of the Visionary," Evangelist Temple House of Refuge for all Nations C.O.G.I.C., accessed June 23, 2017, http://netministries.org/see/churches.exe/ch33684.
45. Ibid.
46. "$242,600 Asked in Church Suit," *Kentucky New Era*, December 15, 1949.
47. J. Howard Dell, *Minutes from the COGIC Elders Council* (Memphis, TN: Church of God in Christ Elders Council, 1950), 19.
48. Bobby Bean, *This is the Church of God in Christ*, 86.
49. Ibid.
50. Church of God in Christ, *The Official Manual of the Church of God in Christ*, 7th ed., (Memphis, TN: Church of God in Christ, 1957), 13.
51. Calvin White, *The Rise to Respectability,* 119.

Chapter 6
Post-Mason Era: The Ascension and Ousting of O.T. Jones, Sr.

1.   The obituary program of Mason added to the glaring controversy surrounding his birth year. The program stated that Mason was born in 1862 while other years have been recorded as 1856, 1866, 1863, and 1864.
2.   Obituary of Charles Harrison Mason, November 28, 1961.
3.   Anthea D. Butler, *Women in the Church of God in Christ: Making a Sanctified World*, 157.
4.   Per the COGIC Manual of 1957, the General Assembly served as the authority to define COGIC doctrine and was the law-making authority of the Church. The General Assembly was composed of a Chairman, ordained elders, Board of State Overseers, Board of Bishops, and prescribed Lay delegation. Ordained elders were preachers without a church and pastors of churches. Overseers and Bishops were preachers who supervised pastors, elders, and church leaders in foreign territories. Lay members do not hold any credentials nor are they licensed to preach.
5.   Bishop Samuel P. Nesbitt, "Constitutional Rights Expose', September 15, 2009," (essay/letter, Jacksonville, FL, January, 2010).

6.   Ibid.

7.   Ibid.

8.   To note with some irony, the dream by Bishop James O. Patterson and the congratulatory remarks by Bishop Otha Kelly would, in the future, offer stark contrasts to their actions after 1964. Both Patterson and Kelly worked against the administration of O.T. Jones and was successful in ousting him by declaring the office of Senior Bishop, a ceremonial title with no official power in COGIC.

9.   "Bishop Jones New Head of Church of God in Christ," *Chicago Defender*, December 15, 1962.

10. Samuel P. Nesbitt, "In Retrospect: 57th Annual Convocation and Events Which Followed," *The COGIC Voice*, March 1, 1965, 7-8.

11. Ibid., 9.

12. Robert R. Owens, *Never Forget: The Dark Years of COGIC History* (Fairfax, VA: Xulon Press, 2002), 84.

13. Pearl R. McCollum, *Historical Sketches of Pioneering Women of the Church of God in Christ*, Inc., 17.

14. Ibid., 47.

15. Bobby Bean, *This is the Church of God in Christ*, 158.

16. Lucille J. Cornelius, *The Pioneer*, 85-86.

17. Samuel P. Nesbitt, *The COGIC Voice*, 13.

18. Ibid., 19.

19. Ibid.

20. Church of God in Christ of America, Inc., "COGIC ORG 1895 A.D., RE-ORG 1969 A.D." Church of God in Christ of America, Inc. http://netministries.org/see/churches.exe/ch33714 (accessed November 8, 2016).

21. Samuel P. Nesbitt, The COGIC Voice, 20.

22. Ibid.

23. Robert Owens, *Never Forget: The Dark Years of COGIC History*, 91.

24. Samuel P. Nesbitt, The COGIC Voice, 20-21.

25. Ibid., 28.

26. Ibid., 21.

27. Ibid.

28. Robert Owens, Never Forget, 127.

29. The Sunday service of the Holy Convocation in Memphis was characterized by the national leader, the senior bishop, preaching the Sunday morning sermon. After the conclusion of the official sermon by the senior bishop, he traditionally receives an offering (monetary donations) from the attending members and clergy.

30. Lucille J. Cornelius, *The Pioneer: History of the Church of God in Christ*, 81.

31. Ibid., 84.

32. Robert Owens, *Never Forget,* 148.

33. "Ala. Court Scolds Church in Test Case," Chicago Defender, April 2, 1966.

34. R.E. Ranger, "Always Liars" (letter, Church of God in Christ, Fort Worth, Texas, April 4, 1966).

35. Ibid.
36. Robert R. Owens, *Never Forget: The Dark Years of COGIC History*, 136.
37. Church of God in Christ 59th Annual Holy Convocation Souvenir Booklet, 1966.
38. According to the Official COGIC Manual, Jones' tenure was not mentioned after the death of Mason. The historical writing only mentioned the development of the Executive Board and the advancement of Bishop J.O. Patterson to the office of presiding bishop. In the book, *History and Formative Years of the Church of God in Christ,* edited by J.O. Patterson, German Ross, and Julia Atkins, summarized the years between 1961-1968 as the Years of Wilderness Wandering or The Dark Ages. Again, O.T. Jones, Sr. was snubbed, and his tenure was not mentioned. Dr. Bobby Bean in his book, *This is the Church of God in Christ*, mentioned Senior Bishop Jones, but referred to his tenure as the Dark Ages of the Church of God in Christ. Bean praised Patterson's leadership which brought the church out of the Dark Ages.
39. Robert Owens, *Never Forget: The Dark Years of COGIC History*, 156-157.
40. Ibid., 157.
41. Ibid., 152.
42. Ibid., 138.
43. Patterson is referring to the National Baptist Convention, USA, Inc. (NBC) convention incident in 1961. According to C. Eric Lincoln's book, *The Black Church in the African American Experience*, a team of preachers led by Rev. Gardner Taylor wanted a four-year term limit to set on the leadership of the NBC, USA. Rev. J.H. Jackson, president of NBC, USA took the matter to court and won a decision for him to have no term limits set on the president of NBC, USA. The "Taylor Team" composed of Gardner Taylor, M.L. King, Sr, M. L. King, Jr., Ralph Abernathy, Benjamin E. Mays saw Jackson's authority as autocratic, so those who opposed Jackson wanted Taylor to be the new NBC, USA president. Furthermore, the "Taylor Team" supported King's social change strategies as Jackson condemned King's actions as injurious to racial advancement and harmony. In 1961, at the NBC, USA convention in Kansas City, the "Taylor Team" was initially denied access to the convention. However, when the Taylor delegates were allowed into the convention, physical confrontations occurred as the Taylor delegates moved to take control of the platform. J.O. Patterson felt that the Jones faction, during the Holy Convocation of 1966, was acting just like the "Taylor Team" of 1961.
44. Robert Owens, *Never Forget: The Dark Years of COGIC History*, 138-139.

Chapter 7
The End of The O.T. Jones Era and the 1968 COGIC Convention

1. Ibid., 156.
2. Lucille J. Cornelius, *The Pioneer: History of the Church of God in Christ*, 86.
3. Ibid., 87.
4. Ibid.

5. Jonathan Chism, "'The Saints Go Marching': The Church of God in Christ and the Civil Rights Movement in Memphis, Tennessee, 1954-1968" (PhD diss., Rice University, 2014), 139-144, accessed June 22, 2017, https://scholarship.rice.edu/bitsream/handle/1911/76423/CHISM-DOCUMENT-2014.pdf.

6. Ibid., 145.

7. Ibid., 147-149.

8. Calvin White, Jr., *The Rise to Respectability: Race, Religion, and the Church of God in Christ*, 128.

9. Ibid.

10. Ibid., 273.

11. Ibid., 122.

12. David W. Dunlap, "Harlem Church Where Malcolm X was Eulogized Faces its own Final Days," New York Times, March 30, 2016, under "Building Blocks," http://www.nytimes.com/2016/03/31/nyregion/harlem-church-where-malcolm-x-was-eulogized-faces-its-own-final-days.html.

13. Bobby Bean, *This is the Church of God in Christ,* 106.

14. Lucille J. Cornelius, *The Pioneer: History of the Church of God in Christ*, 88.

15. Church of God in Christ International, "Our History," Church of God in Christ International,http://cogicinternational.com/new/our-history/ (accessed November 13, 2016).

16. The Church of God in Christ International, "The History of the Church of God in Christ International," Church of God in Christ International, http://www.cogic.international.org/about_us (accessed November 13, 2016).

17. Church of God in Christ International, "Our History," Church of God in Christ International.

18. The Church of God in Christ United, "The History of the Church of God in Christ United," Church of God in Christ United, http://cogicuiwc.org/index.html (accessed November 14, 2016).

19. James Whitehead, Jr., ed., "Church of God in Christ History Series." *Y.P.W.W. Senior Quarterly 33*, no. 1 (December 1996 – February 1997): 43.

20. Ibid., 43.

21. Ibid., 43.

22. Ibid., 44-45.

23. Ithiel Clemmons, *Bishop C.H. Mason and the Roots of the Church of God in Christ*, 129.

24. U.S. Bureau of Census, "1920 United States Federal Census," http://search.ancestry.com (accessed November 19, 2016).

25. Church of God in Christ, Inc, *From the Beginning of Bishop C.H. Mason and the Early Pioneers of the Church of God in Christ*, 41.

26. Dr. Mattie McGlothen Library/Museum, "Dr. Mattie Mae Carter McGlothen," Dr. Mattie McGlothen Library/Museum, http://mcglothenlibrarymuseum.org/mcglothen-bio.html (accessed on November 19, 2016).

27. Ibid.

28. United Churches of God in Christ, "Brief Historical Sketch of the United Churches of God in Christ," United Church of God in Christ, http://www.ucogic.org/history.html (accessed November 28, 2016).

29. Ibid.

30. Church of God in Christ, Inc., *Diamond Jubilee Celebration: 75th Anniversary, Flyer and Program*, November 9, 1982.

31. David Hall, "To Be or Not to Be," *The Whole Truth* 17, no. 5 (1985): 2.

Chapter 8
Bishop Louis Ford Era, 1989-1995, and Successive Bishops

1. James Whitehead, Jr., Church of God in Christ History Series, *YPWW Quarterly*, 46.

2. Ibid.

3. Calvin White, Jr., *The Rise to Respectability*, 134.

4. James Whitehead, Jr. "Church of God in Christ History Series," *YPWW Quarterly*, 46.

5. Ibid., 47.

6. Church of God in Christ, *The First National Holy Ghost Conference Program* (Memphis, TN: COGIC Publishing House, 1990), 1.

7. Ibid., 7.

8. James Whitehead, Jr., Church of God in Christ History Series, *Senior YPWW Quarterly*, 47.

9. Note: The United Church of God in Christ should not be confused with the Church of God in Christ, United. The United Church of God in Christ was founded in Georgia in 1980 by Bishop Marshall Carter. The Church of God in Christ, United was founded by Bishop James Feltus, Jr., of New Orleans in 1973.

10. Jean Lewis-Dell to AUC Archives, August 4, 1998, J. Howard Dell Papers, Atlanta University Center Library, Atlanta, GA.

11. Leroy James, interview by author, Augusta, September 19, 1998.

12. Ithiel Clemmons, *Bishop C.H. Mason and the Roots of the Church of God in Christ*, 133.

13. Full Gospel Baptist Church Fellowship International, "Who is Full Gospel," Full Gospel Baptist Church Fellowship International, 2016, accessed June 8, 2017, https://www.fullgospelbaptist.org/about/

14. Lighthouse Churches of God in Christ of Canada, "About LCOGICOC," Lighthouse Churches of God in Christ of Canada, accessed December 2, 2016, http://lcogicoc.homestead.com/About-Us.html .

15. Bobby Bean, *This is the Church of God in Christ*, 164.

16. Ibid.

17. Obituary of Mother Emma Frances Searcy Crouch, January 10, 1997.

18. Ibid.

19. Obituary of Bishop Chandler David Owens, March 10, 2011.

20. James Whitehead, Jr., COGIC History Series, Senior *YPWW Quarterly*, 49.

21. Obituary of Bishop Chandler David Owens, March 10, 2011.

22. Ibid.

23. Bobby Bean, *This is the Church of God in Christ*, 187.

24. Obituary of Bishop Gilbert Earl Patterson, March 29, 2007.

25. Ibid.

26. Ibid.

27. Larry G. Britton, ed., "Bishop G.E. Patterson Named Chief Operating Officer for National Headquarters," The Whole Truth, Spring 1996, 9.

28. Bobby Bean, *This is the Church of God in Christ*, 114-115.

29. Phil W. Petrie, "The Church of God in Christ: New Directions for a new Century!" Gospel Today, November/December, 1995, 34-35.

30. Ibid.

31. Obituary of Bishop Chandler David Owens, March 10, 2011.

32. Church of God in Christ, "Mother Willie Mae Rivers," Church of God in Christ, October 2012, accessed December 7, 2016, http://www.cogic.org/holyconvocation/files/2012/10/Mother-Willie-Mae-Rivers-Bio.pdf.

33. Billy Bruce, "COGIC Removes Orlando Pastor.," Charisma, August 31, 2000, accessed June 11, 2017, http://www.charismamag.com/site-archives/134-peopleevents/people-events/123-cogic-removes-orlando-pastor.

34. Ibid.

35. Ibid.

36. Author's personal notes. The author was an elder in COGIC and was a member of the General Assembly of COGIC voting in the 2000 presiding bishop election.

37. Ibid.

38. Ibid.

39. Ibid.

40. Ibid.

41. Ibid.

42. Ibid.

43. Ibid.

44. Obituary of Bishop Gilbert Earl Patterson, March 29, 2007.

45. Ibid.

46. Church of God in Christ, "Bishop Charles E. Blake Biography," Church of God in Christ, 2008, accessed December 9, 2016, http://cogic.org/pdf/General-Media-Packet.pdf

47. Ibid.

48. Charles Blake, "From the Desk of Presiding Bishop Charles E. Blake, Sr." (letter, Church of God in Christ, 2017), 2.

49. Charles E. Blake, interview by The Whole Truth, Los Angeles, September 1, 2014.

Epilogue

1.   In the African-American Church experience, a person, generally, claimed to be anointed by God to preach. The experience is usually characterized by a personal talk or sign from God approving that person as an anointed servant to preach the Gospel to those who have not confessed to believing in Jesus Christ.

2.   Robert L. Johns, Black Heroes (2001), in the Georgia State University Digital Library, accessed June 25, 2017,http://eds.a.ebscohost.com.ezproxy.gsu.ed.

3.   Marie W. Dallam, Daddy Grace: *A Celebrity Preacher and His House of Prayer* (New York: New York University Press, 2007), 125.

BIBLIOGRAPHY

Archival Sources

Bishop J. Howard Dell Papers, Atlanta University Center Archives, Robert Woodruff Library, Atlanta, Georgia.

Church of God in Christ History Collection, Flower Pentecostal Heritage Center, Springfield, Missouri.

Pentecostal and Charismatic Research Archive (PCRA), University of Southern California Digital Archives, USC Library, Los Angeles, California.

Personal Collection, Church of God in Christ Historical Papers and Documents 1985-2017, Douglasville, Georgia.

Government Documents

Bureau of Investigation. Mason-Colored Preacher Alleged Openly Advised Against Registering........., Treasonable & Seditious Remarks Against United States Government. Lexington, MS, 1917.

Bureau of Investigation. "Re: Rev. Charles Harris Mason, Lexington, Holmes County, Miss." Jackson, MS: Agent Palmer, 1918.

U.S. Bureau of Census. *1920 United States Federal Census*. n.d. http://search.ancestry.com (accessed November 19, 2016).

War Department. "Re: In Case of C.H. Mason, Henry Kervin, and Other Suspects." Paris, TX: Office of Chief of Staff., 1918.

Church of God in Christ Primary Sources

Bryant, J.E. and O.T. Jones, ed. *Manual of the Church of God in Christ*. Memphis, TN: Church of God in Christ, 1944.

Church of God in Christ. *Church of God in Christ 59th Annual Holy Convocation Souvenir Booklet*. Memphis, TN: Church of God in Christ, November 7-17, 1966.

Church of God in Christ. *The Official Manual of the Church of God in Christ*, 7th ed. Memphis, TN: Church of God in Christ, 1957.

Church of God in Christ, Inc. *The First National Holy Ghost Conference Program*. Memphis, TN: COGIC Publishing House, January 16-18, 1990.

Church of God in Christ, Inc. "Women's Page." *The Whole Truth*, February 1968: 3.

Church of God in Christ, Inc. *60th Annual Holy Convocation of the Church of God in Christ Souvenir Book and Official Program*. Memphis: Church of God in Christ Publishing House, November 7-17, 1967.

—. *Minutes of the 12th General Convocation*. Memphis, TN: Church of God in Christ, Inc., December 10, 1919.

—. *Minutes of the 13th General Convocation*. Memphis, TN: Church of God in Christ, Inc., December 8, 1920.

—. *From the Beginning of Bishop C. H. Mason and the Early Pioneers of the Church of God in Christ*. Memphis, TN: COGIC Publishing House, 1991.

COGICC. *Manual of the Church of God in Christ Congregational*. East St. Louis, IL: COGICC, 1946.

Cornelius, Lucille J. *The Pioneer: History of the Church of God in Christ*. Memphis: Self published, 1975.

Dell, J. Howard. *Minutes from the COGIC Elders Council*. Memphis, TN: Church of God in Christ Elders Council, 1950.

Mason, Charles H. "The Kaiser in the Light of the Scriptures." Memphis, TN: Elder William B. Holt, Secretary to General Overseer Mason, June 23, 1918.

Mason, Elsie. *The Man, Charles Harrison Mason (1866-1961)*. Memphis: COGIC Publishing House, 1979.

Mason, Mary and others. *The History and Life Work of Elder C.H. Mason and his Co-laborers from 1893 to 1924*. Memphis, TN: Church of God in Christ, 1924.

McBride, Calvin. *Frank Avant vs. C.H. Mason: Mason and the Holy Ghost on Trial*. Bloomington, IN: IUniverse, 2009.

McCullom, Pearl Roberts. *Historical Sketches of Pioneer Women of the Church of God in Christ, Inc.* Memphis, TN: COGIC Publishing House, 1975.

Nesbitt, Samuel P. "Constitutional Rights Expose' September 15, 2009." Jacksonville, FL, January 2010.

—. "In Retrospect: 57th Annual Convocation and Events Which Followed." The COGIC Voice, March 1, 1965: 18-22.

Obituary of Bishop Chandler David Owens, Sr. Marietta, GA, Turner Chapel AME, Woolard/Jordan Innovative Design, March 10, 2011.

Obituary, Bishop Gilbert Earl Patterson. Memphis, TN, Temple of Deliverance COGIC, March 29, 2007.

Obituary, Charles Harrison Mason. Memphis, TN, Mason Temple, 1961, n.d.

Obituary, Mother Dorothy Webster Exume. Atlanta, GA, Cathedral of Faith COGIC, January 15, 2011.

Obituary, Mother Emma Frances Searcy. January 10, 1997.

Patterson, J.O., Julia Atkins, and German Ross,. *History and the Formative Years of the Church of God in Christ*. Memphis, TN: Church of God in Christ Publishing House, 1969.

Pleas, Charles H. *Fifty Years Achievement: A Period of History of the Church of God in Christ from 1906-1956*. Memphis, TN: Church of God in Christ, 1956.

Range, C.F and Clyde Young, eds. *Church of God in Christ Official Manual*. Memphis, TN: Board of Publications of COGIC, 1973.

Whitehead, James, Jr., ed. "Church of God in Christ History Series." *Church of God in Christ YPWW Senior Quaterly*, 1996-1997: 40-50.

Interviews

Blake, Bishop Charles E., interview by The Whole Truth. Los Angeles, CA. (September 1, 2014).

Dell, Bishop J. Howard., interview by the author. Atlanta, GA. (October 4, 1991).

James, Pastor Leroy., interview by the author. Augusta, GA. (September 19, 1998).

Owens, Bishop Chandler D., interview by Joan Woolard. Marietta, GA. (October 10, 2000).

Williams, Bishop Adrian D., interview by author. Fayetteville, GA. (September 14, 1998).

Court Cases

A.B. McEwen, et al., vs. O.T. Jones, R.E. Ranger, and O.T. Jones, Jr. 69683-2 (Chancery Court of Shelby County, Tennessee, October 13, 1967). Mailed from the Memphis Public Library to the author.

Bishop H. Jenkins Bell as Jurisdictional Bishop of Western Florida Ecclesiastical Jurisdiction, The Church of God in Christ, Inc., v. Board of Trustees, Malone Memorial Church of God in Christ, a/k/a Orlando Institutional Church of God in Christ and Derrik W. Hutchins. 99-7908 (Circuit Court of Orange County, Florida, April 19, 2000). Information was faxed to author by Elder Quintin Robertson of the Lutheran Theological Seminary in Philadelphia, Pennsylvania.

Bishop R.E. Ranger v. Bishop J.O. Pattersn et al., (District Court of Harris County, Texas, September 7, 1967). Information cited from the newspaper, Chicago Defender.

Emmitt Jackson, et al., v. John F. Key, et al., (Circuit Court of Birmingham, Alabama, April 2, 1966). Information was cited in the newspaper, Chicago Defender.

Frank Avant v. C.H. Mason. 14770 (Chancery Court of Shelby County, Tennessee, July 28, 1908). Information cited from the book writtend by Calvin McBride, Frank Avant v. C. H. Mason: Mason and the Holy Ghost on Trial.

Newspapers

Chicago Defender Press. "Bishop Jones New Head of Church of God in Christ." *Chicago Defender*, December 15, 1962.

Chicago Defender Press Service. "Bishop and Pastor Lose Court Fight." *Chicago Defender*, March 31, 1934.

Chicago Tribune Press. "500 Church of God in Christ Women Gather for First National Meet." *Chicago Tribune*, May 5, 1951.

Kentucky New Era. "$242,600 Asked in Church Suit." December 15, 1949.

Dunlap, David W. "Harlem Church Where Malcolm X was Eulogized Faces its own Final Days." *New York Times*, March 31, 2016. Accessed November 19,2016. http://www.nytimes.com/2016/03/31/nyregion/harlem-church-where-malcolm-x-was-eulogized-faces-its-own-final-days.html.

Internet Sources

Bishop Charles E. Blake Biography. 2008. http://cogic.org/pdf/General-Media-Packet.pdf (accessed December 9, 2016).

Bruce, Billy. "COGIC Removes Orlando Pastor." *Charisma*, August 31, 2000. Accessed June 11, 2017. http://www.charismamag.com/site-archives/134-peopleevents/people-events/123-cogic-removes-orlando-pastor.

Church of God in Christ. "Mother Willie Mae Rivers. October 2012." AccessedDecember 7, 2016. http://www.cogic.org/holyconvocation/files/2012/10/Mother-Willie-Mae-Rivers-Bio.pdf.

Church of God in Christ International. "Our History." Accessed November 13, 2016. http://cogicinternational.com/new/our-history.

Church of God in Christ International. "The History of the Church of God in Christ International." Accessed November 13, 2016. http://www.cogic.international.org/about us.

Church of God in Christ of America, Inc. "COGIC ORG 1895 A.D., RE-ORG 1969 A.D."Accessed November 8, 2016. http://netministries.org/see/churches.exe/ch33714.

Church of God in Christ, Mennonite. "Who We Are." Accessed July

14, 2016. http://churchofgodinchristmennonite.net/en/who we are.

Church of God in Christ United. "The History of the Church of God in Christ United."Accessed November 14, 2016. http://cogicuiwc.org/index.html.

COGICA. "Bishop Ralph L. Johnson." Accessed January 22, 2014. http://bishopdrralphljohnson.webs.com.

Dr. Mattie McGlothen Library/Museum. "Dr. Mattie Mae Carter McGlothen."Accessed November 19, 2016. http://mcglothenlibrarymuseum.org/mcglothen-bio.html.

Evangelist Temple House of Refuge for all Nations C.O.G.I.C. "Brief Autobiography of the Visionary." Accessed June 23, 2017. http//netministries.org/see/churches.exe/ch33684.

First Church of God in Christ. "The First Church of God in Christ, Fort Smith, Arkansas."Accessed November 25, 2014. http://www.first-cogic.org/history.html.

Johns, Robert L. "Black Heroes." (2001). Accessed June 25, 2017. http://eds.a.ebscohost.com.ezproxy.gsu.edu.

Lighthouse Churches of God in Christ of Canada. "About LCOGICOC." Accessed December 2, 2016. http://lcogicoc.homestead.com/About-Us.html.

National Baptist Convention, USA, Inc. "About Us." Accessed March 15, 2016. http://nationalbaptist.com/about-us/index.html.

Northern Mississippi Ecclesiastical Jurisdiction Church of God in Christ. "Northern Mississippi Ecclesiastical Jurisdiction Church of God in Christ." Accessed July 30, 2016. http://nmcogic.org/about-us/history.

PBS. "Sister Rosetta Tharpe: The Godmother of Rock and Roll." Accessed November 1, 2016. http://www.pbs.org/wnet/americanmasters/sister-rosetta-tharpe-full-episode/2516.

Rehoboth Church of God in Christ, Jesus Apostolic. "History of Rehoboth." Accessed October 2, 2016. http://www.rehoboth1.com/history-of-rehoboth.html.

RootWeb.com, Inc. "James Logan Delk."Accessed October 11. 2016. http://wc.rootsweb.ancestry.com/cgi-bin/igm.cgi?.op.

Southern California Second Jurisdiction Church of God in Christ. "About Southern California Second."Accessed July 25, 2016. http://socal2nd.org/about.

Texas Northwest Ecclesiastical Jurisdiction COGIC. "History." Accessed October 13, 2016. http://www.texasnwcogic.org/history.htm.

The Assemblies of God. "The Assemblies of God Faith." Accessed March 3, 2014. http://ag.org/top/About/History/index.cfm.

The Historical First Ecclesiastical Jurisdiction of Michigan. "Our History." Accessed March 23, 2015. http://www.nemichigan.org/nemhistory.htm.

United Churches of God in Christ. "Brief Historical Sketch of the United Churches of God in Christ." Accessed November 28, 2016. http://www.ucogic.org/history.html.

Primary Book Sources

Bean, Bobby. *This is the Church of God in Christ*. Atlanta, GA: Epic Publishing, 2001.

Butler, Anthea D. *Women in the Church of God in Christ: Making a Sanctified World*. Chapel Hill, NC: University of North Carolina Press, 2007.

Clemmons, Ithiel C. *Bishop C.H. Mason and the Roots of the Church of God in Christ*. Bakersfield, CA: Pneuma Life Publishing, 1996.

Hill, Elijah L. *The 1917 FBI Files of Bishop Charles Harrison Mason.* Atlanta, GA: Self-Published, 2015.

Mason, Mack C. *Saints in the Land of Lincoln.* Hazel Crest, IL: Faithday Press, 2004.

McBride, Calvin. *Walking into a New Spirituality: Chronicling the Life, Ministry, and Contributions of ElderRobert E. Hart* (Lincoln, NE: iUniverse), 2007.

Morris, Elias C. *Sermons, Addresses and Reminiscences and Important Correspondence, With a Picture Gallery of Eminent Ministers and Scholars* (Nashville, TN: National Baptist Publishing Board), 1901. Accessed June 22, 2017. http://docsouth.unc.edu/church/morris/morris.html.

Owens, Robert R. *Never Forget: The Dark Years of COGIC History.* Fairfax, VA: Xulon Press, 2002.

Penn, Marthene Talley. *The Early Years C.O.G.I.C. North Georgia: Before there were Jurisdictions.* Columbus, GA: Brentwood Christian Press, 2003.

White, Jr., Calvin. *The Rise to Respectability: Race, Religion, and the Church of God in Christ.* Fayetteville, AR: University of Arkansas Press, 2012.

Theses and Dissertations

Chism, Jonathan. " 'The Saints Go Marching': The Church of God in Christ and the Civil Rights Movement in Memphis, Tennessee, 1954-1968." PhD diss., Rice University, 2014. Accessed June 22, 2017. https://scholarship.rice.edu/handle/1911/76423.

Articles

Britton, Larry G. "Bishop G.E. Patterson Named Chief Operating Officer for National Headquarters." *The Whole Truth*, Spring 1996: 9.

Bradford, Sonya D. "Highlight of Arizona Juanita Dranes: COGIC's Music Ministry." *The Whole Truth*, September 1, 2014, 37-39.

Hall, David. "To Be or Not to BE." *The Whole Truth*, 1985: 2.

Petrie, Phil W. "Church of God in Christ: New Direction for a New Century." *Gospel Today*, November/December 1995: 34-35.

Secondary Works

Anderson, Allan. *An Introduction to Pentecostalism*. New York: Cambridge University Press, 2004.

Dallam, Marie W. *Daddy Grace: A Celebrity Preacher and His House of Prayer*. New York: New York University Press, 2007.

Frazier, E. Franklin. *The Negro Church in America*. New York: Shocken Books, 1975. —. The Negro Church in America. New York: Schocken Books, 1974.

Genovese, Eugene D. *Roll, Jordan, Roll*. New York: Vintage Books, 1976.

Gilkes, Cheryl Townsend. *If it Wasn't for the Women*. New York: Orbis Books, 2001.

Harvey, Paul. *Freedom's Coming: Religious Culture and the Shaping of the South from the Civil War Through the Civil Rights Era*. Chapel Hill, NC: University of North Carolina Press, 2005.

Jefferson, Anita Bingham. *Charles Price Jones: First Black Holiness Reformer*. Florence, MS: Stephens Printing, 2011.

Lincoln, C. Eric and Lawrence Mamiya. *The Black Church in the African-American Experience*. Durham, NC: Duke University Press, 1990.

MacRobert, Iain. *The Black Roots and White Racism of Early Pentecostalism in the USA*. Eugene, OR: Wipf and Stock Publishers, 2003.

Martin, Larry E. *The Life and Ministry of William J. Seymour and a History of the Azusa Street Revival*. Pensacola, FL: Christian Life Books, 2006.

Payne, Jr., Leonard M. *My People Yesterday, Today and Forever*. St. Clairsville, OH: Xlibris Corporation, 2008.

Preobrazhensky, Evgeny and Nikolai Bukharin. *The ABC of Communism: A Popular Explanation of the Program of the Communist Party of Russia*. Ann Arbor, MI: University of Michigan Press, 1966.

Raboteau, Albert J. Slave Religion: *The "Invisible Institution" in the Antebellum South*. New York: Oxford University Press, 1978.

Stephens, Randall J. *The Fire Spreads: Holiness and Pentecostalism in the American South*. Cambridge, MA: Harvard University Press, 2008.

Synan, Vinson. *The Holiness-Pentecostal Tradition: Charismatic Movements of the Twentieth Century*. Grand Rapids, MI: William B. Eerdmans, 1997.

Woodward, C. Vann. *The Strange Career of Jim Crow*. New York: Oxford University Press, 2002.

APPENDICES

FINAL DECREE OF THE MEMPHIS, SHELBY COUNTY, TENNES-
SEE CHANCERY COURT-July 28,1908

FRANK AVANT

vs.

C. H. MASON

This cause came to be heard this day before the Honorable F. H. Heiskell, Chancellor, upon the hold recording the cause. Including the order of reference and the Master's report made in obedience thereto, which report is the final decision of the Chancery Court of Memphis, Shelby County, Tennessee, Frank Avant vs. C. H. Mason:

And the defendant having accepted to said report the same came on for argument. The exceptions taken by the defendant to the report of the Master made in the cause to the present term of the Court and the Court having heard read the report and proof referred to therein, and the exceptions and being of the opinion that all of the said exceptions taken as a foresaid are not well taken and the same are hereby overruled and disallowed, and said report is by the Court on motion of the Complainant, in all things confirmed. It is therefore ordered adjudged and decreed, by the Court that the

Complainants to this suit Frank Avant et al, as adherents to the original faith and order are entitled to the use, occupation and enjoyment of Saints Home Church of God in Christ, called the Sanctified Church which is situated on the east side of Wellington Street near Vance Street in the city of Memphis, Tennessee together with the lands and improvements belonging or in any wise appertaining to the same and the defendants there agents, friends and sympathizers and each of them are hereby perpetually enjoined from in any matter trespassing on same, and the said C.H. Mason, his agents, friends and sympathizers and each of them are hereby perpetually enjoined from preaching or attempting to preach in said church or on said church property. The defendant C.H. Mason, J.I.J. Prophet, Billy Frazier, Allie Frazier, Sam Jones, Eddie Rogers, S.T. Samuel, George Taylor, and Noah Deberry will pay the cost of this suit for which will issue as at law. To which said action of the Court the defendants then and there excepted, and now except, and have hereby prayed an appeal to the next term of the Supreme Court to be held over for the Western District of Tennessee at Jackson on the Monday in April 1909, which said appeal is granted by the Court upon the defendants giving an appeal bond as required by law.

APPENDIX B

THE TENNESSEE SUPREME COURT DECISION

-May 24, 1909

FRANK AVANT

vs.

C. H. MASON

Be it remembered that this cause came on this day to be heard on the record from the Court below, assignments of Error and arguments of Counsel, whereupon the Court is of opinion and doth accordingly adjudge and decree that there is error in the degree of the Chancery Court, and it is therefore reversed.

The Court is further of the opinion and doth accordingly adjudge and decree that the defendants, C.H. Mason and those adhering to him, are entitled to the use, occupation and enjoyment of the Saints Home Church of God in Christ, called the Sanctified Church, which is situated on the east side of Wellington Street near Vance Street, in the City of Memphis, Tennessee, together with the land and improvements belonging, or in any wise appertaining to the same, and the Complainants, their agents, friends and sympathizers and each of them, are hereby perpetually enjoyed from in any manner, trespassing on the same.

It is further adjudged and decreed that the defendants recover of the complainants, and of I.L. Jordan, their surety on the prosecution bond, all of the costs of this Court and of the Court below.

On motion of the complainants, the cause is remanded to the Court below for a reference for damages on the injunction bond.

Note: The Tennessee Supreme Court judge(s) that heard the arguments from both sides in the case gave a memorandum opinion or decision in favor of C.H. Mason, which meant a court decision that gives the ruling (what it decides, and orders done) but no opinion (reason for decision).[1]

---

1   *Calvin McBride, Frank Avant v. C.H. Mason: Mason and the Holy Ghost on Trial, 15.*

APPENDIX C

Bishop and Pastor Lose Court Fight
The Chicago Defender (National edition) (1921–1967); Mar 31, 1934;
pg. 13

Bishop and Pastor Lose Court Fight

Judge Rules Members Can Select Their Own Leader

31 Mar 1934

Ala. Court Scolds Church In Test Case
The Chicago Defender (National edition) (1921-1967); Apr 2, 1966;
ProQuest Historical Newspapers: Chicago Defender
pg. 46

Ala. Court Scolds Church In Test Case

APPENDIX E

Controversy To Get New Court Date
The Chicago Defender (National edition) (1921-1967); Aug 27, 1966;
ProQuest Historical Newspapers: Chicago Defender
pg. 13

CHURCH OF GOD IN CHRIST

Controversy To Get New Court Date

BIRMINGHAM, Ala. — (UPI) The growing controversy over who is the legal authority in the International Church of God in Christ is due for another airing in the courtroom sometime in August.

It has been widely circulated throughout the Negro press that a final decree has been rendered in the case of Emmitt Jackson, et al vs. John F. Key, et al, pending in the Circuit Court of the tenth judicial Circuit of Alabama, in equity, No. 157-949. Nothing could be farther from the truth. On March 15, a decree was rendered in which the court reserved jurisdiction for certain purposes, including an election to be held by the church membership of the East Birmingham Church of God in Christ.

The question of who actually leads the vast church organization came up when the so-called executive board headed by Bishop A. B. McEwen of Memphis, Tenn. and Bishop J. S. Bailey of Detroit, Mich., assisted by the General Church Secretary, Bishop J. O. Patterson of Memphis, Tenn., aided by other board members, decided to establish diocese number two and appoint Elder J. M. Bailey of Mobile, Ala., the brother of Bishop J. S. Bailey, as presiding bishop.

Elder John F. Key, pastor of the East Birmingham C.O.G.I.C. decided to transfer to the so-called number two diocese without proceeding according to due process as set forth in the church constitution or by proper authority.

The presiding bishop of diocese one, Bishop C. A. Ashworth, removed pastor Key constitutionally upon the request of local membership.

When elder Key refused to vacate the pulpit, an injunction restraining Elder Key was obtained from the Circuit Court by Deacon Emmitt Jackson, chairman of the board of trustees of the East Birmingham Church, and other trustees considered loyal to the constitution and to the senior bishop of the church, Bishop O. T. Jones, Sr., of Philadelphia.

Judge Barber's ruling is described by Elder W. E. Greer, C.O.G.I.C. information and communication officer, as irrelevant and unrelated to the case in point; namely actions taken by Rev. Key in the East Birmingham Church only.

Elder Greer further stated that Judge Barber's sweeping ruling which states that the title of senior bishop held by Bishop O. T. Jones, senior bishop of Philadelphia is "honorary" is in fact, based on falsified documents and testimony that were presented in court by a member of the so-called executive board of the Church of God in Christ, and which could lead to the arrest, conviction and possible confinement of certain national church figures.

"Because of the general confusion, and because the Judge ruled the East Birmingham Church's action in joining the new diocese 'null and void' the litigation is scheduled to continue at an early date at which time the Judge will be asked to reassess the evidence and will certainly result in a reversal of his original ruling", declared W. E. Greer.

"We merely want the general public to know that all is not resolved and the case is not closed as some executive board members have led the people to believe in erroneous news releases", said Elder Greer.

APPENDIX F

"Always Liars": a letter from Bishop R.E. Ranger

Part 1 Author's CAPS

For there are many unruly and vain talkers and deceivers, specially they of the circumcision: Whose mouths must be stopped, who subvert whole houses, teaching things which they ought not, for filthy lucre's sake. One of themselves, even a prophet of their own, said, the Cretans are always liars, evil beasts, slow bellies. Titus 1:10-12

Peace be unto you my Brethren partakers of the same faith, nurtured by the same love, standing in the consciousness of the same judgment, and for this cause animated by the same hope of eternal life.

The year 1965 has died since we were last together in our National Headquarters in Mason Temple, 938 Mason St. Memphis, Tenn. Another New Year has been born and is, as of the present date April 4, 1966, now well on its way to its appointed terminus, once the circle of its existence has brought it, too like 1965, and all of its predecessors, back to the Garden of Eden, to the valley marked for its determined end, THE VALLEY OF DECISION.

Its seems that physically many of us, if not the most of us have been blessed to enjoy the favors of our God over the period over which we have been permitted to come since we were last together in our NATIONAL CONVOCATION in November 1965. With a significantly few of us, the passage of this particular period of time has marked the END OF OUR EARTHLY JOURNEY. With others our journey of life has come upon problems of sickness and accident, all in the consequential will of our God. It is he who knows the way that we all take and hath said When he hath tried me, I shall come forth as gold." Job 23:10 We must notice however that the "Pure Gold" does not emerge until after the trials by God. The dross must be burned away by TRIAL.

Our NATIONAL CONVOCATION, last November brought to us many experiences foreign to the history of the CHURCH OF GOD IN CHRIST. It is disagreeable to all of us to contemplate the fact that it did occur. We do not even now feel ourselves comfortable in its contemplation.

(1) We saw a display of hatred and evil purpose among the brethren.

(2) We looked upon the deliberate "Rape of the Rights" of the highest of all OFFICIALS of the CHURCH OF GOD IN CHRIST, Sunday Nov 14, 1965.

(3) We witnessed the attempted seizing of the entire machinery of financial power and government of the CHURCH OF GOD IN CHRIST by violence.

(4) We saw the beginning of a coalition of men in the Elders Council and the so-called "EXECUTIVE BOARD" designed to destroy the BOARD OF BISHOPS, THE GENERAL ASSEMBLY and the OFFICE OF THE SENIOR BISHOP.

(5) We have observed the development of a NATIONWIDE CAMPAIGN of lies and attempted intimidation, directed through the channels of the only NATIONAL MEDIA published within the CHURCH OF GOD IN CHRIST, THE EVANGELIST SPEAKS. (allegedly bought for that purpose) and by addressing slanted new releases to publications of national circulation, with the Racial Press group, all over the nation.

(6) We have seen the forcible entry of this so-called "EXECUTIVE BOARD" into the jurisdictions presided over by certain state BISHOPS, who did not show themselves sufficiently frightened by "Threats and attempted intimidations" that were addressed to them by this BOARD with but one purpose and that was to destroy.

(7) We have seen the EDICT addressed to Dr. OT Jones, Jr as President of the Youth Department, that he ceases all activity as President of this DEPARTMENT and appear before this group who seek to serve as accusers (with no accusation) Judges (plainly without judgement) Persecutors (without a valid charge) and intimidators without law at the APRIL CALL MEETING convening April 12-14, 1966 in

Memphis, Tenn. No Charge is made! Just answer before us but before we even see you or give one word of accusation, CEASE YOUR WORK! How many of this group can stand the examination of even the last twelve years of their lives? Answer, those live where they have lived and where they live now.

(8) We have received a SPECIOUS CALL for a SPECIAL GENERAL ASSEMBLY IN THE APRIL SPRING CALL of the CHURCH OF GOD IN CHRIST, in Memphis, Tenn. The purpose of this call is to "RAPE THE CONSTITUTION of the CHURCH OF GOD IN CHRIST" as the RIGHTS OF THE SENIOR BISHOP were stripped from him by "RAPE AND VIOLENCE" November 14, 1966. The CONSTITUTION calls for one General Assembly each year held at the time of the NATIONAL CONVOCATION. The BOARD OF BISHOPS alone is empowered to call an extra session. The BOARD of BISHOPS is now composed of all who are Bishops in good standing in the CHURCH. THE BOARD OF BISHOPS HAS NOT EVEN MET. THE CALL IS A FAKE!

"Always Liars": A letter from Bishop RE Ranger, part II

Part 2 CAPS are the Author's

(9) We are now being told that the so called "EXECUTIVE BOARD" alone composes the BOARD OF BISHOPS. The others of you who are State Bishops must just pay your money and take "ORDERS". Tell me, can a "baby" become his own father? The BOARD OF BISHOPS gave the authority to the so-called EXECUTIVE BOARD to function for one year in leadership or until another SENIOR BISHOP had been elected. The SUPREME COURT of the STATE of TEXAS holds, since its JUDGMENT was given in 1963, that the power to this group to act ceased December 7, 1962, when Bishop Ozro T. Jones was elected SENIOR BISHOP. Only a Federal Court can overturn that judgment. Now, please tell me "How can a baby" become his own father? Bishop L.H. Ford, of Chicago, IL admitted in his sworn testimo-

ny in Kountze, Texas (Hardin County) when he and Bishop AB McEwen were there as representatives of the so called EXECUTIVE BOARD that the BOARD OF BISHOPS created the EXECUTIVE BOARD. He further admits under oath in court that they were to serve for 1963. COURT RECORDS WILL SHOW THIS! If according to his testimony, the BOARD OF BISHOPS created them for just one year, how have they now become the BOARD OF BISHOPS that created them? Somewhere, there is a dead cat on the line.

(10) If the BOARD OF BISHOPS is nothing, if the General Assembly is only a rubber stamp to validate the illegal actions taken in the Elder's Council which has no legislative CONSTITUTIONAL powers, if the SENIOR BISHOPS office leaves him only as a figure head, why should the STATE BISHOPS who have the leadership of all of the people who compose the state assemblies all over the nation, continue "Fattening Frogs to feed Snakes?" Taxation without representation is tyranny. Suppose every STATE BISHOP just holds back his report until a little sense can percolate through a few of those who have BLOCK-HEADS? BISHOPS you do not have to fear these men. They have already shown themselves to be plain Hitler-Stalin type dictators. What would the CHURCH OF GOD IN CHRIST be like if they held power 10 years? I will answer; we would all be a group of spineless dupes and theological slaves! God told Ezekiel, "Son of Man stand upon thy feet and I will speak to thee." Ezekiel 2:1 If we want God to be among us and bless our labor the time has come for each of us to "stand upon our feet". This little group of twelve to fourteen men are not the BOARD OF BISHOPS. THEY ARE NOT THE GENERAL ASSEMBLY, having sole legislative power in the CHURCH OF GOD IN CHRIST. We are all very certain that no one of them is the SENIOR BISHOP. Although the great trouble that we now must face really hinges on the fact that a great number of them want to be the SENIOR BISHOP THEMSELVES. As SENIOR BISHOP O. T. JONES will not hurry up and die as some of them were so very certain that he would when he was elected December 7, 1962, they are now seeking to seize the office by coldly, calculated, cunningly and determining-

ly designed "RAPE OF THE OFFICE". Your money is being spent to promote this very cohesive and constantly concurring group of conspirators, of evil purpose. Have you been threatened? If you have not, watch it! You may expect to be before your get away from Memphis, Tenn. April 12-14, 1966.

Hear me today! There is no place that I seek in any capacity of leadership in the CHURCH. I have already won the battle in the courts of our State, that many of your states will have to win, if you State Bishops survive as leaders and not serve as SLAVES: HEAR MY WORDS TODAY! "I would rather speak the truth to ten than blandishments and lying to a million. Try it, ye who think there is nothing in it. Try what it is to speak with God behind you—to speak as to be only the arrow in the bow which the Almighty draws" H.W.B.

Bad words are as influential as the plague and the pestilence. They have wrought moreevil than battle, murder and sudden death. They creep through the ears into the heart, call up all of its bad passions and tempt it to break God 's commandments. A few bad words got into the ear of the mother of mankind and they led here on to eat the forbidden fruit and thus to bring death into the world. G. Morgridge

"Always Liars": A letter from Bishop RE Ranger, part III

Part 3 CAPS are the Author's

Paul, the Apostle to the Gentiles, had a very special word to Titus who like Timothy was called "Mine own Son" or "My true child". He set forth his authority as a servant of God and an APOSTLE OF JESUS CHRIST. Titus had been left on an Island called Crete. There was a special purpose in having left him in that one place. The CHURCH was there in that there were many believers in Christ Jesus, but the believers had little organization.

Titus had a job that required activity and judgment. The activity was that he might really know the needs of the people, and the judgment was to be exercised in selecting from among them leaders in sufficient numbers, but the leaders must have the quality of blameless Bishops over the flock. We may be certain that the Cretans had many points of strength that made them acceptable as CHRISTIAN CONVERTS. But the Cretans also had three particular things with which their characters were found to be blemished. (1) There were in reputations as "Always liars" (2) evil beasts (3) slow bellies. Among them were "Many unruly" and "Vain talker and "Deceivers".

What a list of disadvantages to be overcome! Slow bellies; evil beasts, always liars. Deceivers, Wild Beasts, Idle Bellies. Gluttonous, and in all things a sensual people—-always liars! How can we reconcile this to the call of Christ?

What is sin? Wherein may it be found to be indulged? Who fathered it? Ye are of your father the devil, and the lusts of your father ye will do. He was a murderer from the beginning, and abode not in the truth, because there is no truth in him. When he speaketh a lie, he speaketh of his own, for he is a liar and the father of it. John 8:44. This description us if the FATHER OF LIES and the description in Titus, just read from Chapter 1 describes an entire people; a people from whom came CHRISTIAN BELIEVERS! Among them: (1) the unruly (2) Vain Talkers (3) Deceivers, whose mouths must be stopped; those who subvert whole houses, teachers of things that they ought not; wrong teaching being done for FILTHY LUCRE'S SAKE. How many labor not to proclaim the truth, but to subvert hearers for FILTHY LUCRE'S SAKE? Listen while men talk. Know their purposes, not of their words. "Buy the truth and sell it not"

Slow bellies, evil beasts, ALWAYS LIARS!!! Liars in the Cretan Church; liars not to be indulged and excused but to be sharply rebuked for the purpose of producing a soundness in their faith. This is the pattern and purpose of God. He has placed himself on record in Psalms 101:7: He that worketh deceit shall not swell in my house; he that telleth lies shall not tarry in my sight." God is not dead; God has not changed; God will not lie!

CHURCH OF GOD IN CHRIST, MY BRETHREN, let us seek nothing but the truth. You all are aware of the fact that a Senior Bishop of the CHURCH OF GOD IN CHRIST was elected to that position December 7, 1962. The so-called "EXECUTIVE BOARD" now claims by sworn oath that they only elected a SENIOR BISHOP, of the BOARD. ALWAYS LIARS! You know that the so-called "EXECUTIVE BOARD" was chosen to serve in leadership only until another SENIOR BISHOP has been elected for the CHURCH. THEY CLAIM unlimited power. ALWAYS LIARS! You know that the CONSTITUTION provides that the Senior Bishop shall appoint all State Overseers, now State Bishops. The so-called "EXECUTIVE BOARD" claims it now has the power to make such appointments without either CHURCH LAW or custom or practice to support such a claim. ALWAYS LIARS! You know that two years was the time that passed by while Bishop Ozro T. Jones was recognized in all portions of the UNITED CHURCH, by reason of this election. He asked for a financial accounting from all of the DE-PARTMENTS. The so-called "EXECUTIVE BOARD IMMEDIATELY BEGAN A FIGHT CLAIMING ALL THE POWER OF THE OFFICE. to which he was duly elected.; then claiming to be the BOARD OF BISHOPS, THEN CLAIMING THE POWERS OF THE GENERAL ASSEMBLY TO LEGISLATE only as they dictated. ALWAYS LIARS!

Now, they come claiming the power and right to call a SPECIAL CONSTITUTIONAL GENERAL ASSEMBLY. Its purpose has not been announced, but you may be certain that they are only seeking to enhance power for themselves by other false claims. ALWAYS LIARS!

They claimed under oath in Birmingham, Ala. to have held a GENERAL ASSEMBLY November 17, 1965 on YPWW DAY, in which they amended the CONSTITUTION, giving themselves special power to do as they choose and making the OFFICE OF THE SENIOR BISH-OP just a small honor. No discussion, no notice, no announcement. Just, we did it! ALWAYS LIARS!

THE GENERAL SECRETARY [Bishop JO Patterson, Sr.] of the CHURCH SWORE UNDER OATH, in Birmingham, Alabama that Bishop O.T. Jones was not nominated of the CHURCH, only Senior Bishop of this BOARD. A letter which had to admit bore his signature was produced in open court, stating that he had thrown his "Great influence" behind Bishop OT Jones as SENIOR BISHOP of the CHURCH OF GOD IN CHRIST because Bishop AB McEwen had widely circulated certain scandals regarding his moral conduct. ALWAYS LIARS!

The same man swore under oath, in the same COURTROOM that he never signed any Credentials with Bishop OT Jones as SENIOR BISHOP, appointing any man a STATE BISHOPat any time since he had been in OFFICE. Bishop Eurie [James Eure?] of Maryland was able to catch the plane that same night from Baltimore, Md and produce his Credentials in the COURT; its signature had to be admitted to the JUDGE! ALWAYS LIARS! Now caught!!!

Do not be alarmed by certain carefully selected portions of transcript that have been elected for circulation in certain areas from the Birmingham, Ala case. The full record of the transcript is feared. it will show men who are always liars! Lying under oath is perjury, you know. In the State of Alabama, the penalty upon a conviction, is from two to twenty years in the penitentiary. Why must men be ALWAYS LIARS?

APPENDIX G

Bishop J.O. Patterson's letter to Bishop R. E. Ranger

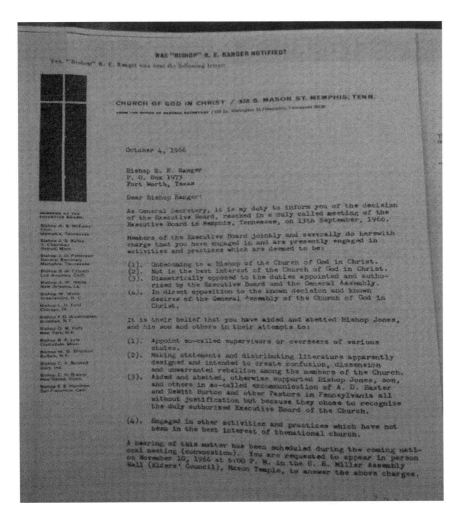

Bishop Ranger's Response to Bishop Patterson's letter

You may consider this to be the official charge. However, a
charge containing the signatures of all Executive Board mem-
except Bishop O. T. Jones is on file.

With deepest personal regards,

J. O. Patterson

BISHOP J. O. PATTERSON,
General Secretary

The registered card from the Post Office Department signed by "Bishop" R. E. Ranger was proof that he received the letter.

WHAT REPLY DID "BISHOP" RANGER MAKE?

"Bishop" Ranger sent the following telegram:

WESTERN UNION
TELEGRAM

251P EST OCT 13 66 CTA395 DB192
CT D FWCO68 NL PD FORT WORTH TEX 13
BISHOP J O PATTERSON
  1774 SOUTH PARKWAY EAST MFS
YOUR LETTER RECEIVED. YOUR MANIFEST EGO IS EVIDENTLY EXPOUNDED
TO THE AIRSHIP LINDENBURG SIZE. HOWEVER BOTH IT AND YOU SEEM
TO HAVE BEEN FILLED WITH THE WRONG GAS. IT BURNED UP
  BISHOP R E RANGER.

**DID "BISHOP" O. T. JONES AND "BISHOP" R. E. RANGER APPEAR BEFORE THE GENERAL COUNCIL
FOR TRIAL, OR HAVE ANYONE TO REPRESENT THEM?**

NO. Both "Bishop" Jones and "Bishop" Ranger ignored the trial. The Council heard the accusations which were substantiated by many reliable witnesses. After hearing the evidence, the Chairman called several times for the defense or their representatives. When ample time had been given and neither of them offered any defense or any excuse for not being present, it was obvious that they were defying and ignoring the General Council and therefore the Chairman entertained the following motion:

"Mr. Chairman, I so move that it is the decision of this Assembly that the charges against Bishop Jones and Bishop Ranger are sustained by the proof given and therefore they are hereby removed from their respective offices as Bishops of the Church of God in Christ, and that after one year if they repent of their wrong, they may apply for reinstatement by sending a written application to the General Secretary."

This motion was seconded by Bishop C. C. Cox, Nevada, Bishop Leroy Anderson, N. Y. and Bishop O. Freeman bid. The motion was carried by a vote of 907 to 5.

It was further voted that all acts done by Bishop Jones and Bishop Ranger during this term will be called null and void.

This motion prevailed by a vote of 907 to 5.

APPENDIX H

COGIC Executive Board Wins Church's Court Case
The Chicago Defender (National edition) (1921-1967); Dec 31, 1966;
ProQuest Historical Newspapers: Chicago Defender
pg. 6

COGIC Executive Board
Wins Church's Court Case

HOUSTON, Texas — Judge Warren P. Cunningham ruled in favor of members of the executive board on the Churches of God In Christ (COGIC), following a hearing in the Harris County District Court here on an application for a temporary injunction filed by Bishop R. E. Ranger, of the Southeast District of Texas.

The decision is regarded by board members as a key victory in the group's fight with a church faction representing Bishop O. T. Jones, of Philadelphia, who was ousted as senior bishop of the Church at the annual COGIC convention in Memphis last November.

Ranger, who was removed from the State Bishop's Board at the same time, is a supporter of Bishop Jones in the factional fight.

Bishop Jones, in defiance of the board's ruling, held what he called a nationwide rally of support in Philadelphia and reported that "a dozen bishops and 300 ministers" of the COGIC attended.

However, the executive board is supported by the more than 70 "bona fide" bishops of the Church and practically all ministers of the denomination's more than 5,000 churches throughout the

Bishop A. B. McEwen

United States and several foreign countries. In addition, the board has the support of all national officers who head auxiliaries, as well as Dr. Arenia C. Mallory, president of the Saints Junior College, Lexington, Miss.

Bishop Ranger had asked the court to issue a temporary injunction restraining the board from interfering with his authority and dispossessing his jurisdiction in the Church of God in Christ of Southeast Texas.

Members of the board named in the suit included Bishop A. B. McEwen, of Memphis, chairman of the executive board and chairman of the general assembly; Bishop J. S. Bailey, of Detroit, vice chairman of the general assembly; Bishop J. O. Patterson, general secretary, Memphis; Bishop S. M. Crouch, of Los Angeles; Bishop O. M. Kelly, of New York City; Bishop Louis H. Ford, of Chicago, international director of public relations; Bishop C. E. Bennett, of Gary, Ind.; Bishop John White, of New Orleans.

Also Bishop Wyoming Wells, Greensboro, N.C.; Bishop C. H.

Brewer, New Haven, Conn.; Bishop F. D. Washington, Brooklyn, N. Y.; Bishop W.G. Shipman, of Buffalo, N. Y., and Bishop E. E. Hamilton, San Francisco.

Among the Bishops on hand to lend moral support to the defendants were Bishop D. Lawrence Williams, chairman of the State Bishops' Board, Norfolk, Va.; Bishop J. H. Dell, of Albany, Ga., secretary of the Elders' Council; Bishop R. Courtney, Trenton, N. J., a member of the State Bishops' staff, and Elder Roger Jones, of Flint, Mich., a member of the Youth Provisional Board.

Also present for the court hearing were the following Bishops assigned to Texas:

Bishop T. D. Iglehart, Bishop F. L. Haynes, Dallas; Bishop J. E. Alexander, Midland; and Bishop C. H. Nelson, of Houston. Together the four Texas Bishops have jurisdiction over a total of 229 churches which support the executive board.

Local Bishops at the hearing were Bishop Tanner Perry, Bishop G. W. Law and Bishop R. J. Darrett, all of Houston. State supervisors of the Southeast Texas District, COGIC, along with hundreds of ministers, were also present.

The board was represented by A. A. Latting and J. O. Patterson, Jr., attorneys of Memphis, Tenn.; Q. T. Wells, of New York City, and Warner Brock, of the law firm of Brock and Williams, Houston.

Following Judge Cunningham's decision, the entire Board went into special session at the Rock Street Memorial Church of God In Christ to weigh the future of the Church in Southeast Texas.

It was decided that the Southeast District will be administered under the jurisdiction of the executive board until a bishop has been appointed.

APPENDIX I

IN THE CHANCERY COURT OF SHELBY COUNTY, TENNESSEE

STATE OF TENNESSEE)
  On Relation of
  A. B. McEwen, et al,)

      Complainants,)

VS.)   No. 69683-2 R.D.

O. T. JONES, R. E. RANGER,)
and O. T. JONES, JR.,
)

      Defendants.)

ENTERED
OCT 1 1967
No. 286-123

CONSENT DECREE

This cause came on to be heard on the Original Bill of the complainants, the Answer and Crossbill of the defendants, the Answer to the Crossbill, statement of counsel representing the respective parties, and upon the entire record in the cause, from all of which it appears to the Court that the parties have entered into the following Settlement Agreement, to-wit:

SETTLEMENT AGREEMENT

That the ultimate question in controversy is where the authority of the Church of God in Christ is placed by its Constitution. This problem generally involves two questions: Namely, the authority and power of Senior Bishop O. T. Jones, and the authority and power of the Executive Board. The parties recognize and agree that the ultimate solution of both of these questions and all related and ancillary questions should be determined by the General Assembly of the Church of God in Christ in a Constitutional Convention called for that purpose.

In order to preserve without detriment or prejudice the respective contentions of the parties until they can be resolved by the General Assembly of the Church of God in Christ, and for no other purpose, the parties agree as follows:

(1) That all rights, powers and duties of the Senior Bishop and the Executive Board shall remain status quo until a final determination by the Constitutional Convention of the General Assembly.

(2) The authority vested in Senior Bishop Mason as spelled out in the Constitution and By-Laws of the Church of God in Christ reverted on Bishop Mason's death to the Board of Bishops.

(3) The Board of Bishops is composed of all Bishops in the Church, whether referred to as "National", "State", "Foreign", or "Staff".

(4) That the Constitutional Convention of
the General Assembly of the Church will be called to
convene on January 30, 1968, as provided by Article 8
of the Constitution of the Church of God in Christ, at
which time any party to this litigation or any other
member of said General Assembly would be permitted to
offer a new Constitution revision and/or amendments to
the end that the General Assembly, by majority vote,
can determine and decide the offices to be created in
the Church, the authority to be vested in each such office, and any other matter that comes within the frame-
work of the Constitution and By-Laws.

(5) The 1967 General Convocation of the
Church of God in Christ shall proceed as planned from
November 7, 1967 through November 17, 1967, inclusive,
without any interference by any party hereto. All
parties further agree that such Convocation shall be
concerned only with spiritual and ecclesiastical matters, and none of the issues herein agreed to be reserved to the Constitutional Convention of the General
Assembly shall be debated, argued, or commented upon
by any speaker and, should such occur, the Presiding
Officer shall rule such speaker out of order and shut
off any further remarks.

(6) There shall be no session of the Board of Bishops or of the General Assembly called or held prior to the aforementioned Constitutional Convention of the General Assembly which would contravene or violate the letter and spirit of this Compromise Settlement Agreement.

(7) No party to this suit, or his agent, designee or representative, shall appoint or remove or participate in the appointment or removal of any Bishop, whether "State" or otherwise, or State Assembly designated by any such Bishop, or any National official prior to the determination by the aforementioned Constitutional Convention of the General Assembly of the parties' respective powers, except that the Board of Bishops may fill vacancies in the event of death, resignation, or good faith emergency, which emergency is not designed or calculated to be a breach of this Agreement.

(8) That prior to the aforementioned Constitutional Convention of the General Assembly no party to this suit, either directly or indirectly, shall attempt to change or affect the status or position in the Church of any other party except as herein provided.

(9) That all persons shall be seated as delegates or alternates to the aforementioned

Constitutional Convention of the General Assembly who
are certified by their respective State Assemblies,
and which shall be limited to the following: All ordained elders, State Bishops, members of the Board of
Bishops, and one State Supervisor and one lay delegate
from each State Assembly.

(10) The foregoing points of agreement represent a good faith compromise of the respective parties' contentions in an effort to preserve the Church
in its faith and to promote peace and harmony within
the Church, and this Agreement shall not be construed
or argued as sustaining the contentions of any party
or as propoganda before the Constitutional Convention
or during the proceedings thereof.

It is, therefore, by the Court, by and with
the consent of the parties, ORDERED, ADJUDGED and
DECREED as follows:

(1) That the foregoing Settlement Agreement
be, and the same is by the Court, confirmed and approved;

(2) That the temporary injunctions heretofore
issued in this cause be, and the same are hereby, dissolved.

(3) That this cause be, and the same is
hereby, retained in the jurisdiction of the Court for

the enforcement of this Settlement Agreement and for
such further orders as the justice of the cause shall
require.

_____
CHANCELLOR

1-13/67

CONSENTED TO:

For the Complainants and Cross Defendants:

_____
A. A. Latting, Solicitor

For the Defendants and Cross Complainants:

_____
Lucius E. Burch, Jr., Solicitor

For additional copies:

e-mail: contato@upbooks.net.br
+55 (19) 98430-7994

Mailing Address:
Rua Agostinho de Faria, 488 - Cidade Líder
São Paulo, SP - Brazil - CEP 08280-100
C/O: Eneas Francisco

Made in the USA
Columbia, SC
02 June 2021